CHANGING SCHOOL SUBJECTS

CHANGING EDUCATION

Series Editors:
Professor Andy Hargreaves, Ontario Institute for Studies in Education
Professor Ivor Goodson, University of East Anglia

This authoritative series addresses the key issues raised by the unprecedented levels of educational change now facing schools and societies throughout the world.

The different directions of change can seem conflicting and are often contested. Decentralized systems of school self-management are accompanied by centralized systems of curriculum and assessment control. Moves to develop more authentic assessments are paralleled by the tightened imposition of standardized tests. Curriculum integration is being advocated in some places, more specialization and subject departmentalization in others.

These complex and contradictory cross-currents pose real challenges to theoretical and practical interpretation in many fields of education and constitute an important and intriguing agenda for educational change. *Changing Education* brings together leading international scholars who address these vital issues with authority and accessibility in areas where they are noted specialists. The series will commission books from all parts of the world in an attempt to cover the global and interlinked nature of current changes.

Published titles:

David Corson: *Changing Education for Diversity*
Gill Helsby: *Changing Teachers' Work*
Joe L. Kincheloe and Shirley R. Steinberg: *Changing Multiculturalism*
Colin Lankshear: *Changing Literacies*
Kenneth Leithwood, Doris Jantzi and Rosanne Steinbach: *Changing Leadership for Changing Times*
Louise Stoll and Dean Fink: *Changing our Schools*

Forthcoming titles:

Bob Lingard: *Changing Educational Policy*
Peter Tomlinson: *Changing Approaches to Learning and Teaching*
Maurice Galton: *Changing Classroom Practice*

CHANGING SCHOOL SUBJECTS

Power, gender and curriculum

CARRIE PAECHTER

OPEN UNIVERSITY PRESS
Buckingham · Philadelphia

Open University Press
Celtic Court
22 Ballmoor
Buckingham
MK18 1XW

email: enquiries@openup.co.uk
world wide web: http://www.openup.co.uk

and
325 Chestnut Street
Philadelphia, PA 19106, USA

First Published 2000

A catalogue record of this book is available from the British Library

ISBN   0 335 20119 9 (pb)   0 335 20120 2 (hb)

Library of Congress Cataloging-in-Publication Data
Paechter, Carrie F.
    Changing school subjects : power, gender, and curriculum / Carrie Paechter.
      p. cm. — (Changing education)
    Includes bibliographical references and index.
    ISBN 0-335-20120-2 — ISBN 0-335-20119-9 (pbk.)
    1. Curriculum change—Great Britain. 2. Curriculum planning x Social aspects—Great Britain. 3. Feminism and education—Great Britain.
    I. Title. II. Series.

LB2806.I5.P34   2000
375'.001'0941—dc21   00-035991

Typeset by Type Study, Scarborough
Printed in Great Britain by St Edmundsbury Press, Bury St Edmunds, Suffolk

For Mordecai and Zachary

CONTENTS

Series editor's preface   ix
Abbreviations   xi
Acknowledgements   xiii

Part I   Gender, power/knowledge and curriculum change

1   Introduction: studying curriculum change   3
2   Power, gender and curriculum   14
3   Gender, power and school subjects   32

Part 2   Gendered marginality

4   Life in a marginal subject   49
5   Negotiating a new school subject: the case of design and
       technology   63
6   Physical education, sport and the body   91

Part 3   Students, subjects and examinations

7   Students and subjects: power/knowledge and integrated
       curricula   111
8   Discipline as examination/examination as discipline:
       the effects of curriculum codification on teachers,
       students and subjects   130
9   Conclusion   153

       Appendix: Empirical sources   158
       References   163
       Index   179

SERIES EDITORS' PREFACE

Looking at the papers presented at a recent conference on 'Education and Social Justice', it was clear that there was a consensus on a number of issues that went from the far left political spectrum right through to the far right. One form of consensus was that subject knowledge should be unproblematically accepted as a central part of schooling and a central part of the training of teachers. This consensus, embraced by most Western governments, actually stands in the face of most of the work undertaken by sociologists of educational knowledge in the past thirty years. Their work shows that in a sense much subject knowledge is a form of structured exclusion for many of its students. As social justice has been banished from the discourse, so subject knowledge as *given*, has once again been established. It is the great virtue of Carrie Paechter's book that not only does she seek to rehabilitate the challenge to this normative position, but she also extends the analysis of school subject knowledge in a number of crucial ways.

Writing in 1994, one of the series editors had ruminated about the dangers of poststructuralist and postmodern discourses, with specific regard to school subjects.

Given the deconstructionist and poststructuralist impulse at the moment, it is possible to doubt that the contest over curriculum and the institutionalized categories that comprise curriculum sites of action is really important. For curriculum can indeed be reinterpreted, text can be deconstructed, every prescription can be subverted, inverted, converted or perverted. These are vital truths but the deconstructive impulse complements but does not contradict the impulse that studies the social construction of prescription. Such work does not contradict the scholarly impulse to study the processes of definition and delineation which are central to the preactive construction of curriculum and the social priorities embedded within that curriculum. Prescriptions do indeed set parameters for schooling and curriculum; here the definitions and delineations circumscribe what is 'cultural' or 'social', what is of status and significance. The dissident, it is true, can transcend but the conformist majority is more likely to bend. In Foucault's sense, schooling and curriculum do remain successful disciplinary devices, managing populations and subjectivities with considerable dexterity. The social construction of the preactive curriculum is a vital and still substantially unexplored element of these devices and desires.

(Goodson 1994: 13)

Whilst, herself, much inspired by postmodern impulses, the supreme virtue of Carrie Paechter's book is that it also holds onto the need to challenge the given nature of subject knowledge, if anything at all is to be done in terms of the matrix of social exclusion/inclusion. What we particular recommend about the central core of the text is the way that the relationship between school subjects and subjectivity is persistently interrogated and highlighted. The relationship between subject identities and issues of marginality and subjectivity are explored with great precision in a number of case studies at the heart of the book.

The text, however, goes beyond these paramters to extend our analysis, both in terms of issues of gender and issues of power. Paechter is quite right to extend the brief here and push the analytic framework further with regard to issues of gender and power. Particularly rewarding, is the way that existing sociological portraits of school subjects are linked to Foucault's notion of power/knowledge. In a very elegant way, she shows how a good deal of existing power/knowledge analysis is itself gendered and how this issue can be analytically resolved.

In the final sections, these analyses are brought to bear on examination as a disciplinary device. The effects of this on the school subjects themselves, as well as on the teachers and students involved in their transmission, negotiation and reception, provide a vital counterpoint to the mindless accountability and assessment strategies currently being pursued. In this sense, and others, the book is a timely reminder about the lessons that have been learnt and are to be learnt about the nature of subject knowledge. As it stands, most subject knowledge can be seen as a means of distributing disciplinary inequality. Until the heartland of subject knowledge is itself renegotiated, any talk of redrawing the boundaries of social exclusiveness is simply political polemic. Paechter's book reminds us of this essential truth.

Reference

Goodson, I. F. (1994) *Studying Curriculum: Cases and Methods*. Buckingham: Open University Press.

ABBREVIATIONS

AT	attainment target
BS	business studies
CDT	craft, design and technology
D&T	design and technology
GCSE	General Certificate of Secondary Education
GNVQ	General National Vocational Qualification
HE	home economics
HMI	Her Majesty's Inspectorate of Schools
IT	information technology
LEA	local education authority
NCC	National Curriculum Council
NVQ	National Vocational Qualification
PE	physical education
PoS	programme of study
PSE	personal and social education
RoA	record of achievement
SATs	Standard Assessment Tasks
SCAA	School Curriculum and Assessment Authority
SEAC	School Examinations and Assessment Council
TES	Times Educational Supplement
TVEI	Technical and Vocational Education Initiative

ACKNOWLEDGEMENTS

In carrying out the empirical work for this book and in writing it up in this form I have had help and support from a number of people. First of all, I am enormously grateful to all the teachers, students and advisory staff who took part in the three research projects discussed in this book; without their generosity my own work would be impossible. Second, for their help at different times over the past ten years, in my attempts to formulate and express my ideas, I should like particularly to thank Stephen Ball, Paul Black, Maud Blair, Richard Bowe, Richard Edwards, John Head, Gabrielle Ivinson, Meg Maguire, Patricia Murphy, Robin Murray, Gary Spruce and Gaby Weiner. I would also like to thank Shona Mullen of Open University Press and the series editors, Ivor Goodson and Andy Hargreaves, for their help with the final draft. Pip Eastop read and commented on much of the text and has, as always, been unfailing in his support.

part 1

GENDER, POWER/KNOWLEDGE AND CURRICULUM CHANGE

one

INTRODUCTION: STUDYING CURRICULUM CHANGE

Why study curriculum change?

> Conflict over the written curriculum has both 'symbolic significance' and also practical significance – by publicly signifying which aspirations and intentions are to be enshrined in written curriculum[,] criteria are established for the evaluation and public estimation of schooling.
>
> (Goodson 1988: 12)

What happens in the school curriculum is fundamental to people's lives. Schools are meant to educate the next generation, and to do so through the curriculum. If the curriculum excludes or marginalizes some groups or discounts their ideas, it will make it harder for members of those groups to benefit from the education system. If a high status curriculum is only offered to or accessible by some groups (males, middle-class students, the 'more able'), social divisions will be perpetuated; conversely, if we want a future significantly different from our present, we will need to educate our future citizens differently. Studying what goes on in schools, how a written curriculum is realized in classrooms, is therefore very important for anyone interested not just in educational, but in social change. Furthermore, in a period in which the curriculum within schools is constantly subject to change from outside, studying the impact of these changes on teachers and students is an important means through which we can see how future changes might be better planned and implemented. At a time when boys and girls are seen to be performing differentially across a wide range of subjects, we also need to focus in particular on the gendered nature of curriculum, on how curricular forms act to include or exclude certain groups, and on how curriculum change affects male and female teachers and students. We need in particular to consider the relationship between power, gender and knowledge and how this relationship translates into the school curriculum. In this book I look at how networks of power, gender and knowledge intersect to determine how school knowledge is constructed, what knowledge is made available to which students, who is permitted to supply that knowledge and how they are allowed to do so.

In the past 30 years there has been an increased interest, in the West, in the study of curriculum change. This has happened for a number of reasons. Curriculum change itself has increased in frequency, pace and, above all, ubiquity. Until quite recently, curricula changed gradually, as a result of initiatives by groups of teachers or academics working together to establish a new school subject or alter the teaching methods of an old one (Layton 1972; Goodson 1983b; Goodson and Ball 1984). Teachers who did not want to engage with change could, by and large, avoid it. This is no longer the case; to refuse to take part in ongoing change is, essentially, to opt out of teaching altogether. This ubiquity is connected with a second reason for the increased interest in curriculum change: the alteration in emphasis from individual or group endeavour to government initiatives and projects, often connected, particularly in England and Wales, with the introduction of mandatory curriculum content and forms. Although in many cases these mandatory curricula differ only in detail from what went before, the move from a position where a subject department within any particular secondary school could have some choice in the topics taught or the order in which they were studied, to one in which all aspects of the subject are prescribed (and tested), feels to teachers like considerable change. Furthermore, with the introduction of mandatory curricula came attempts to change the relative status of a number of school subjects, by making some compulsory and others not for different periods of time in a student's school career (Paechter 1993c). Such changes in the balance of the curriculum as a whole have been destabilizing for teachers and schools.

At the same time there has been an increased interest in the social processes of schooling, and curriculum is a central aspect of this. Increasingly, the relationship between teachers, students and the curriculum has been seen as an important area for investigation. As Young (1971) points out, school subjects vary in status in the eyes of teachers, students and the outside world. Ball (1987) notes that the status of a particular subject within a specific school can have an enormous impact on the resources available to teachers and students working in that area. Furthermore, what goes on in schools is now recognized as being intimately connected with and reflecting what goes on in wider society; the two are not separate. As Hamilton points out:

Schooling and society must be examined in terms of the reciprocal relationships that hold them together across time and space. From such a perspective, the day to day practices of schooling are deemed to be both socially-constructed and historically-located. Their shape derives as much, for instance, from the changing expectations of priests and politicians as it does from the pre-given circumstances of school architecture and textbook availability. Necessarily, then, the practices of schooling are both 'in' and 'of' society.

(1989: 151)

Consequently, curriculum change often goes hand in hand with and reflects social change; how we as a society choose to educate our children reflects what we think is important.

We need to study curriculum change in its social context because such studies help us to see why we have the curricula that we do. We need to understand how they came to be, and get to grips with their contingent nature. Once we can start to unpick the relationship between social processes and curriculum forms, we have a better chance of changing each through the other, and once we have a grasp of how particular curricula have come to dominate our schooling systems, we can have a clearer insight into the ways in which things might change.

The negotiation of curriculum is also a key area for studying the change process in educational contexts. Because curriculum is so central to schooling, and because schooling is, and is seen to be, fundamental to the structuring and restructuring of social relations (Young 1971), curriculum change on a national scale involves extensive contestation and debate at both macro and micro levels. Thus we can follow the public debates about the introduction, for example, of the new National Curriculum for design and technology (D&T) in the UK, and at the same time examine in detail the processes of change as teachers in specific school settings tried to come to terms with the results of those debates. What we see when we carry out these studies is that conditions of change uncover and make clearer the assumptions that underlie both curriculum forms and schooling more generally; by examining curriculum change we are better able to understand the wider processes of schooling. The ubiquity and pace of change, in the past 15 years in particular, has meant that all aspects of schooling have been exposed and contested. What is seen as important in curriculum terms reflects both what are perceived to be fundamental aspects of schooling, and what are considered to be key underpinnings of a particular social formation.

Starting points

The 'new sociology of education'

The conceptual point of origin for this, and many other, studies of the sociology of curriculum, is the publication in 1971 of Young's edited collection,

Knowledge and Control: New Directions for the Sociology of Education.
This book was and remains enormously influential and brought about a
radical change in the approach to the study of what is taught in schools.
While previously the field had been dominated by philosophers of education, who took the broad subject areas of the curriculum for granted as
'forms of knowledge' (Hirst and Peters 1970), Young argued that these
needed interrogating, and that, rather than being based on fundamental
knowledge forms, the content and structure of the curriculum resulted from
power struggles both within and outside of schools: 'Education is not a
product like cars and bread, but a selection and organization from the available knowledge at a particular time which involves conscious or unconscious choices' (Young 1971: 24).

In considering the selection and organization of curricula, Young argued,
we should ask both by what criteria different approaches to knowledge are
given value – that is, how some curriculum areas attain high status and some
do not – and how this relates to wider social structures. Thus, the importance given to particular curriculum contents and forms within any society
both reflects and is reflected by what is considered important more generally
within that society. We can therefore use the study of curriculum to discover
more about what is valued by the dominant groups in a particular social formation. Young further argues that intervention in curriculum forms might
be a productive means to social change: by changing the curriculum, by
choosing to educate children differently, we might be able to change society.
At the same time, however, he appreciates that such attempts at change are
likely to be strongly contested by dominant interest groups: 'As we assume
some patterns of social relations associated with any curriculum . . . changes
will be resisted in so far as they are perceived to undermine the values, relative power and privileges of the dominant groups involved' (Young 1971:
34).

In the same volume, and complementary to Young's analysis of the curriculum as socially organized knowledge, was a paper by Bernstein (Bernstein 1971), developed in his subsequent writings (Bernstein 1971, 1975,
1977, 1990, 1996), in which he focused in particular on the selection and
organization of knowledge by developing a typology of school knowledge
codes.

Bernstein sees the curriculum as organized into units of time, each of
which has a certain content. These contents can be seen to differ in status,
as demonstrated by the amount of time they are given and whether they are
compulsory or optional. They can also be considered in terms of their
relationship to each other and to the non-school world, and this is where
Bernstein puts his emphasis. He uses the concepts of classification and framing to consider the various ways of organizing curricula and of teaching the
subjects within them. These concepts are then used to analyse the differences

between strongly classified 'collection' curricula, where the contents are well insulated from each other, and those of the weakly classified, 'integrated' type, in which the contents stand in a more open relationship to each other, and in which separate subject areas are subordinated to some form of unifying idea (Bernstein 1971). The degree of classification between a set of categories, such as a school curriculum made up of subjects, matters because it is the maintenance of these boundaries that not only makes such a collection curriculum possible but also perpetuates the power relations between different curriculum areas:

> I want to argue that the crucial space which creates the specialization of the category – in this case the discourse – is not internal to that discourse but is the space between that discourse and another. In other words, A can only be A if it can effectively insulate itself from B. In this sense, there is no A if there is no relationship between A and something else.
>
> (Bernstein 1996: 20)

The implication of this is that in order for a school subject to retain its identity, strong boundaries have to be maintained between it and other subject areas. This is particularly important to teachers of high-status subjects, who go to great lengths to avoid 'pollution' from lower status areas (Whitty *et al.* 1994). These boundaries between subjects therefore become important sites of struggle and resistance. Both teachers and students actively support and resist particular curriculum definitions through disputes concerning boundary strength and what is included and excluded on each side of particular boundaries. Furthermore, as Bernstein points out, 'Attempts to change degrees of insulation reveal the power relations on which the classification is based and which it reproduces' (1996: 21).

Consequently, the study of curriculum change, especially of attempts to introduce interdisciplinary work, becomes particularly important for understanding power relations between teachers and between school subjects.

Classification, then, refers to the boundary strength between different categories. Framing, on the other hand, is concerned with the means by which a learner acquires a pedagogic message. It refers to who controls what, within a particular pedagogic relationship. It focuses in particular on what is considered appropriate within that situation, in terms of what is learned and how it is learned. Where framing is strong, the teacher explicitly controls all aspects of the situation, including the selection of subject matter, its sequencing and pacing, what may or may not be brought into the learning situation, and the relationship between teacher and learner. Where framing is weak, the learner has more apparent control over some aspects of the situation, although, as Bernstein points out, this does not mean that the

of instructional discourse do not exist, rather that they are rendered
ible to the student (Bernstein 1996).

Both Young and Bernstein lay particular emphasis on the distinction
between school and non-school knowledge. They, and others writing at that
time, believed that breaking down the barrier between the two could act as
a catalyst for social change. Young suggests that a particular feature of academic curricula is their 'unrelatedness . . . which refers to the extent to
which they are "at odds" with daily life and common experience' (1971:
38), while Bernstein notes that 'in a sense, educational knowledge is uncom-
monsense knowledge' (1971: 58) and argues that children are taught to separate school and non-school knowledge from an early age:

> I suggest that the frames of the collection code, very early in the child's
> life, socialize him [*sic*] into knowledge frames which discourage con-
> nections with everyday realities, or that there is a highly selective
> screening of the connection. Through such socialization, the pupil soon
> learns what of the outside may be brought into the pedagogical frame.
> Such framing also makes of educational knowledge something not ordi-
> nary or mundane, but something esoteric which gives a special signifi-
> cance to those who possess it. I suggest that when this frame is relaxed
> to include everyday realities, it is often and sometimes validly, not
> simply for the transmission of educational knowledge, but for purposes
> of social control of forms of deviancy. The weakening of this frame
> occurs usually with the less 'able' children whom we have given up edu-
> cating.
>
> (1971: 58)

This distinction between school and non-school knowledge, especially for
'more academic' students, became an important theme for subsequent writers tracing how a subject went from being concerned with everyday realities
to being fully incorporated into academic abstraction. In 1972, Layton, for
example, in a key paper, suggested that:

> It is possible to discern three stages in the development of school sub-
> jects. In the first, the callow intruder stakes a place in the timetable,
> justifying its presence on grounds such as pertinence and utility. During
> this stage learners are attracted to the subject because of its bearing on
> matters of concern to them. The teachers are rarely trained specialists,
> but bring the missionary enthusiasm of pioneers to their task. The dom-
> inating criterion for the selection of subject matter is relevance to the
> needs and interests of learners.
>
> In the second stage, a tradition of scholarly work in the subject is
> emerging along with a corps of trained specialists from which teachers
> may be recruited. Students are still attracted to the study, but as much

by its reputation and growing academic status as by its relevance to their own problems and concerns. The internal logic and discipline of the subject is becoming increasingly influential in the selection and organization of subject matter.

The third stage is characterised by a further advance along the road of specialization and expertise. The teachers now constitute a professional body with established rules and values. The selection of subject matter is determined in large measure by the judgments and practices of the specialist scholars who lead inquiries in the field. Students are initiated into a tradition, their attitudes approaching passivity and resignation, a prelude to disenchantment.

(1972: 11)

In the period that followed, a number of researchers, (for example Goodson 1983b, 1998; Cooper 1984, 1985; Ball 1985; McCulloch *et al.* 1985; Goodson *et al.* 1988) fleshed out this structure with a series of studies suggesting that for a subject to become securely established in schools it was necessary for it to become less focused on utilitarian considerations and develop a university base. The form and content of the subject so established was also heavily influenced by the universities that trained the teachers, and set the examinations; they had an important role in boundary maintenance. Goodson notes, for example, the very successful strategy of early geography educators, who explicitly set out to establish university departments of geography, which would in their turn produce specialist geography teachers for schools, who would be responsible for setting examinations in their subjects (Goodson 1985). As he remarks, 'this strategy reads very much like a plea for monopoly rights or for a closed shop' (Goodson 1988: 168). It was strikingly successful, however, and geography was able to establish itself as an academic subject in both school and higher education, able to fend off challenges from more 'relevant' subjects such as environmental studies (Goodson 1983a). Goodson (1985) compares the success of geography with the failure of rural studies, which did not manage to establish a presence in tertiary education, in gaining a long-term foothold in the school curriculum. Rural studies remained a low status, practically based subject justifying its place in schools by its utility to students rather than academic considerations. Similarly, for the practically based subject of craft, design and technology to become securely placed in the English and Welsh National Curriculum (in the form of design and technology) without a power base in the universities (Penfold 1988), it has been necessary for the subject to become far more academic, giving more emphasis to planning, evaluating and design. Despite this, the subject retains a comparatively low status (see Chapter 5).

Subject subcultures

'Subjects are not monolithic entities but shifting amalgamations of sub-groups and traditions. These groups within the subject influence and change boundaries and priorities' (Goodson 1983b: 3).

An important aspect of the developments during the late 1970s and 1980s that arose out of the work of the 'new sociology of education' was the idea that the particular manifestation of any one school subject is developed and maintained through the work of competing interest groups. Although in many cases the nature of the subject is a matter of fierce debate within the group (Ball and Lacey 1980; Cooper 1984), it is in the interests of each subject group as a whole to preserve strong classification between itself and other groups, in the interests of providing a distinct identity and thus focus for resources both in a particular school and within the education system as a whole. To this end, teachers, and (at least at the more academically advanced levels) students are socialized into a supposedly unified culture, based on the fiction of the subject as discipline. This was, for example, how Goodson's pioneer geographers managed to establish their subject so successfully. Originally vulnerable because it straddled the boundary between science and humanities, geography's practitioners worked hard to promote its 'disciplinary' status. Having set up university departments to ensure that specialist geography teachers would be socialized into the university-led subject culture during their undergraduate degrees, they then fiercely defended their territory.

> Once geography was established as a separate subject in its own right in the early years of the twentieth century, geographers began to obsessively patrol their subject borders. They sought to ensure that no other integrated subjects could follow their route into separate subject status.
> (Goodson 1983a: 92)

Although, as Ball and Lacey (1980) point out, these subject subcultures are strongly internally contested, the public face of unity preserves the fiction that they are based on something more fundamental than the successful dominance of a particular interest group, such as Hirst and Peters' (1970) 'forms of knowledge'. This fiction is important for promoting and sustaining the presence of an individual subject as part of the taken-for-granted curriculum.

A key arena for struggles between the various segments (Cooper 1984) competing for dominance of a particular subject subculture, is the school subject department (Siskin 1994). Although in England and Wales in recent years the introduction of the National Curriculum has meant that teachers within schools have had less freedom than before to choose a curriculum reflecting their personal or departmental philosophies, the way in which a subject is approached remains in significant respects subject to negotiation between teachers in any particular school department. Thus subject departments form an important arena both for the development of subject subcultures and for the embracing of or resistance to imposed curriculum change (Bowe *et al.* 1992). Ball and Lacey note that:

> Rather than being a cypher of subject knowledge for the teacher the subject department is in itself an arena of competition in which individual social strategies are organised on the basis of biography, latent culture and situational constraints. It is an arena of competing paradigms and definitions, defining and defending boundaries externally and 'demanding allegiance from its members internally and conferring a sense of identity upon them' (Musgrove 1968) . . . the extent of agreement and allegiance within subject departments cannot be taken for granted.
>
> (1980: 151)

By studying the detail of these internal departmental struggles, in which teachers compete for dominance in the definition of what is central to their subject at that particular school, and by looking at the relationship between these internal struggles and those taking place in the wider political arena, we can gain a better understanding of how change takes place. In particular, we can get a clearer idea of what drives, and what inhibits, change processes, and how best to ensure that changes (or at least the ones we ourselves favour) succeed.

This study of the sociology of curriculum, through the examination of the micro and macro processes of curriculum change, is an ongoing tradition to which this book itself offers a contribution. However, much of the empirical work reported on here is unusual in that it arises from the study of important curriculum changes as they occurred. Researchers studying curriculum change in the 1990s were fortunate to be working in a period in which teachers in England and Wales were having imposed on them a new National Curriculum, which contained some elements that were radically different from what had gone before. We were thus able to study some of the processes of curriculum history as they were taking place; a luxury not afforded to many scholars in this area. So while being part of the tradition of sociology and history of curriculum, this book is in some senses a development of it. Unlike previous researchers in this area, whose studies of struggles over specific innovations used a combination of archive research and interviews with those seen, after the event, as 'key actors', I was able to look directly at what was happening between teachers in specific schools as they attempted to deal with large-scale curriculum change. This has allowed the collection of participants' opinions and actions as they were formed, rather than as *post hoc* rationalizations. It has also meant that the views and actions of 'ordinary actors' in curriculum development, the teachers in the classroom and staffroom, have been central to the research, making it much easier to bring together the macro and micro aspects of the change process.

Power and gender

The corpus of work focusing on the sociology of school knowledge and in particular on the nature and negotiation of the curriculum is very important but lacking in two significant respects. First, the analyses in almost all cases ignore both the gendered nature of school subjects and the genders of those teachers involved in the struggles for subject definition (Whitty 1985). Although these writers are clearly concerned to consider the ways in which different groups gain differential access to the curriculum, this is understood almost exclusively in terms of class. Measor points out that:

> it is clear that there is a 'sexual division of knowledge; and that it ties up with notions about gender-appropriate subjects for both boys and girls' (Deem 1980: 7). This means that we need to take account of gender in any work on curriculum or curriculum innovation, and equally to attempt to grasp the very powerful forces which militate against change.
>
> (1983: 190)

This injunction has, however, been widely ignored until very recently, except by those concerned about the resistance of girls to 'masculine' subjects such as mathematics and science. In any case, even Measor's approach assumes that the key issues in what might be called 'gender-risky' curriculum innovation are concerned with the differential responses of male and female students, and not with the impact of gender on the micropolitical forces that shape the curriculum itself; Datnow's recent work (Datnow 1998) is a notable (but in my view undertheorized) exception to this. That segmental struggles within subject subcultures are in some cases struggles between male and female traditions and approaches has only really been addressed in the subject area in which it is most unavoidable, physical education (PE), where there has been considerable research (for example Fletcher 1984; Scraton 1986; Dewar 1987; Sherlock 1987; Flintoff 1993), ignored for the most part, however, by sociologists of curriculum. Curriculum historians, concerned as they have to be with the accounts of 'key actors', have dealt almost entirely with the actions of men, but this has rarely been noted or analysed.

Second, although struggles over the curriculum are fundamentally concerned with power, power has itself not been well theorized in much sociological and historical research into curriculum change. The earlier studies arising directly from the 'new sociology of education' were underpinned by implicit views of power arising from liberal or Marxist socialism; this was not generally, however, very clearly articulated. Subsequent studies, while referring to the power of the various interest groups, give little indication of how that power is understood, although it is likely that most follow Cooper's view that 'power must be conceptualized in terms of the resources available to actors' (1984: 54). However, this loose definition does not really get us very far in thinking about how power relations operate either within schools in general or in the specific conditions of educational change. Without a clear understanding of the operation of power relations in school settings, we are also unable to make connections between research into educational change and, for example, the micropolitical manoeuvrings of other professional groups.

This book is an attempt to move on from this largely untheorized position by using Foucault's work on power/knowledge to give an underpinning and explicit theorization to work on struggles over curriculum content and form. My intention is to develop Foucault's analysis of power to encompass the relationship between power and gender, and then to apply this theoretical lens to the situation of curriculum negotiation and contestation. Thus I focus much more explicitly than previous authors have on the role of gendered power/knowledge relations in curriculum change; the empirical sections of the book are rooted in this theoretical standpoint.

First, however, I need to make my position explicit. This is done in detail in Chapter 2 in which I explain Foucault's concept of power/knowledge, suggest how it is gendered and discuss some of the current debates about Foucault's work, particularly as it applies to education. I then go on to take a broad look at the relationships between gender, power and school subjects. These two chapters set the scene for the subsequent sections, in which I examine how this relationship is played out in practice.

two

POWER, GENDER AND CURRICULUM

Perhaps, too, we should abandon a whole tradition that allows us to imagine that knowledge can exist only where the power relations are suspended and that knowledge can develop only outside its injunctions, its demands and its interests. Perhaps we should abandon the belief that power makes mad and that, by the same token the renunciation of power is one of the conditions of knowledge. We should admit rather that power produces knowledge (and not simply by encouraging it because it serves power or by applying it because it is useful); that power and knowledge directly imply one another; that there is no power relation without the correlative constitution of a field of knowledge, nor any knowledge that does not presuppose and constitute at the same time power relations.

(Foucault 1977: 27)

One always has to start with some assumptions, with a basis beyond which one does not go in tracing back causes and connections. The theoretical framework of this book begins with power/knowledge; with the idea, originating in the work of Foucault, that these two concepts are so intertwined that there can be no knowledge without power, no power without knowledge. This goes alongside a belief that the gendered nature of both power and knowledge is fundamental to our understanding of the relationship between power, knowledge and gender. Furthermore, although education presents itself as being about the communication and transfer of (disembodied) knowledge, it is at the same time about (embodied) gendered relations of power and issues in the transfer of that power. What this involves, if and how that transfer comes about, and how it is resisted, are therefore issues to be addressed if we are to gain an understanding of the relationship between power and knowledge as they operate in schools and other educational institutions (Marshall 1990). Addressing these issues is also essential for an understanding of how the education system is used to support power relations within the wider society, both through differentiations in the kinds of knowledge offered to different cohorts of students, and, in elite schools, through the initiation of a particular group of children into a discourse that privileges ruling-class values and mores.

All social arenas are threaded through with multiple power relations, and educational institutions are no exception. These power relations are composed of and organized by the relationships between individuals and social groups on the basis of many interweaving factors: age, race, gender, social position, etc. In this context, the relationship between the participants in the social structures of education and the knowledge that is the commodity and currency of schooling are also important. Some students, for example, are not given access to some forms of curriculum, and some teachers are not permitted to teach some student groups or some curriculum areas; different groups and forms of knowledge are protected from cross-contamination. Although in some cases this cultural quarantine is overt, in others the segregation between individuals and groups is embedded in the structure of institutions, and is more difficult to perceive and hence to resist.

My aim in this book is to show how the gendered power/knowledge relation operates in the formation of curriculum structures. I shall address this issue mainly by looking in detail at a number of recent attempts to change both the content and processes of schooling, focusing on the impact on and implications for power/knowledge relations in this context. Examination of such issues under conditions of change is particularly productive, as alterations and challenges to the status quo, by their very nature, make what is usually taken for granted present to consciousness (Paechter 1995b). Furthermore, the stresses caused by disequilibrium can exaggerate the reactions of actors in a situation, making more manifest existing underlying tensions (Datnow 1998).

Many proposed curriculum changes have included attempts to alter prevailing power/knowledge relations, and have often failed due to insufficient understanding of the complexity of such relations and to the gender-blindness of those leading the innovation (Datnow 1998). Examples include the UK government's assault, in the early 1990s, on the low status of D&T education, through changes in the content and composition of the subject and its position in the core of the new National Curriculum. This largely failed because of a lack of understanding of the investment of teachers, both within and outside the D&T subjects, in the prevailing power/knowledge relations (see Chapter 5). Attempts, at the beginning of the twentieth century, to establish domestic science as an alternative, 'female' science, were also doomed to fail because the power/knowledge relations supported other, more 'masculine' forms of science education in a position of seniority, ensuring that girls aiming at high level qualifications would always have to study these forms (Manthorpe 1986). The introduction, in the late 1980s, of a significant coursework element into the General Certificate of Secondary Education (GCSE)[1] examination in England and Wales, although having some success in challenging a situation in which boys tended to outperform girls in examinations, came under fire precisely because this effect challenged public and political assumptions about the relative ability of young men and women (Weiner 1993; Younger and Warrington 1996).

Before we come to look at the specifics of the role of gendered power/knowledge relations in the negotiation of curriculum forms in schools, a clearer theoretical framework is needed. In the remainder of this chapter I am going to outline my understanding of the nature of the relationships between gender, power and knowledge, and suggest how this relates to the negotiation of curriculum. In the rest of the book I will show how this is manifested in practice.

Gender, power and knowledge

The nature of power

> A society without power relations can only be an abstraction. Which, it be said in passing, makes all the more necessary the analysis of power relations in a given society, their historical formation, the source of their strength or fragility, the conditions which are necessary to transform some or abolish others. For to say that there cannot be a society without power relations is not to say either that those which are established are necessary, or, in any case, that power constitutes a fatality at the heart of societies, such that it cannot be undermined.
>
> (Foucault 1982: 222)

Central to Foucault's conception of the relationship between power and knowledge is the idea that power is to be found throughout society in a complex network of micro-powers, with corresponding micro-resistances. Power, in this formulation, becomes distributed, built into the minutiae of human relations, the assumptions of our discourses, the development of our bodies and the fabric of our buildings. This view of power undermines traditional liberal views of power relations and of the relationship between knowledge and power (Blacker 1998; Ingólfur Ásegir Jóhannesson 1998). First, rather than being located in a few individuals and institutions, power is seen as existing everywhere, as inhering in the multiple and complex relations between all individuals, groups, institutions and even spaces in a given society. Power, in this conception, 'means relations, a more-or-less organised, hierarchical, co-ordinated cluster of relations' (Foucault 1980: 198).

In suggesting that there can be no society without power relations, Foucault is explicitly claiming that the liberal, juridical view of power is inadequate. Instead of seeing power as emanating from a conception of state power derived from that of the sovereign, he offers an alternative. In this, power does not derive from a single source, but instead is everywhere, constituted by a complex network of relations between people and institutions:

> the classical liberal normative contrast between legitimate and illegitimate power is not adequate to the nature of modern power. The liberal framework understands power as emanating from the sovereign and imposing itself upon the subjects. It tries to define a power-free zone of rights, the penetration of which is illegitimate.
>
> (Fraser 1989: 26)

Such a 'power-free zone of rights' may be found, for example, in Rawls' (1972) 'original position', in which individuals are invited to debate the rules by which a society is to be governed, from behind a 'veil of ignorance' concerning their position within that society. It sets up a moral and judicial framework in which moral questions become 'like a math problem with humans' (Gilligan 1982: 26) and in which actual human relations are not seen to play a role. Such a framework has been challenged by Gilligan and her collaborators (Gilligan 1982; Gilligan and Attanucci 1988), working in the field of moral development, and by the philosophical writing of Hekman (1995), who develops Gilligan's psychological work to suggest alternative approaches to moral theory. These writers suggest that we are able to use a variety of different moral voices, and that the dominance of judicially based paradigms is gender related. Males have been found to use justice based judgements more readily than females, who tend to prefer to think in terms of the effects of their actions on others to whom they are connected. This 'caring perspective' (Gilligan 1982) has only recently been worked through philosophically, and its historically low and unformulated status is an important example of the way the gendering of power/knowledge relations relates to the androcentric nature of Western thought.

Second, if there is no society without power relations, there is also no knowledge without them either, which again has implications for the traditional liberal view of the power/knowledge relationship. Concomitant to the idea of a power-free zone of rights, the liberal view of knowledge also takes for granted that it is possible to have knowledge (for example that of pure mathematics) that is independent of power configurations. As we shall see later, such knowledges are not only imbued with power relations, but also deeply gendered.

Foucault's view of power has a number of implications both for analyses of power and for strategies of resistance (Sheridan 1980; Blacker 1998; Gore 1998; Ingólfur Ásegir Jóhannesson 1998). In the first place, because power is not a unified force, a separate entity, it cannot be held or accumulated. 'Power is not something that is acquired, seized or shared, something that one holds on to or allows to slip away; power is exercised from innumerable points, in the interplay of nonegalitarian and mobile relations' (Foucault 1978: 94). Power is not something that is held solely by the state or by a dominant social group; it is something that is exercised (although not equally) by all. Power is conceived of as coming from below; it is exercised in micro-situations, in relations between individuals. Foucault sees power as beginning in small interactions and spreading to the wider social arena, rather than the other way round. This in turn has implications for our approach to the analysis of power, which has to start from the small and local and work outwards to the global, rather than in the reverse direction: Foucault talks about 'an *ascending* analysis of power' (1980: 99). Such a conception of power affects both how we analyse its operation and how we think of resistance. Resistance is within, rather than opposed to power, and powerful in itself. Seeing power as a local, multiple networked phenomenon highlights the importance of micro-studies, of the detailed examination of the power relations between small groups of individuals. At the same time it makes clear that even small resistances are important: 'each localized struggle induces effects on the whole network' (Sheridan 1980: 139). Furthermore, by focusing on the *exercise* of power, Foucault is laying stress on the mechanisms through which this exercise takes place, rather than on who, in particular, is wielding power at any one time. What we have to consider, he argues, is the process, not who is benefiting from it at any one moment.

> Of course we have to show who those in charge are . . . But this is not the important issue, for we know perfectly well that even if we reach the point of designating exactly all those people, all those 'decision-makers,' we will still not really know why and how the decision was made, how it came to be accepted by everybody, and how it is that it hurts a particular category of person, etc.
>
> (Foucault 1988: 103–4)

This emphasis on processes allows us to see that power can be inherent in structural mechanisms to the extent that it does not matter who operates them. For example, the design of Bentham's Panopticon, a prison constructed in such a way that its inmates are kept under constant, unobserved surveillance, assures the application of power independently of who is operating the mechanism. Because the central observation tower is in darkness, while the cells on the perimeter are illuminated, the prisoners cannot tell when they are being watched. Since their freedom depends on them being seen to have reformed, they therefore have continually to police their own behaviour. The power relations are created by the way the Panoptic space is arranged, irrespective of the persons involved:

> It is an important mechanism, for it automatizes and disindividualises power. Power has its principle not so much in a person as in a certain concerted distribution of bodies, surfaces, lights, gazes; in an arrangement whose internal mechanisms produce the relation in which individuals are caught up ... There is a machinery that assures dissymmetry, disequilibrium, difference. Consequently, it does not matter who exercises power. Any individual, taken almost at random, can operate the machine.
>
> (Foucault 1977: 202)

In the Panopticon, the power relations inhere and are enacted in and through the literal space of the building and the symbolic space of the prison. This is also the case in schools, where power relations are deeply bound up with the disciplining of students' bodies (Corrigan 1988; Gore 1998). In the early nineteenth century, school architecture followed an explicitly Panoptic pattern. Under the monitorial systems devised by Bell and Lancaster, large groups of children, subdivided into smaller clusters instructed by monitors, were observed and controlled by a single teacher (Hamilton 1989). Children, as individuals and in groups, moved within the instructional space according to fixed hierarchies, and the practice of 'place-capturing', whereby one's position in class was literally marked by one's physical location in the schoolroom, spatialized pupil and teacher hierarchies while translating pupil learning directly into spatial terms. Later, this was combined with the introduction of 'simultaneous teaching' of a class of children selected for their equal attainment, spatializing achievement still further as classes were taught in separate rooms. Within these separate classrooms, fixed, forward-facing desks allowed the teacher overtly to control pupils through constant surveillance. This move, from the single schoolroom to separate, smaller classrooms, formed the class group into a more cohesive whole, and enhanced the status and privacy of the individual teacher; while students became more controlled and homogeneous, and teachers became more individualized and independent. The playground, also invented during the same period, allowed for a more covert and thus more fully Panoptic surveillance (from the master's window) of supposedly free play (Markus 1996).

The fixed-desk, formal classroom went almost unchallenged in state schooling for 150 years. It was only in the 1960s that alternative school designs were proposed, in the context of attempts to change primary school pedagogy (Palmer 1971). The reaction against whole-class teaching that took place during this period brought with it a reaction against more formal uses of school space. Walkerdine (1984), for example, quotes two representations of classrooms from the Nuffield Mathematics project: one of a 'conventional junior classroom' showing desks in rows with the teacher at the front, and another of a classroom 'rearranged to make better provision for active learning' (1984: 156–7). In the latter classroom the desks have been replaced by tables, different areas of the room are available for different activities and the space is, on the face of it, more flexible. That flexibility does not, however, include the possibility of whole-class teaching without significant rearrangement, and the pupils have lost the one piece of personal space they could previously lay claim to; their own desk. The importance of personal desks to children, who are otherwise without ownership of classroom space, is highlighted by Nespor:

> Desks were one of the few spaces kids could claim as their own within the classroom, although the claim was not absolute: One of the worst humiliations a teacher could inflict was to force a kid to empty his or her desk. At Thurber, the desks were moveable tables with metal legs, plastic tops, and little cubbyholes underneath, which kids filled with enormous amounts of clutter.
>
> (1997: 132)

Moreover, with the move to less formal seating arrangements, the teacher's surveillance of the classroom has changed from being overt (sitting at the front and clearly seen by all) to being, by comparison, covert, as she or he moves around the room from one group to another. This more covert observation represents an increase in its Panoptic nature, as students, no longer always able to perceive the direction of the teacher's gaze, have (as in the nineteenth-century playground) to be continually aware of its possibility and therefore to keep a check on their actions at all times. School science laboratories still present a sort of compromise between these two spatial arrangements. Although the layout of the furniture is more-or-less fixed and formal (it is often possible to re-arrange the benches, but seldom done in practice), and there may be a raised demonstration/surveillance bench at the front, the teacher moves from group to group, while observing the whole.

This way of looking at power, as residing in relations, including spatial relations, rather than in persons or institutions, brings with it a complementary view of resistance, which is seen by Foucault as being within power. Power and resistance become mutually dependent:

> Their existence depends on a multiplicity of points of resistance: these play the role of adversary, target, support, or handle in power relations. These points of resistance are present everywhere in the power network. Hence there is no single locus of great Refusal, no soul or revolt, source of all rebellions, or pure law of the revolutionary. Instead there is a plurality of resistances, each of them a special case.
>
> (Foucault 1978: 95–6)

Resistance does not depend, therefore, principally on the existence and action of large revolutionary movements, and it is not necessary, or even possible, to aim at the overthrow of a whole power/knowledge matrix at once (Sheridan 1980; Blacker 1998; Ingólfur Ásegir Jóhannesson 1998). Resistance can and does take place in micro-situations; there are innumerable, local points at which power chains can be broken. As there are 'local centres' of power/knowledge (Foucault 1978: 98), so there can be local centres of resistance to the way that power/knowledge is exercised in a particular case. This opens up the possibility not only of considering in detail the ways in which power/knowledge relations are exercised in classrooms and staffrooms, but also of working out resistances to these. By rejecting a unified conception of the school as a repressive state institution (Bowles and Gintis 1976; Harris 1979) we have a way of resisting some of its more oppressive features without waiting for widespread social revolution (Whitty 1985). It remains open to teachers and groups of teachers to work with their students to alter the operation of the power/knowledge matrix within their own situations.

Power/knowledge

Although I take as given the mutual implication of knowledge and power, this should not be seen as simple or straightforward. It is not enough to say that power is knowledge and knowledge is power and leave it at that (Hoskin 1990). In fact Foucault himself takes too simplistic a view when he talks of abandoning a tradition in which 'knowledge can exist only where the power relations are suspended' (1997: 27). This tradition has dominated Western thought at least since the Enlightenment, and it is also deeply embedded in our 'thinking-as-usual' (Schutz 1964), a fundamental part of the language of knowledge and of truth-claims (Hekman 1995). Walkerdine (1988) notes that in the case of the paradigmatic form of decontextualized knowledge, that of pure mathematics, it is precisely that decontextualization that renders the 'possessor' of such knowledge so powerful. Reason is seen as lying outside of power relations and thus as having access to ultimate and unassailable truths, and it is this that confers power on those who are seen to have 'mastered' it. Although on one level it is an illusion that absolute, decontextualized knowledge will bring with it absolute and impartial power and control, this illusion in itself confers power. While power emanating solely from reason remains a chimera, the discourse surrounding it still confers on those that are seen as possessing knowledge a real (in the sense of exercisable) power that comes from its possession, rather than from the knowledge directly. Walkerdine refers to this belief in the power of reason as 'reason's dream', describing it as a:

> fantasy of a discourse and practice in which the world becomes what is wanted: regular, ordered, controllable. The imposition of this discourse

onto the world therefore renders to the mathematician, scientist, psychologist, linguist or whatever an incredibly powerful position. For s/he produces statements which are taken to be true. The result of a fantasy is lived as a fact.

(1988: 188)

This view of the power of mathematical discourse is echoed by that of Chalmers with regard to science: 'The naming of some claim or line of reasoning or piece of research "scientific" is done in a way that is intended to imply some kind of merit or special kind of reliability' (1982: xv).

Walkerdine points out that although this power to control the world is in itself illusory, the discourse of the power of reason results in a situation in which those claiming such knowledge are given the power anyway. While the belief that pure, decontextualized knowledge brings power over an ultimately comprehensible universe is itself a fantasy, we nevertheless use it explicitly to open up routes to power within the wider society. Because we believe that those who have attained the 'mastery of reason' that comes with 'real understanding' (Walkerdine 1988) already possess knowledge related power, we allow them to develop this further, by giving them, for example, preferential access to higher level certification. Walden and Walkerdine document how girls in one school were directed towards lower level mathematics examinations, on the grounds that the girls' performance arose from 'rote-learning' rather than from 'real understanding', even though their attainment was equal to or better than that of boys who were given the opportunity to obtain higher status qualifications (Walden and Walkerdine 1985). Such practices, if repeated nationally, can have the effect of restricting girls' access to certain areas of higher level study, as has been noted by Gipps and Murphy, again with regard to mathematics:

there is evidence that some 1 percent of students (about 5000) who were entered for the intermediate grade tier [at GCSE] could have achieved a higher grade and that this affects more girls than boys. This 'misclassification' restricts their ability to continue their study of mathematics to A level.[2]

(Gipps and Murphy 1994: 224–5)

The differences in perceived power between contextualized and decontextualized knowledges is also apparent, in the UK at least, in the academic/ practical divide that lies behind the low status of traditional technology education; the ability to build and maintain working machines is considered to be of lesser value than the understanding of the scientific principles according to which such machines operate (Goodson 1992). Thus the fantasy of power and control vested in the understanding of the 'truths' of mathematics and science is translated into actual power within the wider social system. Connell *et al.* (1982) note that the emphases of what they refer to as the 'hegemonic curriculum', whose key features are 'hierarchically-organized bodies of academic knowledge appropriated in individual competition' (1982: 122), parallels, and thus reinforces, the practices of the middle-class professional and business world. At the same time, hegemonic processes operating on subject disciplines also affect the sort of knowledge that is permitted to count and that which is not. The curriculum consists of both what students have the opportunity to learn and what is forbidden them (Cherryholmes 1988; Popkewitz 1997), and it is the operation of power that governs this knowledge distribution. This involves not only the restriction of certain subjects (or aspects of subjects) to certain students, but also what is permitted to count as knowledge within a subject (Harding 1990), and the severity of the penalties for breaching these boundaries (Bernstein 1971). For example:

> It is not enough to say that science is a set of procedures by which propositions may be falsified, errors demonstrated, myths demystified, etc. Science also exercises power: it is, literally, a power that forces you to say certain things, if you are not to be disqualified not only as being wrong, but, more seriously than that, as being a charlatan.
>
> (Foucault 1988: 107)

The fantasy of the power of decontextualized knowledge also pervades relations within schools, affecting in particular the balance of 'knowledge possession' between teacher and taught. This is not to suggest that students are ignorant; it is rather that the knowledge that they have tends not to be that which is legitimated by the schooling system, largely because it is not of the form that is traditionally associated with power. Informal, everyday knowledge is not concerned with transcendent truths, but the latter are regarded as power-bearing and are thus more highly valued. Furthermore, Marshall (1990) has pointed out that a further aspect of teacher–student power/knowledge relations is the imbalance in the knowledge each has of the other. He notes that within such institutions as the prison, the hospital and the school:

> knowledge has been developed about people, and their behaviour, attitudes, and self-knowledge have been developed, refined, and used to shape individuals. These discourses and practices have not only been used to change us in various ways but are also used to legitimate such changes, as the knowledge gained is deemed to be 'true'. Foucault identifies this knowledge, developed by the exercise of power and used in turn to legitimate further exercises of power, as power-knowledge.
>
> (Marshall 1990: 15)

Although I think that Foucault's use of the term is wider than this, such a definition is useful in pointing to the way that 'pastoral power', a concept found in Foucault's later work, is used within schools and other institutions to discipline its objects in the name of working for their well-being (better health, literacy, access to jobs, etc.). For one of the main features of pastoral power is that it 'cannot be exercised without knowing the inside of people's minds, without exploring their souls, without making them reveal their innermost secrets' (Foucault 1982: 214).

The idea that pastoral power is used to justify and reinforce other power/knowledge relations is important in pointing up the way that such relations can have both positive and negative aspects. Within schools, the interaction between power and knowledge is thus not only concerned with the imbalances between teacher and taught in the amount and importance of the knowledge that they have, but it is also about the power invested in the teacher by virtue of his or her knowledge of the student, a knowledge that is further stressed as an important pedagogic, as well as a disciplinary, tool (Walkerdine 1984).

Before going on to look at how gender interacts with the power/knowledge dyad, it is worth pausing to consider the purpose of such theoretical investigations. Is it enough to outline the complexity of gendered power/knowledge relations in, for example, the education system, without taking a position on whether they are just and caring, and without looking for ways in which injustices and failures to care can be resisted? One criticism of Foucault is that he does just this (Said 1986; Hartsock 1990; Soper 1993). Fraser, for example, points to what she sees as a 'normative one-dimensionality' in Foucault's work:

> Foucault vacillates between two equally inadequate stances. On the one hand, he adopts a concept of power that permits him no condemnation of any objectionable features of modern societies. But at the same time, and on the other hand, his rhetoric betrays the conviction that modern societies are utterly without redeeming features.
>
> (1989: 33)

Fraser is certainly correct as regards Foucault's rhetoric, even if she somewhat overstates his position. For he is quite explicit in his belief that power has to be resisted; indeed this is part of his very conception of power: 'as soon as there is a power relation, there is a possibility of resistance. We can never be ensnared by power: we can always modify its grip in determinate conditions and according to a precise strategy' (Foucault 1988: 123).

It is not so immediately clear whether Fraser is also correct regarding Foucault's theoretical position. It is tempting to see in his painstaking and often seemingly dispassionate display of micro-powers a certain philosophical disengagement, a retreat into the neutrality of description (Soper 1993). On the other hand, that very 'neutrality', that refusal, for example, to start from the liberal assumption that the prison is an instrument of reform, is what allows Foucault to make so explicit his alternative reading. In discussing Foucault's view that the rhetoric of the reforming prison bears no relation to its carceral manifestation, Patton suggests that

> It is at this point, with the role of the discourse of prison-reform in the carceral device, that the immediate political stakes of Foucault's genealogy become apparent. For genealogy is not content to be an academic tool; it is supposed to be also a weapon against the power it describes, a discourse which takes the side of its victims and works to unmask the techniques and operations of power in all their savagery and inhumanity. Certainly it is scholarly: 'Genealogy is grey, meticulous and patiently documentary'. It 'demands relentless erudition'. Yet it is a weapon precisely because of this patience. The latter is a condition of its producing truth-effects subversive to the social economy of truth.
>
> (1979: 143)

Foucault's dispassionate and detailed illustrations of his thesis thus themselves act to arouse passion and an outcry against the practices he describes (Smart 1986). He was himself active in the prisoners' rights movement (Sheridan 1980), and it is clear that he believes that moral judgements should be made (Blacker 1998). But what Fraser is arguing is that he does this from within a theory that asserts that such judgements are impossible. She suggests that because Foucault regards power as inescapable, he has to see it as normatively neutral, and cannot distinguish between power that should, and power that should not, be resisted. Hartsock characterizes Foucault as a 'coloniser who refuses' (1990: 164), resisting the ideology of a culture while continuing to live within and prosper from its discourses. As a member of the ruling class, she argues, he is unable to see, let alone condemn, the power relations within society, and that as a result, power 'disappears' in his work.

Hekman, on the other hand, argues that such a reading of Foucault ignores his rejection of the Cartesian unitary and unchanging rational subject. She argues that, by seeing human subjects as constantly in the process of reinventing ourselves, Foucault allows the possibility of resistance through the construction of alternative discourses:

> The resistant subject is one that refuses to be scripted by the dominant discourse and turns instead to subjugated knowledges to fashion alternative discourses of subjectivity. Foucault's understanding of the resistant subject is informed by his concept of 'local resistance'. Against those who claim that his approach entails political quiescence, Foucault argues that it is not necessary to appeal to universal concepts of truth and knowledge in order to ground political action.
>
> (Hekman 1995: 84)

Furthermore, Blacker (1998) points out that what Foucault is arguing is not that the ideals associated with humanism are inherently contradictory, but that genealogy reveals that the deeds of humanism belie its words; the grand ideals of humanism are accompanied by inhuman realities.

Critiques of Foucault that require either that he somehow detach himself from his position as a white male intellectual, or that he produce definitive moral judgements about the practices he exposes, seem to me to stem from a position that has itself been influenced by the seductive belief in the power of reason, in a belief that if we can expose the 'truths' about oppression this will empower us to become free from it (McNeil 1993). Fraser, for example, seems to suggest that it would be possible to make objectively neutral (and therefore 'correct') judgements about the acceptability or otherwise of particular uses of power. But this, again, is to assume that there is some knowledge that is independent of power, and it is this, Foucault says, that is impossible. Although it remains possible for us to make moral judgements and to act accordingly, we cannot expect such judgements to carry the force of universal truths. Our ethical standpoints will themselves be constituted by the power relations in which we ourselves are caught up, which is why, for example, we are so easily convinced by the liberal rhetoric of prison reform (Foucault 1977; Patton 1979). What Fraser seems to be doing is accusing Foucault of inconsistency while at the same time retaining a view of the objective 'provability' of moral judgements that is outside Foucault's conception of knowledge and power. This is not to say that Foucault is refusing to make moral judgements, or act upon them (Hekman 1990); it is rather to assert that although we may believe passionately that something is right or wrong, we can have no conception of what this might mean that can stand outside the power/knowledge relations within which our experience is constituted and our subjectivity constructed. Furthermore, Foucault does seem to provide the most that is possible, in the form of an implied rule of thumb: as power is generally perceived as repressive, and as it can and clearly has been used to oppress, we should give our energies to finding the points of resistance, and thus enable ourselves to experience and take hold of the positive aspects of power. This is my aim in examining gender/power/knowledge as it is manifested in education and schooling.

Power/knowledge and gender

It has often been argued that Foucault ignores gender in his analysis of power, and more specifically, that his analysis of power is androcentric (Morris 1979; Hartsock 1990; Soper 1993). My own view is that this is an incorrect reading of his ideas, although it is only in his later work that he seems to acknowledge that the power/knowledge relation has a gender dimension (Foucault 1978, 1984). Foucault's approach to power, however, is a fertile starting-point for the examination of the connections between power, knowledge and gender. His genealogical unpicking of power relations at the micro level not only allows us to make sense of the injunction to make the personal political but also to undercut power/knowledge structures by considering both their positive and their negative aspects.

One area in which this is important is in looking at the pleasurable side of what Foucault terms our 'will to knowledge' (Foucault 1978), and Walkerdine (1988) refers to as 'Reason's dream'; the pleasure that comes from the illusory power of pure reason. While liberal theories of power have regarded it simply as repressive, Foucault points out not only that power is pleasurable, but also that this pleasure is an important factor in the successful operation of power relations; we are held in power networks in part precisely because of this positive aspect:

> power would be a fragile thing, if its only function were to repress, if it worked only through the mode of censorship, exclusion, blockage and repression, in the manner of a great Superego, exercising itself only in a negative way. If, on the contrary, power is strong this is because, as we are beginning to realise, it produces effects at the level of desire – and also at the level of knowledge.
>
> (Foucault 1980: 59)

Power is not simply repressive, but is bound up with our desire, the desire to know and to understand: 'power is pleasurable. It is the power of the triumph of reason over emotion, the fictional power over the practices of everyday life' (Walkerdine 1988: 186). Consequently, in considering the relationship between power and knowledge, we cannot conceive of power as simply a great negative, only to be resisted, but must also see it as emancipatory, as producing pleasure and a sense of mastery, which, even if based on an illusion, allows us a glimpse of freedom. And it is this positive aspect to power which goes some way towards explaining our 'will to knowledge' (Foucault 1978), our desire to understand, and our attempts to pass this knowledge on to succeeding generations, even as such attempts are constantly frustrated by power's negative aspects.

At the same time, however, this pleasure, as well as the power it accompanies, is gendered, and often, especially for women, comes at a price. Although what is seen as 'pure' knowledge, worth knowing for its own sake, has varied over time, whatever has this label has generally been given a masculine[3] marker and concomitant higher status. Currently the paradigms of knowledge particularly associated with 'the fantasy of possession of total power and control' (Walkerdine 1988: 207) are those of pure mathematics, and, to a lesser degree, science.[4] Such decontexualized knowledges have been constructed to exclude women (and, until relatively recently, working-class men (Goodson 1992)) in a number of ways. In the early twentieth century, for example, girls spent less time on mathematics and science than did boys, making their entry into the higher reaches of these subjects extremely difficult. At the same time, this exclusion has meant that the subjects themselves have had their stereotypically masculine characteristics reinforced; non-objectivist science, for example, has not made much headway in the academy (Harding 1990). This dominance of masculine-labelled forms of thought is not confined to these areas. As indicated above, for example, the dominant paradigm of moral reasoning, derived from Kant and Rawls, is a rationalist one that tries to operate independently of the particularities of human relationships. This paradigm has been used by Kohlberg to set up a developmental progression from bounded and particular to abstract and generalizable moral decisions. Women and non-white or non-Western males, however, have been found to score only at the lower and intermediate levels of this sequence. Gilligan (1982) has challenged this model on empirical grounds, arguing that any theory of moral development that excludes females from the higher levels must be built on an androcentric model of ethical thought (Hekman 1995). She produces evidence to suggest that in practice women tend to favour alternative models when making moral decisions although both genders, when prompted, are able to use a variety of 'moral voices' (Gilligan 1982; Gilligan and Attanucci 1988).

Because powerful forms of knowledge are those that are decontextualized, in order to have access to the pleasure associated with them both women and men have to relinquish the personalized, contextual aspect of the self. The paradigm of decontextualized knowledge requires the suspension of subjectivity and a denial of the body. Both of these are problematic for females. First, emphasis on human interconnectedness and the contingencies of human relationships makes women and girls take more account of context in a variety of situations (Gilligan 1982; Gilligan and Attanucci 1988; Murphy 1990; Gipps and Murphy 1994; Murphy and Elwood 1997). Second, femininity is produced in Western society as fundamentally embodied, so that to ignore or deny the body is to disregard a fundamental aspect of the self.[5] At the same time, those disciplines in which the power–pleasure relationship is particularly strong are constructed as masculine against a femininity that is constructed as unable to access them. Thus, for women and girls to become involved with such disciplines, to engage with them successfully, requires a denial of femininity, of part of one's (albeit socially constructed) identity. This, in turn, undercuts one's sense of personal power. Furthermore, Brown and Gilligan (1993) suggest that adolescent girls experience a period of crisis that stems from conflicts between speaking out about their knowledge of themselves and others (and thus demonstrating their pastoral power) and preserving the quality of their relationships. Here the pleasurable aspect of power, the sense of connection through intimate knowledge of oneself and others, is undercut by the realization that to speak out about what one knows goes against accepted norms for female behaviour and threatens the girls' relationships with those close to them. If human connectedness is, as Gilligan (1982; Gilligan and Attanucci 1988) suggests, more central to female thinking than to that of males, this is an important, and gendered, limitation on women's ability to use pastoral power/knowledge.

Gender, power/knowledge and curriculum

We have seen, then, that knowledge is gendered in a number of ways. Furthermore, because powerful knowledges are generally gendered masculine, power/knowledge is gendered in its turn. What bearing does this have on the school curriculum?

What ends up as part of the curriculum arises from gendered power/knowledge relations. It is the product of negotiation, some of which itself has a gender dimension (Paechter and Head 1995). Decisions about both what is taught and what is not (Cherryholmes 1988) are taken within gendered power/knowledge relations; they reflect the levels and types of power accorded to different forms of knowledge and different actors in the decision-making process. Monaghan and Saul (1987) note, for example, that in the USA the continued predominance of the teaching of reading over the teaching of writing is partly due to social control issues in settler times. At this period, reading, especially of the Bible, was seen as an important way of transmitting social mores to young children. Writing, on the other hand, was not only regarded as less socially necessary, but also brought with it the freedom to write for and of oneself; it was accordingly played down.

What is taught, and how, can also be governed more directly by power/knowledge relations. In the UK, the founders of the nineteenth-century Mechanics Institutes saw scientific education as a means to the control of dissent among skilled (male) artisans. The institutes provided a limited scientific curriculum in which all conflicts and questions were removed and the provisional nature of scientific knowledge was played down or excluded. The emphasis was on practical demonstrations of the wonders of science, the desired result being moral improvement and a law-abiding artisan class, their time spent reading scientific literature rather than radical tracts. Furthermore, it was hoped that by giving skilled artisans further schooling opportunities this would distance them further from the labouring classes and make them less likely to join with the latter in social revolution (Shapin and Barnes 1977). By permitting a potentially rebellious group some sense of power acquired through knowledge, the possibility of a bid for greater power, through rebellion, was avoided.

As well as being governed by power/knowledge relations related to class and gender in wider society, the curriculum is also gendered as a result of its application to teachers and students as embodied beings, and bodies are overtly gendered. Some aspects of the curriculum (physical education most especially, of course) apply directly to the body, and it is noteworthy that these can be the most gendered (Fletcher 1984; Bryson 1987; Sherlock 1987; Scraton 1993; Talbot 1993; Paechter and Head 1996a). However, this is not the only way in which bodies are disciplined by the school curriculum (Corrigan 1988; Nespor 1997). In my own study of interdisciplinary initiatives in secondary schools (see Chapter 7), students repeatedly characterized the differences between subjects in terms of physical freedom or constraint; subjects were marked as those in which one could talk or move around or, conversely, in which one had to stay still at one's desk. In this way, the (subject) discipline disciplines the embodied subject; the gendered nature of the latter has its effect upon the former.

Finally, those areas of knowledge perceived to be more powerful are able to augment their power through greater access to curriculum time and institutional space. Pre-eminent among these are mathematics, science and information technology, although (in English-speaking countries) English can command time (but not so easily space), partly due to its legacy of equipping the nation's youth with the skills to read improving literature (Monaghan and Saul 1987). Science, pre-eminently, is able to make powerful bids for both time and space; for example, when the English and Welsh National Curriculum was first introduced in 1989 most 14–16-year-olds were expected to take 'double science', meaning that they would have to cover twice as much ground as they would in subjects like geography or modern foreign languages. The amount of curriculum time and the number of teachers required combined with the use of specialist rooms mean that science departments, which are often male-dominated, take up large areas of school space and can resemble semi-independent fiefdoms, with the staff remaining in the preparatory rooms during breaks rather than mingling with their colleagues in the common staffroom, again emphasizing the 'separateness' of this powerful domain.

Gender, power, knowledge and curriculum are therefore intimately interrelated. Gendered access to positions of power arises, through the curriculum offered or denied to particular groups, from differential access to knowledges which are themselves marked differentially with relation to power. At the same time, and partly because of this, some forms of knowledge are quite clearly labelled by gender, and, of these, those signified as masculine are usually the more powerful. Women and girls have traditionally been excluded from such forms, initially simply through curriculum exclusion, and, more recently, by their being marked in ways that adolescents in particular find difficult to reconcile with their sense of self. Boys are also excluded from some areas of knowledge in this way, but the domains to which they have less access also confer less power, so they do not lose so much, at least in this respect. Meanwhile, curriculum decisions, taken as a result of micropolitical struggles that are themselves located in gendered power/knowledge networks, perpetuate an inequality that stretches right through schooling and from teacher to student. It is this relationship, between gender/power/knowledge and the processes and content of the school curriculum, that I explore in the rest of this book.

Notes

1 The main school-leaving examination, usually taken at age 16+.
2 A level is the most prestigious university entrance level examination in England and Wales.
3 By 'masculine' I mean commonly and stereotypically associated with the male gender. I do not wish to imply any essentialism in my use of the term or of its conventional opposite, 'feminine'.
4 This has not always been the case. In the nineteenth century in the UK classics dominated the curriculum for men; women were expected to study science, then of lower status (Delamont 1994).
5 I am not suggesting here that women and girls are 'naturally' like this, or that embodiment and giving emphasis to human interconnectedness are essential attributes of those gendered female. Rather, I would argue that the ways in which females are constructed by the discourses of Western society lead them to think and act in these ways (Paechter 1998a).

three

GENDER, POWER AND SCHOOL SUBJECTS

It was quite common in the nineteenth century to exclude women from higher education and the professions on the grounds that they were swayed by their emotions and not, therefore, invested with the capacity to make rational judgments. It is by arguments like this that the sexed body (the seat of 'nature') becomes the site for the production and explanation of mind. Since the very differentiation between men's and women's bodies is central to this approach, there is no way reason can ever be gender-neutral.

(Walkerdine 1990: 67–8)

If we accept that the power/knowledge relation is gendered, then examining the ways in which it is used to construct a gendered school curriculum should help us to understand power/knowledge effects in other areas. Conversely, by looking more closely at the gendered operation of power/knowledge, we may be able to see how the school curriculum has become gendered and what we can do about this. In this chapter I am going to look broadly at the way power/knowledge relations are illuminated and exemplified in the gendering of school subjects. In the next section of the book I then consider in more detail how change has affected the power/knowledge relations involved in a number of marginal areas.

When curriculum changes take place, these highlight a number of taken-for-granted ideas about subject status. For example, in the late 1980s and early 1990s the UK government attempted to raise the status of D&T, by making it compulsory throughout 5–16 schooling (see Chapter 5). The decision to elevate the position of what were very marginal areas highlighted not only their marginality but the power/knowledge relations that underpinned them; these also, ultimately, led to the failure of the project. Examples such as this also show how the processes of change, because they involve a rethinking of what one does, if not what one believes, tend to uncover the assumptions that underlie our 'normal' behaviour. Because schools are social systems, with interlinked and interdependent parts, changing one aspect may have illuminating or devastating effects on other areas. We may find that carrying on as before in one aspect of school life is no longer possible because of changes somewhere else. Kenway *et al.* (1998), for example, found that supporting girls by using single-sex classes for some subjects allowed the development of more macho cultures in the boys' groups, which acted counter to the intention to reduce sexist practices in school. In my own research (Paechter 1995b), teachers at Lacemakers School[1] who wanted to avoid curriculum change found their choices about which groups they wanted to teach, and how, severely restricted as innovation spread throughout the school; rapid curriculum change highlighted the partial illusion of teacher autonomy.

Reason, power and subject status

One way we can look at power/knowledge relations in situations of change is to examine what stays the same. The ability to adapt to a changing environment without losing one's core features is itself an indicator of high status; dominant individuals and subject areas have the power to arrange things so that what is fundamental to them remains relatively unaffected. Goodson *et al.* (1997), for example, note that the key aspect of the curriculum of elite American private schools is not its content but its form; these schools have been able to introduce computers, the arts and international perspectives to their elite classical curriculum without compromising their emphasis on intellectual and abstract knowledge. Goodson *et al.* point out that:

> In effect, one can introduce innovations into the classical curriculum that appear technical, or even egalitarian, without in any way diffusing the super elaborated code in its abstractness and imperial suppositions. The apparent blurring of the classical curriculum by the introduction of innovation only serves to emphasize that the class relations inherent in differentiated curriculum forms may take a variety of disguises, but the reality is as unalterable as class relations.
>
> (1997: 181)

Successful resistance to change on the part of the relatively powerful may also take place at the micro level. In the 1970s and 1980s in the UK, for example, mathematics departments often continued to teach in homogeneous ability groups in the face of a general move to mixed ability groups. At one school I worked in the mathematicians also managed to retain their departmental worktable when the staffroom was otherwise reorganized into communal areas for work and relaxation.

Similarly, when considering the introduction of the English and Welsh National Curriculum, it is useful to consider what subjects were expected to change radically and which were permitted to remain more or less the same. While the low status areas of home economics (HE) and craft, design and technology (CDT) were expected to radically reformulate themselves into the new subject of D&T, mathematics, science and English teachers found the core of their curriculum largely untouched, even through successive revisions. Where there were some aspects of these subjects, such as using and applying mathematics, which teachers found hard to deal with, the requirements were gradually watered down within a few years to leave relatively minor modifications of the status quo. Furthermore, teachers of these subjects also felt powerful enough to be fairly creative with the statutory Orders[2]. Bowe *et al.* (1992), for example, note that, as departments got to grips with the National Curriculum:

> There is a process of developing a collective reading of the Programmes of Study and the Attainment Targets; making sense by making meaning . . . gaps in the text were identified, and the National Curriculum choices of what was crucial material was set against the collective wisdom and history of the department. The National Curriculum version of what is mathematics was not simply taken over. What this department saw as 'basic' was retained, anything seen as 'redundant' removed.
>
> (1992: 94)

The most radical departure affecting any of the 'big three' subjects was the introduction of a choice between single or double award science for GCSE; since many schools then made the double subject compulsory for all, this had the overall effect of extending science provision and therefore the power of the subject area. Science departments who were uncomfortable with the accompanying move to balanced science could and did find ways of continuing to teach separate science subjects, sometimes with the support of school managements (Bowe *et al.* 1992).

All three of these subjects also remained compulsory as the National Curriculum was revised over the years. Other areas, such as history and geography, were increasingly marginalized as curriculum time became squeezed. For English and mathematics, this pre-eminence has been further underlined in primary schools by the introduction of literacy and numeracy hours, daily structured lessons in each subject for all primary students. Given the pressures on the school day, the setting aside of such a proportion of time for these areas puts a concomitant squeeze on other aspects of the primary curriculum. The *Times Educational Supplement* (Cassidy 1999), for example, reported as its main story on 25 June 1999 that, since the introduction of the literacy hour, resources for primary science, in terms of time, money and in-service training, had been cut to such an extent that Britain's international standing in this area might be in jeopardy. The importance of science remained high enough, however, for these losses to be countered by strategies such as using scientific texts, vocabulary or diagrams as part of literacy hour activities.

At the other end of the age range, and particularly in the two years after the completion of compulsory schooling, we can see clear differences between high and low status curriculum forms in terms of the degree of change to which they have been subjected. Vocational education, in the last 20 years of the twentieth century, was subjected to numerous revisions and reshapings. Meanwhile, the academic 'gold standard' of A level[3] examinations remained untouched, despite successive reports from government and other bodies recommending change.

The case of A level examinations is a particularly interesting example of the way gendered power/knowledge relations are played out in the school setting. In the last decade of the twentieth century, England and Wales saw an increasing gender differential in success in GCSE examinations. Overall, girls outperform boys, although this is not the case in all areas, and the degree to which this happens also varies between subjects. For example, in 1997, while girls gained eight per cent more A*–C grades overall, this gap was increased in English to nearly 17 per cent and reduced in science to 1.2 per cent, while boys outperformed girls by the narrow margin of 0.1 per cent A*–C grades in mathematics (Elwood 1999). By A level, however, although girls still outperform boys overall (1.2 per cent more grades A–C in 1997), the gaps are much smaller than at GCSE; given their GCSE results, girls make less progress in the following two years than do boys (Elwood 1999).[4] Elwood argues that the reasons for this 'crossover' are complex but are partly due to the different styles of expression and communication expected in different subject areas at different levels. GCSE English, for example, values expressive rather than factual writing, which tends to favour girls. At A level this changes and a sparse, definite and analytical writing style is expected of students. This is seen by teachers as reflecting a more masculine writing style.

> Males and females were also acknowledged to show differences in their styles of expression and communication. This was most noticeable, not surprisingly, in English literature where it was felt that the style of expression which tended to be valued at A level was very different to that valued at GCSE and was more commonly shown by male students.

Teachers commented that males tended to write less, keep more ruth-
lessly to the point and have more confidence in their views. Females
were considered to write at length, to lack the courage to discard irrelevant material and to perform less well in A level examinations.

(Elwood 1999: 198)

This analytical, rational approach to English literature reflects the aims and
intentions of the elite curriculum of which, in England and Wales, A level is
one of the remaining mainstays. Given that this has its origins in the education of the eighteenth- and nineteenth-century gentleman (Goodson
1992), it is unsurprising that it is masculine in approach.

The education of the English gentleman, and the higher level curricula
that stem from it, are rooted in ideas from Enlightenment thought that value
reason over emotion, public over private, the mental over the physical or
manual, and, by analogy, masculinity over femininity (Gatens 1991). The
ideal of the eighteenth- and nineteenth-century rational man sees him as
transcending the needs and calls of his body, in contrast to his female counterpart who, unable to separate from her body because of her childbearing
capacity, is seen as unable to attain full, disembodied, rationality (Paechter
1998a). That this dichotomy is reflected in present-day schooling practices
can be seen directly in the differences between GCSE and A level English; the
lower level qualification, taken by the vast majority of students, puts a premium on writing about the personal and emotional, while the more elite A
level leaves this behind to concentrate on a more masculine, analytic, rea-
soned response to literature (Elwood 1999).

I am not arguing that girls and young women are unable to think or act
rationally. However, the ways in which masculinity and femininity have
been and continue to be constructed in Western thought, and in particular
as they are constructed by secondary school (and university) curricula, do
reflect this dualism between reason and emotion as paralleling that between
masculinity and femininity. Brittan (1989) suggests that masculinity and
rationality are both aspects of the construction of the autonomous (male)
self in Western society. Walkerdine and the Girls and Mathematics Unit
further argue that:

Ideas about reason and reasoning cannot be understood historically
outside considerations of gender. Since the Enlightenment, if not before,
the Cartesian concept of reason has been deeply embroiled with
attempts to control nature. Rationality was taken to be a kind of rebirth
of the thinking self, without the intervention of a woman. The rational
self was a profoundly masculine one from which woman was excluded,
her powers not only inferior but also subservient. The 'thinking' subject
was male; the female provided the biological prop both to procreation
and to servicing the possibility of 'man'. Philosophical doctrine was

transformed into the object of a science in which reason became a capacity invested within the body, and later mind, of man alone.

(1989: 27)

The rational man so valued by Enlightenment thought was taught, and expected to excel in, powerful knowledges, particularly those associated with reason, such as mathematics, a subject which could be argued to be the very epitome of disembodied rationality (Walkerdine 1988). Mathematics and the dominant forms of science have become associated with masculinity partly because they are constructed as inherently rational and partly because they are associated with men's attempts to dominate the world, with the perceived power of the mind over the natural world. Given the assumed dominance of males over females, anything so strongly associated with male activity would in any case become labelled as masculine and protected as such. Massey (1995), for example, notes how men working in high technology industries valorize reason and transcendence and construct powerful masculinities around them; they not only see themselves as powerful in their ability to manipulate ideas and highly technical machines, such as computers, but, furthermore, separate out as non-masculine, and deny, expertise in dealing with technology carrying more feminine markers, such as washing machines.

Heckman (1990) notes that since the Enlightenment reason and rationality have been defined in exclusively masculine terms. Since Descartes, she argues, the search for certainty has been grounded in the rationality of the knowing subject; the definition of humanity has become bound up with notions of reason as fundamental to subjectivity. Women, because of their supposed fundamental embodiment, are seen as incapable of full rationality; because science is defined as inherently rational it is therefore not only masculine but at least partially inaccessible to females.

All of this has two effects in the school curriculum, especially in mathematics and science, and at the more prestigious levels. First, girls are seen as less likely to succeed in these areas. Where they do so, this is seen as being as the result of hard work rather than the 'natural aptitude' ascribed to boys (Walkerdine and The Girls and Mathematics Unit 1989). Elwood notes that 'The characteristics of a good A level student tended to be described through words such as 'flair', 'unique' and 'sparkle'; qualities often ascribed to boys' (1999: 199). In subjects such as English, not of themselves marked as masculine, these sort of characteristics are only perceived as coming into play at the higher levels of education; in mathematics they feature much earlier on. Walkerdine and The Girls and Mathematics Unit (1989) note that even in primary classrooms girls who succeed at mathematics are perceived as hardworking, while boys are described as having 'flair' even when objectively less successful. They further argue that:

The idea of 'flair' and 'brilliance' became attached to a certain way of challenging the teacher's power to know. Boys who did this were accorded the accolade 'brilliant'. However, it was not a simple matter of girls behaving more like boys. Girls' challenges were thwarted. Teachers systematically extended boys' utterances and curtailed those of girls, as though girls' challenges were more threatening.

(1989: 203)

All of this has two main effects on the relationship between young women and school subjects. First, girls become socially constructed as less able to succeed at the more rationalist modes of learning, such as mathematics and science. Where they are successful, their success is seen as being in the face of difficulty rather than due to the 'natural' aptitude perceived in boys. Not surprisingly, many become discouraged and see themselves as finding mathematics and science difficult, even when their examination success suggests the opposite (Landau 1994). The perception of 'hard work' as a feminine characteristic, while supporting girls' success at GCSE, leads teachers to undervalue their performance at higher levels, even in arts and humanities, where a culture of 'effortless achievement' may be fostered by high achieving boys working in secret (Walkerdine 1990; Redman 1997). Furthermore, because girls have developed preferred ways of working and expression, particularly in subjects like English where emotional empathy is encouraged at lower levels, they need to make greater changes than do boys to adapt to the more rationalist modes required as they progress through school, while boys, disadvantaged by empathetic and discursive approaches at first, are able to make up lost ground, particularly after the end of compulsory schooling.

High status subjects in schools, then, maintain a rationalist focus, especially at the higher levels, and, as a result of this tend to be marked as masculine. The exception to this, English, while retaining its feminine image, alters its approach post-16, when the minority of boys who take it tend to be very successful (Elwood 1999). Students are compelled to study the 'big three' throughout compulsory schooling, and these subjects are seen as safe academic bets for those aspiring to university entrance. Not surprisingly, this gives them access to other aspects of power within the school world. Mathematics, English and science departments are usually given large allocations of space, time and personnel, making them dominant in other ways. They are likely to have dedicated suites of specialist rooms that other teachers do not use. This is particularly the case in science, where the provision of 'prep' rooms and sometimes technicians means that the science department can operate as a world apart, its members rarely appearing in the general staff common room. High status departments may also use their numerical strength, particularly of male teachers in a female-dominated profession, to dominate communal space. One teacher described the way that the mathematics department in her school had permanently taken over half of the staffroom desk space; note also that one of the other groups claiming this privilege come from the low status but heavily masculine-marked physical education (PE):

> MH: Now these people, the maths department, PE department and some of the English department and the languages department, all have got offices of their own but they feel an incredible need to do their work at those specific places . . . They've got their piles of books and their calendar, their timetable and their equipment, and . . .
>
> CP: Right. You mean they sort of, they claim it like desk space? This is my desk?
>
> MH: Oh yes, oh yes. Oh, very definitely. In fact this is the maths department office here.
>
> CP: Do they have a separate office?
>
> MH: They have a lot of office space throughout the school.
>
> CP: Oh right, but they actually . . .
>
> MH: But they use this one.
>
> > (Martha Hartwell, joint Head of D&T, Knype School)

Shilling and Cousins (1990) similarly note that male students are able to colonize and regulate school spaces, such as the library, for their recreational use. As well as this informal annexing of resources, higher status departments often have preferential access to a whole range of benefits, partly as a result of this status and partly as a part of its construction. As they command large specialized spaces and can claim to need extended teaching periods (for example, to conduct experiments) science departments in particular are likely to have their lessons placed first on the school timetable, with other subjects' requirements arranged to fit in. In primary schools, the dominance of the literacy and numeracy hours has also had an effect on the resourcing of the rest of the curriculum, in terms of time, money and classroom support, affecting even science provision, as reported by the *Times Educational Supplement* (TES):

> More than 10 per cent of science lesson time has already been lost because of the pressure on teachers to boost literacy, [a] survey for the Association for Science Education has found.
>
> Spending on science books and equipment has been slashed since the introduction of the literacy hour, reported one in three teachers in a survey of 525 UK primaries.
>
> > (Cassidy 1999: 1)

In secondary schools, the predominance of English, mathematics and science causes a number of mutually amplifying effects. Because these subjects are seen as important, a higher proportion of student study time is given over to them. This means that more teachers are needed, resulting in large, powerful departments, often with concomitant equipment budgets. Large departments are also perceived to require greater organization, so more promotional posts are attached to them; this means that teachers of high status subjects are more likely to hold promoted posts within the subject area, giving the subject the benefit of more experienced and expert teachers and the teachers the advantage of more clearly mapped-out careers. Teachers in lower-status areas such as physical education (PE), particularly if they are female, may, by contrast, have to move outside their departments, for example into pastoral roles, to gain promotion, and even then they remain less likely to advance to senior management posts (Sikes 1988).

This multiplying of advantage for high status areas is seen by teachers as arising directly from the status itself. Although in practice the status of a subject is at least in part a matter of micropolitics, and it is certainly possible for departments such as English, mathematics and science to be marginalized in individual schools (Ball 1987), being a member of the 'big three' gives a subject area an initial micropolitical advantage. When subjects change, this may affect their perceived status, at least for a while. One teacher, for example, hoped that the re-positioning of the D&T subjects from being distinctly marginal to having extended core status within the National Curriculum, would bring immediate and direct benefits, including access to the higher ability students previously counselled out of this area:

> I was very pleased when the document came out and I read it avidly. I read the official report, the final report, and I thought, yes, I can see a way forward here and I feel it'll really give us some status. This is important from the point of view of getting the right pupils, getting the right money, the right timetable.
>
> (Head of CDT, Stonemason's School)

In practice, most D&T departments, associated as they were with 'lower ability' students and manual rather than mental activities, were unable to shake off their previous low status (see Chapter 5); subject hierarchies are too entrenched to simply be overturned by government fiat. The only subject in recent years to have successfully intruded into the predominance of mathematics, English and science has been the relatively new area of information technology (IT). In many schools (and in the National Curriculum documentation) this has succeeded in breaking away from its origins as an annex of mathematics, business studies or, occasionally, D&T departments, to become a major player in its own right. In this it has, of course, benefited from its association in wider society with technical rationality (Massey 1995), its popularity among young men and the belief of successive governments that technical literacy is essential for life in the twenty-first century.

Teachers, subjects and change

Under conditions of change, teachers are forced to renegotiate the relation-ships between the subjects they teach. In these circumstances, previous or accepted subject status can become the focus of micropolitical struggle (Ball 1987); in this process the gendering of the subject areas as well as gendered power relations between the teachers involved come into play. The greater likelihood of male teachers to hold high level positions and to teach high status subjects may then be set against the greater facility of females in form-ing strong interpersonal alliances that can undercut this positional power (Paechter and Head 1996b). When change takes place, subjects and the indi-viduals who teach them are forced to jockey for position in the new order; the more radical the change, the greater the potential for micropolitical upheaval. The introduction of the English and Welsh National Curriculum in the late 1980s and early 1990s, for example, marked a shift from a liberal humanist curriculum in which humanities subjects were positioned fairly firmly after the 'big three', to one in which technical subjects, represented by D&T and IT, were accorded greater priority, particularly after the Dearing curriculum review (Dearing 1994) made humanities subjects no longer compulsory after age 14. This could lead to attempts to reposition these subjects; at Stitchers School, the head of geography used his interdisciplinary project work with the powerful subjects of mathematics and science to distance his department from its presumed ally, history. Meanwhile, at Lacemakers, the head of history was in no doubt about his subject's position in the pecking order, pointing out that its very need for public support pointed to its marginal status:

> Within this school and certainly within other schools, I think that the humanities subjects are regarded as being not on a par with the science subjects, and with maths and English . . . [The head] goes out of his way to say, look, you know the humanities people are valued members of staff and all like that, etc. You do get a gut feeling that if you are teaching technology, maths, physics, no one questions what you do, whereas in humanities everybody seems to question what humanities do.
>
> (Paul Barker, Head of History, Lacemakers School)

In this school, the survival of both history and geography as compulsory subjects at Key Stage 4 depended on students taking GCSE humanities, which, although taught in subject based modules, was examined (after a complex process of accumulating appropriate modules) as an integrated subject. Although Paul Barker did not like this system, he accepted it as the lesser of two evils. His department was regarded as overstaffed, and willing-ness to cooperate with this interdisciplinary initiative was one of the few things he had to bargain with:

I've got this sort of dichotomy, that, is a course really worth while? Well, if it keeps old so and so in a job, because he's doing twenty per cent of his timetable in this, then it's worth doing because he's a good teacher; which is a hell of a way to run an educational organization.

(Paul Barker, Head of History, Lacemakers School)

To some extent, teachers' public and occupational identities are bound up with the subjects they teach; mathematics and science teachers (male and female) are expected to be masculine, rational and objective, English teachers more feminine, emotional and empathetic, and PE teachers, especially the males, seen as ' "Thick Jocks", with brawn but little in the way of brains' (Sikes 1988: 26). When curriculum negotiation takes place between teachers, these stereotypes influence the process, acting as part of the complex of gendered power/knowledge relations. Sparkes *et al.* for example, note that, at least early on in their careers, PE teachers tend to operate as 'restricted professionals', concentrating on teaching rather than taking part in staffroom micropolitics, and that this leaves them as marginalized as individuals as their subject is in the curriculum:

Early on in their teaching careers, few seemed to acknowledge or understand the significance of the educational context in schools, such as the staffroom or staff meetings. This . . . is the context for the discussion of school politics, which draws selectively and consciously on educational theory and research. It provides one of the primary sites of struggle for the finite resources of the school, and many of the physical educators indicated a lack of awareness of how to operate within this domain.

(Sparkes *et al.* 1990: 16)

Women teachers can be particularly disadvantaged in the struggle for staffroom dominance; powerful groups of males may use sexist jokes or other put-downs to make it difficult for them to assert their authority or have an equal say in decision making (Cunnison 1989). Datnow (1998), for example, describes how in one school a group of 'good old boys' effectively prevented moves towards change led by a group of women teachers. They used a number of gender political strategies, including labelling assertive women 'aggressive', making them the butt of jokes, defining them as less committed to their jobs than men and classifying the proposed reforms (which were largely concerned with the pastoral care of students) as 'women's work'. In such circumstances, those subjects stereotypically seen as feminine and largely staffed by women are unlikely to be able to hold their own against the male domination of the masculine subjects of mathematics and science. At the same time, women working in science, mathematics and IT may be able to 'borrow' the masculinity of their subjects and use it to their advantage in staffroom power relations.

Students in changing times

Students have some awareness of power/knowledge relations between school subjects, and this may influence their choices and behaviour. For example, students may selectively truant from some classes and not others, may work harder or behave better in some areas and, when under pressure, may make choices based on their perceptions of which subjects are important for their future careers. A teacher at Lacemakers School, working on an environment GCSE course, had no illusions about why some of his students dropped out of the course towards the end:

> more important I think is the fact that *they* start to realize that eight good ones is better than eleven not so good, and if it means they don't get their English and their maths at grade Cs, well, hang on, someone will say, well, you haven't got English or maths, so what you've got your environment or you've got geography or whatever, you ain't got your English and maths, and I think that's what they begin to appreciate.
>
> (Roy Saunders, Head of Geography, Lacemakers School)

At the same time, students' interaction with school subjects is mediated by gender. Because some subjects are perceived as masculine and some feminine, student responses to these will vary accordingly. This is particularly the case during adolescence, when young people are very much in the midst of working out for themselves what it means to be a man or a woman. Consequently, where there is some choice about what subjects a student may study, these choices will tend to be made at least in part along gender lines; for boys whose masculinity feels precarious, 'feminine' subjects will be perceived as a threat, while for girls unsure of their femininity, 'masculine' areas will be seen as undesirable (Head 1997). This is clear, for example, in the case of GCSE D&T, where students have to follow a core course in resistant materials but can gain a GCSE by combining this with another course in food technology or textiles technology, or extended work in resistant materials. As was the case before the National Curriculum, girls are overwhelmingly choosing to study food and textiles, and boys resistant materials.

At A level, course choice is again split on gender lines. Male students are overwhelmingly present in the physical science subjects (although they are outnumbered by females in biology). This difference is most extreme in physics, where female students were outnumbered by a ratio of nearly four to one in 1997, and in computer studies, where males outnumbered females by nearly seven to one. In the same year, nearly twice as many males as females took mathematics but more than twice as many females as males took English (although a greater percentage of males attained grade A) (Department for Education and Employment 1998). These gendered choices have implications for other choices students may want to make in the future; in particular, by rejecting the physical sciences and IT/computer studies, girls are closing off pathways to university and occupational futures in a variety of areas. While boys are also closing doors, these tend to be those with fewer implications for access to high status careers later in life. Girls suffer more from the results of gendered subject choices because they choose against areas seen as powerful in wider society.

This effect is particularly important when it comes to vocational education, particularly since it has been possible for students to take some vocational courses at age 14–16. This option has been introduced into schools in England and Wales in an attempt to address the perceived underachievement of boys, particularly at GCSE level. Although, as I argued above, the comparatively poor performance at this level with respect to girls is almost removed by A level, to the extent that male improvement in attainment between GCSE and A level is greater than that of females (Elwood 1999), the discrepancy has steadily increased at GCSE level. Furthermore, it is particular groups of boys who are performing comparatively poorly at GCSE. Although both male and female students from manual working-class backgrounds perform less well than those from the intermediate or middle classes, within this former group white males and Afro-Caribbean males and females gain the lowest average examination scores at GCSE (Arnot *et al.* 1998). As the white working-class male group is large enough to be noticeable throughout the country, it has been a particular focus of attention; the suggestion has been made that these students may be better motivated by vocational courses.[5]

Vocational course choice, however, is overwhelmingly gendered at all levels. Among courses available during the period of compulsory schooling (GNVQ level 1),[6] the entry is predominantly male except for courses in health and social care, in which 88 per cent of students in the first two years were female. It has been suggested that these differences are due to a range of factors extrinsic to the courses themselves: careers guidance, school options guidance, peer pressure, societal stereotyping, 'washback' of employment patterns into schools and colleges, parental views and students' own predilections (Equal Opportunities Commission 1999). The Equal Opportunities Commission argues that the gender segregation found is not surprising given that 'vocational options were introduced with no supportive measures to assist non-stereotyped decision-making and choice' (1999: 216). Vocational courses in the non-compulsory sector are also heavily gender segregated, with women not only mainly taking courses in traditional female areas but at lower levels than men. The Commission concludes that:

> Gender, rather than individual achievement, potential and informed choice, is the key determinant of the vocational education and training

experiences of young people. There are negative implications of this sex stereotyping for subsequent career destinations and life chances. Women are particularly disadvantaged because stereotyping in education and training from 14 onwards secures progression into occupational sectors and jobs where the pay is low, with little opportunity for career development.

(Equal Opportunities Commission 1999: 224)

Increased choice before age 16, while it may enable some young men to respond positively to school, may therefore bring with it decreased long-term opportunities for young women, as they use the new freedoms to opt out of higher status, more occupationally flexible areas.

Conclusion

The changes to the school curriculum with the introduction of the National Curriculum for England and Wales left the basic hierarchy of subjects unaltered; Goodson *et al.* (1998) note the resemblance between the list of National Curriculum subjects from 1998 and those established for secondary schooling in 1904. The government's attempt to raise the status of D&T did succeed for a brief period, but in most schools after a couple of years it reverted to the marginal status of its component areas (see Chapter 5). The extension of the range and time allocation of science (students taking double award science GCSE might spend 20 per cent of their time in this area) consolidated its claim to be one of the dominant subjects, while history and geography, particularly once neither was compulsory after age 14 (Dearing 1994), became slightly more marginal. Apart from the increased importance of IT, arguably inescapable because of developments in wider society, it has been very much business as usual in the school pecking order.

Those subjects most affected by the introduction of the National Curriculum were and remain those in the most marginal positions. HE and CDT were turned upside down and reassembled into a new, complex and supposedly gender-neutral subject. PE and music, both marginal, although in different ways, have been the focus of public and hotly contested debates about their nature, pedagogy and curriculum form (Penney and Evans 1994; Shepherd and Vulliamy 1994; Evans and Penney 1995a, b), some of which remain unresolved (see Chapter 4).

These subjects are also among the most gendered, and, in the case of D&T and PE, that gendering has taken a particular form. Unlike dominant subjects, where the form and content of the subject, particularly at the higher levels, has remained based on the curriculum of the nineteenth-century elite boys' schools, these marginal areas have developed distinct gendered forms

(Paechter 1998a). Whereas, for example, attempts to develop domestic science into a 'female' form of science in the late nineteenth and early twentieth centuries failed in the UK due to the insistence of the heads of the elite girls' schools that their students required the same curriculum as their brothers (Manthorpe 1986), the physical and practical subjects, being seen as less important, were not forced into a single mould. Consequently, until the early 1980s boys studied CDT and its precursor subjects, girls HE, and the forms of PE taught to each group only really came together with the advent of the National Curriculum. Even so, different team games may be provided for boys and girls, and the revisions introduced in 2000 (Qualifications and Curriculum Authority 2000) are likely to make it easier for older male students to opt out of dance and females out of competitive sports.

In considering how gender and power/knowledge interact in the development and maintenance of particular curriculum forms, the position of marginal subjects is particularly salient. Examining how they developed, in what ways they are gendered and what it is like to teach and learn in these areas is crucially important for our understanding of the interaction of gender and power relations in schools. In the next section of this book I develop this theme by focusing on the nature of subject marginality and how it affects three specific subjects: PE, music and D&T.

Notes

1 The data sources for the research cited in this book are explained in the Appendix. All schools, teachers, students and local advisors and administrators have been given pseudonyms.

2 The Order for a National Curriculum subject specifies the curriculum to be followed and what is to be assessed.

3 A levels are the main examination taken by students at 18+ and, despite attempts to make vocational qualifications equivalent, remain the main route to university entrance.

4 It needs to be borne in mind here that because A level entry is much more selective than GCSE, and because routes post-16 are themselves gendered, the two populations may not be strictly comparable (Paechter 1998a; Elwood 1999).

5 It is worth remarking in this context that for more academic students, A levels and the forms of study they involve themselves fulfil vocational purposes (Keddie 1971)

7 For more detail on GNVQ and NVQ see Chapter 7.

part 2

GENDERED MARGINALITY

four

LIFE IN A MARGINAL SUBJECT

I expect that the status that [D&T] holds in other teachers' opinions is quite the same as it was 20 years ago . . . I still feel that people probably feel the same way towards us as they do towards, say, PE. I never minded that, that was never a problem for me. I actually think that technology is of a lower academic status anyway.

(Ravi Korde, CDT teacher, Bursley School)

In school, as in the wider world, some forms of knowledge are more powerful and confer more status than others. Central to the school curriculum, alongside reading and writing in the national language, are disciplines concerned with reason, such as mathematics and science. More peripheral are subjects like history, geography and modern foreign languages. Finally, those areas of the curriculum that involve the use of the body, such as physical education (PE), while often compulsory, are given much less status in the academically focused world of the school. Technology, meanwhile, has a somewhat contradictory position, as government attempts to raise its status for national economic reasons (Black and Atkin 1996) come up against teachers' resistance to the curriculum changes that accompany this, and against students' perceptions about what the subject is really supposed to be about.

In this chapter I consider the position of teachers and students working in subjects that for one reason or another are marginal in the school curriculum. In it I focus on three superficially different areas: D&T (a subject that, in England and Wales, incorporates work with food, textiles and resistant materials such as wood, metal and plastics), PE and music. The first two are compulsory in England and Wales, and the third optional after age 14. All three, despite attempts to raise their profiles, have subjugated but in some ways contradictory positions in school, although the knowledge with which they are concerned varies in status. I will argue that their apparent differences obscure commonalities that are features of, and in part contribute to, their marginal positions.

Teaching and learning are generally thought of as being about the mind. It is only in some of the more marginal school subjects, such as PE, that the body is seen as having a role. As we shall see, the body is also important in both D&T and music, and forms an aspect both of their gendered nature and of their curricular marginality. Furthermore, aspects of the body are incorporated into the professional identities of teachers of both D&T and PE and implicated in the gendering of musical knowledge. Consequently, the inscription of gendered bodies into these subjects affects and is affected by the professional identities of those who teach them. In this process, issues of gender, identity, subject status and the body intersect to give a complex picture of gendered marginality.

Gender issues in the approaches to and takeup of high status school subjects have long been treated with concern both within and outside the specific subject communities and a number of studies have taken place, particularly focusing on mathematics and science (Burton 1986, 1989; Walkerdine 1988; Manthorpe 1989; Walkerdine and The Girls and Mathematics Unit 1989; Burton and Weiner 1990; Head and Ramsden 1990; Jones and Kirk 1990; Murphy 1990; Thomas 1990; Riddell 1992; Stables and Wikeley 1996; Boaler 1997). In more marginal subjects, however, gendered attitudes and approaches are still important, but have only been seen as of concern by a relatively narrow group of practitioners. Furthermore, although it is now recognized that it is important to study the lower status areas of schooling, such studies have generally been carried out in isolation from each other by specialists in each field (Dyhouse 1977; Penfold 1988; Attar 1990; Evans 1990b; Kirk 1990; Sparkes 1990; McCormick 1992; Scraton 1993; Green 1997). Little comparison has been made across areas, so that it is difficult to see if they have features and experiences in common. Consequently, we can read about what it is like to work in or study a particular marginal subject, but we do not have any more general picture of marginality. This chapter draws on a number of studies in an attempt to address this gap in the literature. To do this I shall use my own work with D&T departments (Paechter 1993a, b, c, 1995a, c; Paechter and Head 1996a, b), set against the rather more extensive literature on the subject culture and history of PE (Fletcher 1984; Leaman 1984; Bell 1986; Scraton 1986; Burgess 1988; Evans 1990a, b; Kirk 1990; Sparkes 1990; Shilling 1992; Evans and Davies 1993; Flintoff 1993) and the relatively small amount of work done on the position of school music (Vulliamy 1976; Shepherd and Vulliamy 1983; Hargreaves 1994; Hodge *et al.* 1994;

Sloboda *et al.* 1994; Elliott 1996; Swanwick 1996; Walker 1996; Green 1997).

My own findings come from two empirical studies of the development of D&T in the English and Welsh National Curriculum. The first examined the first year in which D&T was taught in secondary schools, focusing on the experiences in two schools within the same local education authority (LEA) (Paechter 1992a, 1993a, 1995a). The second (Paechter 1993b, c, 1995c; Paechter and Head 1996a, b) was a study of the power and gender issues involved in the negotiation of the D&T curriculum,[1] and took the form of case studies of five schools in the London area.[2] I set this work against empirical studies of PE and music, both in schools and (in the case of PE) in initial teacher education.

Gendered legacies

The English and Welsh versions of the three subjects have had rather different recent histories. D&T as such is a relative newcomer to the curriculum, being assembled, when the National Curriculum was first established in 1988, from HE, CDT and, to a lesser extent, business studies (BS), IT and art. It has been taught as a more or less unified subject since 1990, although, particularly since 1995, in most schools teachers have continued to specialize in particular materials and to think of themselves as teachers of CDT or HE. The subject only became compulsory with the introduction of the National Curriculum; before that CDT and HE tended to be dropped by more academic students at the end of the third year of secondary schooling. With the new curriculum came an increased emphasis on design and a concomitant downplaying of craft skills, something that has been a focus of regret for CDT teachers in particular. It also made the subject feel much more academic, with the result that the traditional constituency of the 'less able', academically disaffected students was seen as no longer being so well served.

> Technology now comes across as just a subject within the curriculum that is in no way different except that you start to use your hands a little bit. And, for me personally, that is the wrong approach. It means that another subject has been removed from the curriculum that kids look forward to, if they do look forward to it, for enjoyment and pleasure. And now, the underachievers in academic subjects underachieve in Technology as well . . . And I find that the kids that achieve well in the other subjects achieve well in this one.
>
> (Ravi Korde, CDT teacher, Bursley School)

This increased academic emphasis with the introduction of D&T has militated against the increased status that the subject might have been expected to gain as a result of becoming compulsory. In the past, CDT and HE had been the source of some of the highest examination grades in some inner-city schools. As the focus moved to the design process and to being able to write about and describe one's work, examination results declined, removing one previously important source of status (Paechter 1993c). There has been a similar, although less marked, move to the academic within secondary school PE, with the establishment of an external examination at 16+ bringing a concomitant requirement for students to be able to write about physical processes.

Music's position is somewhat different. Not only is it compulsory only up to age 14, but, compared to other marginal subjects, it is moderately academic in orientation. The status of D&T and PE within school mirrors the class positions of technicians and sportspeople in the outside world. Music, or at least the classical music that, despite the inclusion of popular and world musics, remains dominant in the school curriculum, is seen, on the other hand, as an intellectual and middle-class pursuit. Musical knowledge is a much more powerful form of cultural capital (Bourdieu and Passeron 1977) than is the ability to play or understand football, to devise electronic circuits or to cook a nutritious meal. Furthermore, while in recent years D&T and PE have become more academic in focus, music has moved in the opposite direction, with an increasing role for performance, improvisation and composition as opposed to purely theoretical study, a less exclusive emphasis on notated work, and attempts to incorporate popular and world musics into the formal curriculum (Shepherd and Vulliamy 1994; Elliott 1996; Swanwick 1996; Walker 1996; Spruce 1999). It remains, however, a minority subject, with few teachers in any one school and instrumental teaching treated as an extra-curricular activity pursued by comparatively few students. In a study comparing music and mathematics teachers in terms of work-related stress, Hodge *et al.* found that there were a number of factors that made the position of music teachers particularly difficult:

> The work role of the secondary music teacher may include uniquely stressful activities. They teach a sizable number of large classes each week, decreasing opportunities to develop close contact with students. They are pressured to incorporate substantial amounts of practical content in lessons (which promotes increased noise levels in classrooms). Music teachers, compared with mathematics teachers, tend to work more from unstructured curricula and without the assistance provided by subject texts. The small number of music compared with other teachers in schools allows for little immediate direct, collegiate support. Also, there is the effect of the political–ideological swing 'back to basics'. This has re-established mathematics and the sciences in contrast

with music and the humanities as the pre-eminent subjects in the educational system.

(Hodge *et al*. 1994: 74)

Although they see the small size of music departments as an important
additional factor, Hodge *et al*. suggest that such increased stress is also likely
to be common among teachers, such as those working in D&T and PE
departments, who:

teach non-academic, 'practical' as opposed to 'academic' subjects; . . .
who are marginalised in terms of their power within the school system;
and who feel that their contribution to the process of education in held
to be relatively unimportant, both from within and outside the school.

(1994: 74)

These findings are echoed by my own two studies of D&T teachers, who,
although working in a large, core area, had little power in the school as a
whole. Work carried out by Sparkes *et al*. (1990), looking at teachers in PE
departments, also supports this view. They found that PE staff were regarded
by others in the school as having little to contribute to curriculum debate, PE
being seen as so marginal as to be almost extra-curricular. Furthermore,
younger PE staff were not sufficiently micropolitically astute to be able to
have an impact on this situation, being unaware of the importance of operating within the whole school arena rather than just within their subject area.

Both PE and D&T remain overtly under the influence of deeply gendered
histories, despite attempts to move them towards more neutral identities.
Although D&T now has an officially integrated curriculum, until the mid-
1970s and beyond, CDT and HE were usually taught only to one gender.
They also incorporated key aspects of masculinity and femininity into their
curricula. HE was originally set up to train working-class girls in house-
wifery and mothering, and education in femininity remained until recently a
key aspect of the subject (Wynn 1983). With CDT the situation is more
subtle, but the all-male atmosphere and the association of physical skills
with working-class forms of hegemonic masculinity (Connell 1987) made it
unmistakably a boys' subject (Equal Opportunities Commission 1983).
With the move to D&T, there has also been an increasing tendency for work
with resistant materials, traditionally associated with the male gender, to
dominate the new area (Paechter 1993c). However, more recent changes
have meant that students now have the opportunity for specialization within
D&T for the last two years of compulsory schooling; this has restored the
gendered split between girls following food/textiles courses and boys opting
for resistant materials.

The gendered nature of PE is also long-standing. For most of the twentieth
century, male and female PE teachers were trained at separate institutions

which incorporated and developed very different traditions (Fletcher 1984). Within schools, boys' and girls' PE departments are still often led by different people, with the head of boys' PE often on a higher pay level and in overall charge (Evans and Williams 1988; Scraton 1993). Since the 1980s some schools have introduced mixed-sex classes, a move which, as in D&T, has resulted in the masculinization of the subject as a whole, with the previously strong culture of girls' PE becoming increasingly marginalized (Scraton 1993). Although the rise of the 'new PE', with its emphasis on non-competitive games and an increased stress on health and fitness, might suggest that there are significant moves in the opposite direction, there are indications that this is more rhetoric than reality (Sparkes 1987) and that it is in any case not a radical departure but more a process of accommodation (Evans 1990a). It has also been pointed out (Evans 1990b) that the debate about the 'new PE' has itself been conducted within the masculine subject paradigm of team games, ignoring the female PE tradition of educational gymnastics. Interventions by the UK government during 1994, in particular by the Minister for Sport, advocating the increased role of team games, have further pushed the subject paradigm towards what is traditionally male PE. There is also evidence to suggest that, despite coeducation since 1976, gender divisions remain within some PE colleges, whose curricula have also undergone masculinization in the face of male student resistance to aspects of the subject which they see as feminine, such as dance (Flintoff 1993). This may be partly connected with ambivalences about their femininity among female PE students (Lenskyj 1987; Dewar 1990); Sherlock found that many attempted to resolve this threat to their identity as women by pressurizing their male counterparts into taking on explicitly macho roles (Sherlock 1987).

In the case of music, the situation is more complex. Music itself has generally masculine connotations in all Western traditions, including classical, popular and other forms, such as jazz. The Western 'canon' of important classical works contains few, if any, written by women, and most famous performers are also male. Where women are visible as musicians, it is as performers, and Green (1997) points out that such roles for women either bring with them connotations of sexual availability and super-femininity (as in the 'canary' of the jazz band, employed to sing and be decorative but not considered a musician) or cut across and interrupt the social expectation for musicians to be male, particularly when playing large or loud instruments such as the trombone or drum kit. In this latter case, she argues, not only do women point up the taken-for-granted masculinity of the musical (and particularly orchestral) performer, but they cause the audience to hear not just music but music-as-played-by-a-woman; that transgressiveness enters into the musical experience, even for the female musician herself. On the other hand, most students taking an active and conformist part in school music are girls, particularly playing plucked and bowed string instruments and keyboard instruments. Although boys do study music at school, they tend to approach it transgressively, rejecting its classical focus (particularly school singing) and concentrating on improvised work with electronic equipment and drums. Green argues that only those boys who are particularly expert in the classical realm are able to transcend the gendering of school music as female, and that this contributes to teachers' perceptions of male students as being more successful and adventurous than female, particularly at composition, which, compared to the rest of school music, is strongly marked as male (Green 1997). This perception of boys as creative risk-takers counterposed to girls as conformist, conventional and hard-working, echoes Walkerdine's (1988) and Walkerdine and The Girls and Mathematics Unit (1989) research on teachers' perceptions of boys' and girls' performance in a high status, masculine, subject; mathematics. Girls were seen as succeeding due to hard work, and boys due to innate ability. In the case of school music, where the subject as a whole is marked as female, the higher status aspects are seen as the preserve of males.

Status contradictions

All three subjects are similar in a number of important respects. D&T and PE hold a rather paradoxical position in the overall power structure of the school, being both marginal and compulsory throughout secondary education (Bell 1986). As a result, and in contrast to the situation in music, the departments are often sizable; in my studies the pay of the heads of D&T reflected this, being in every case higher than that of heads of smaller but more academic areas such as history and geography. In terms of size alone, the D&T and PE departments might be expected to rival those of mathematics and English, but this numerical equality is offset by their traditionally non-academic basis (Bell 1986). Both subjects have (historically, at least, in the case of D&T) been concerned principally with the teaching of physical skills rather than with the transmission of academic knowledge. This has given both areas a concern with the body as an instrument, as well as a 'natural' constituency of the 'less able' and the academically disaffected. At the same time, the perceived ability of teachers of these subjects to keep such students occupied and out of trouble (Carrington and Wood 1983; Paechter 1993c) has given them a special status and purpose in many schools, particularly in the inner-cities; their importance to the school in this respect flows directly from their academically low status position:

> in this school, that whole area [CDT and HE] certainly gave [us] the best results in examination level. It also kept [us] out of an awful lot of trouble because a large number of the less able children for example were pushed into that area because it was practical.
> (Sue Pennington, Head of Technology, Turnhill School)

Some aspects of both D&T and PE also, at specific times of the year, play important roles in the 'public face' of the school. Sports days and inter-school matches are times when PE departments can demonstrate a school's success and 'all-roundedness' (Bell 1986; Sparkes 1987; Thomas 1993). The food aspect of D&T has also been important in this regard, with students and staff catering for school functions and sometimes entertaining visitors (Attar 1990). Displays of craft work are often a major feature of the public areas of schools.

Again, music has a different but equally contradictory status. It shares with D&T and PE a role in the 'public face' of the school, in the form of school orchestras, bands and concerts. Its low status is also connected not only with its minority interest and small department size, but with its practical approach as far as GCSE level. Beyond this, however, whereas D&T and PE depart-ments usually perpetuate their practical focus by providing vocational courses, music, by contrast, remains within the more traditional A level framework. Furthermore, because school music has become defined (what-ever its actual content) as 'classical' in counterposition to the 'popular' music preferred by students, the traditionally disaffected students often to be found at their best in D&T and PE may be particularly alienated from the music cur-riculum. Green (1997) argues that this is difficult to avoid; because popular music defines itself as, by its very nature, oppositional, the incorporation of it into school music, as suggested by some authors (Vulliamy 1976; Shepherd and Vulliamy 1983) simply converts it into school, or 'classical' music:

> The mere fact that music is in the curriculum affects pupils' judgments of its style, such that any music which the teacher requires them to study is taken to be classical. Popular music, contrastingly, is *by defi-nition* music which the teacher does not require them to study, and in the minds of many pupils, as soon as the teacher does make this require-ment, the music will cease to be popular.
>
> (Green 1997: 146)

This problem is compounded by deep student loyalties to particular forms of popular music and by the tendency of classically trained music teachers to apply analytical frameworks from their own background to music from other traditions (Shepherd and Vulliamy 1983; Green 1997). Different kinds of music are not just about different preferences; they almost encompass different identities:

> Not only is rock music (much more than jazz used to be) an integral part of the life of many people, but it is a cultural initiator; to like rock, to like a certain kind of rock rather than another, is also a way of life, a manner of reacting; it is a whole set of tastes and attitudes.
>
> (Foucault 1988: 316)

The interests and focus of school music teachers are thus implicitly and explicitly distanced from those of the majority of students, making relationships difficult, particularly with those students who already lack interest in school (Green 1997).

Teachers of both D&T and PE, on the other hand, have a longstanding reputation of unusually close relationships with students, particularly disaffected and working-class boys, due to their more informal teaching arenas (Carroll 1986; Sherlock 1987; Sikes 1988; Templin *et al.* 1988).

> Now, I've always worked *with* the children, and I hope the children, when they come to me, they enjoy what they're doing, and that's why I like it to be at least 50 per cent practical. Got to be, because the children enjoy it . . . I think that's very important. I think you get the best from the kids if they enjoy doing the stuff. And discipline as well, you don't get the problems that maybe you get in a purely academic subject.
> (Tom Harty, CDT teacher, Turnhill School)

This sense of informality and enjoyment is further developed in the case of PE because of the staff's involvement in extra-curricular activities; the fact that for some students it is the only aspect of school that they enjoy also plays an important part (Templin *et al.* 1988). Carrington *et al.* further point to the 'colonization' of school sports teams by black students already 'cooled out' of the academic mainstream (Carrington and Wood 1983). In consequence, PE teachers often enjoy considerable informal power in the school (Sikes 1988), a situation again enjoyed until recently by their D&T colleagues, who had few discipline problems even with the most disaffected students. As well as the link with student enjoyment, this sort of informal power is also connected with working-class male student images of masculinity as being related to working with one's hands (Willis 1977) and the sort of physical prowess often demonstrated by young male PE teachers (Sherlock 1987).

The body

A key issue in this respect, and one in which there are surprising similarities with D&T and music, is the importance of the body in PE. Kessler and McKenna (1978) note the way in which the social construction of gender identifies it with physical attributes; although gender is primarily a social construct, it is attributed on the basis of physical signs and forms (Kessler 1990). Sherlock (1987) notes the social pressures on male PE teachers to be big and physically strong. Differential treatment of the gendered body is also embedded in current practice in PE teaching, for example the exclusion of young women and girls in most schools and colleges from contact sports, with the protection of the female reproductive organs (in fact safely located in the natural defensive structure of the pelvis) sometimes cited as a reason for this (Scraton 1986; Flintoff 1993).

PE, in particular, is a site used by boys and young men to assert and demonstrate hegemonic masculinity: 'A particular variety of masculinity to which others – among them young and effeminate as well as homosexual men – are subordinated (Carrigan *et al.* 1985: 587). This is done through displays of physical strength and the marginalization (often through bullying under the cover of sporting activity as well as exclusion) of their less successful peers (Askew and Ross 1988; Walker 1988; Parker 1996). Meanwhile, adolescent girls may use rejection of PE and work in resistant materials as a way of asserting a passive femininity in the face of stereotypes of the active, technologically manipulative body as masculine (Leaman 1984). In parallel with the association of PE with masculinity is the importance of physical labour to working-class hypermasculinities (Willis 1977; Pyke 1996). Although practical craftwork is now less central than it used to be to work with resistant materials, this remains a factor in the appeal of this aspect of D&T to otherwise disaffected male students. At the same time, the food/textiles aspect of D&T is focused around women's physical labour in the service of others (Attar (1990) points out that female service labour is all that the components of HE – food, textiles and household management – had in common); the female body is used to provide for (feed, clothe) the bodies of unnamed, but presumably male, others.

In music the body is very distinctly gendered. Green (1997) notes that while the female body is so obvious in musical performance that it may get in the way of our perception of intrinsic musical value, the male body disappears to the extent that it is seen as ungendered. In singing, in particular, in which the body itself is the instrument, there is an element of bodily display that renders the singer subject to a gendered and often sexualized gaze. The body of the female singer becomes itself sexualized; it enacts the dichotomy of the madonna/whore as the woman either sings privately to her infant or publicly to a (traditionally male) audience. As the music becomes more distanced from the body through the use of various technologies, from musical instruments to devices such as computers, it becomes more masculine. Green notes, for example, that the boys in her study did much of their work using high-tech equipment and that, while neither gender was particularly happy to use musical notation, the boys were far more comfortable than the girls with its technical aspects.

The special emphasis given to the body in PE means that PE teachers' careers tend to have different trajectories from others in the profession, with teachers moving out of the subject as they get older. PE shares with D&T and music a focus on skills residing in the body as much as in the brain, and a resulting preference for teaching by demonstration and example. This means that PE teachers who lose their ability to perform to a high level may also lose part, if not all, of their identity as PE teachers. As one former PE teacher now working in D&T described it:

> I . . . was skiing in the Easter holidays . . . and I broke my leg . . . And I can remember myself speaking to my head and saying, 'I can't teach PE again, that's it, my PE career's over'. And it actually wasn't that dramatic but it felt like it for me.
>
> (Claudia Nightingale, Deputy Head, Longshaw Girls' School)

The possession and demonstration of such skills are bound up with personal identity; many former craft teachers have found the loss of identity a particular issue in the move to the less skill-based D&T. The importance of the ability to teach by demonstration and example also partly explains the reluctance of many PE and male D&T teachers to support students working in aspects of their subjects in which they are not personally highly proficient (Flintoff 1993; Paechter and Head 1995). It is interesting to note, however, that this loss of identity is itself gendered. The HE and female CDT teachers in my study seemed to locate their professional identity in teaching in general rather than their subject skills in particular, making them more able to adapt to changes in their subjects.

Female teachers

At the same time, the association between physical prowess and particular forms of masculinity points to the somewhat anomalous position of the female PE teacher. Promotional posts within PE remain male-dominated, with most schools having an overall male head of PE, with a head of 'girls' PE' on a lower salary scale (Sikes 1988). In the literature on PE in general, 'sporty girls' are generally treated as anomalous (Carroll 1986; Sherlock 1987; Sikes 1988; Bloot and Browne 1996; Paechter 1998a). To become a successful sportswoman (and therefore potentially a PE teacher) one has to be able to withstand considerable social pressure, due to the challenge posed to hegemonic masculinity by strong, fit women (Johnston 1996). Taking sports seriously also brings a degree of threat to one's femininity, partly because one is no longer able to display a stereotypically feminine body (Lenskyj 1987; Coles 1994–95). In resisting such pressures, athletic girls may explicitly be supported by a peer community that channels them towards careers in PE. An example of this comes from the former PE teacher quoted earlier, talking about how sporty young women are inducted into the PE teachers' world:

> I was one of the sports set at school . . . I was sort of virtually adopted by the PE teacher . . . I was to follow in her footsteps or whatever . . . I think when you're sort of sporty as a young woman you spend a lot of

time with other women [in local sports teams] . . . The seniors coach and some of them umpire, they take you to your matches, and most of them are teachers of the schools anyway. So when you go and play another match, you know, you come across them and, I don't know, you just feel like you're in the crowd or something. In with them, and they tell you what their college is like and you go there.

(Claudia Nightingale, Deputy Head, Longshaw Girls' School)

The reluctance of most adolescent girls to take part in PE, particularly in competitive sport, has been a focus of concern for some time (Inner London Education Authority 1984). Unlike young men, who use physical prowess to establish their masculine status, young women assert their femininity by an explicit rejection of PE. While the stereotyped masculine role is consonant with that of the male PE teacher, women involved in PE are often seen as being outside the feminine, although there is also an alternative super-feminine role associated with gymnastics and dance (Sikes 1988; Thomas 1991). Sherlock (1987) notes in this context the importance of Berger's suggestion that a man's presence depends on the promise of power that he embodies, whereas women represent themselves as something to be surveyed (Berger 1972). Women PE teachers' self-presentation and generally muscular physique are closer to those associated with power and therefore with masculinity. Similar issues arise in the contrast between the celebration of sexualized femininity in the female solo singer and the presentation of strength and power involved in playing instruments like the drum kit or tuba. Female music teachers with skills and knowledge in areas such as bass guitar playing may be seen as so anomalous that what they know is discounted (Green 1997).

Similar issues arise when we look at the two groups of women working in D&T. Female CDT teachers are still very much a minority group, pioneers in what remains a male world. One teacher described her experiences when she first started, as recently as 1985. Although both boys and girls studied CDT, in this school they were taught in single sex groups:

There were these third year[3] boys lining up and one of them looked in there and went, 'Cor, there's a woman in there!', as if I was from the moon. And they couldn't believe it. I mean, even the second years[4] were taken aback when I was waiting for them, because they had been male dominated completely.

(Helen Cartwright, CDT teacher, Bursley School)

Another found that students used her anomalous position as a trigger for speculation about her sexual orientation. A third, who had previously worked in the extremely male world of the building industry, felt that her career as a CDT teacher had been dogged by sexism, and that, after 13 years in male arenas, it was time to leave.

Although the move to integrated D&T made things easier for this group, if only through increased contact with and therefore collegial support from other women staff, for some HE teachers it raised issues about the nature and purpose of their subject. Nationally, HE staffing is almost exclusively female, and there were no male HE teachers in my sample. As was described earlier, the subject ethos has traditionally encompassed a range of stereotypically feminine concerns focused around the home and family. HE teachers were until recently inducted into this world through separate training institutions, and often saw their role as encompassing the feminine side of education (Attar 1990). To some extent this has led to the development of a similar ultra-feminine ethos to that of dance, with HE being used as a way of inducting girls into middle-class, feminine ways of behaving:

> Afternoon tea should be a leisurely meal served at four o'clock . . . It is a gracious meal. Use lace or fine linen cloths on a small table or tea trolley. Small tea napkins should be provided. This is the opportunity to use your best china and to show your silver to advantage.
> (Cullen 1973, quoted in Wynn (1983: 203))

Although some HE teachers, particularly in recent years, have resisted this super-feminine stereotype, pockets of it remain (Attar 1990) and the area as a whole remains focused around aspects of traditionally female service to others.

HE classrooms have also often been regarded by teachers working in the area as safe havens where girls can escape the male-dominated atmosphere of the rest of the school (Attar 1990). One woman, describing how she felt about the subject when she was at school, echoed this idea of HE as being safe, in academic as well as in other respects:

> I suppose, like many girls, I feel that it's a comforting image. It's something you're used to. We all come from homes. We all have mothers that cook. You see it so you say, 'Oh, that's something I can do really well.
> (Paula Tomson, HE teacher, Bursley School)

Although most HE teachers have taught boys for some time, the area has remained female in staffing and orientation. The move to integrated D&T undercut this in a number of ways. A more interdisciplinary approach led, in some schools, to male CDT teachers starting to do some of their work in food and textiles, so that the area was no longer a largely female preserve. At the same time, the homemaking focus of HE has had to give way to a more technological outlook, with an emphasis on design processes and on food and textiles as industries. Although this is welcomed by many HE teachers, others regret the loss of femininity that is part of their own identity as well as that of their subject. In the same way as dance has been threatened by the National Curriculum for PE, so 'female' aspects of D&T are being played down, leading some teachers to lament that 'it's not fair on the girls; 80 per cent is traditional boys' subjects' (fieldnotes).

Conclusion: gender and the marginal subject

D&T, PE and music are three of the most marginal subjects on the curriculum. They are also the three most bound up with the body, bodily display and physical labour. It should not be surprising, therefore, to find that their marginality is deeply gendered. Marginal positions seem increasingly to be associated either with extremes of femininity or with the physical aspects of hegemonic masculinity, Music has been increasingly marginalized, while D&T and PE are, once again, increasingly aimed at potentially disaffected, often black and/or working-class boys. Given that many schools are finding that, without the outlet of the former craft subjects, and with PE restricted to a small proportion of curriculum time, disaffected students are becoming more noticeable, it is not surprising that there is pressure for at least the former CDT side of D&T departments to revert to their former role of keeping this group happy working with their hands. This leaves female CDT staff, many of whom have a design rather than a craft background, marooned, with their female students, in what is once again becoming a man's world. For HE teachers things are even worse; until the upper secondary level their subject has been incorporated into one dominated by men, and much of what they used to teach has disappeared from the curriculum.

In both D&T and PE the move to coeducation has not served women and girls well. Given that there are long-standing and very different male and female subject paradigms, integration was bound to lead to conflicts over the nature and pedagogy of each subject. In both cases, the women seem to be losing, with the dominant conception of the curriculum being that developed, over years of segregation, by men in an exclusively male environment. In higher status areas, such as mathematics and science, this is recognized outside the narrow group of practitioners, and pressure groups have been established that are working to remedy the situation. In marginal areas, however, while teachers are often very clear about the way their subjects have become gendered, they remain unsupported in their struggles for greater equality and opportunity, both for themselves and for their students. Life in a marginal subject can be a constant fight against gendered stereotypes, one which is insufficiently supported by those outside.

Notes

1 ESRC award number R000233548, directed by myself and John Head, based at King's College, London and carried out between September 1992 and August 1994.
2 For further details of both these studies see Appendix.
3 Age 13–14, usually referred to as Year 9.
4 Age 12–13, usually referred to as Year 8.

five

NEGOTIATING A NEW SCHOOL SUBJECT: THE CASE OF DESIGN AND TECHNOLOGY

Innovations are rarely neutral. They tend to advance or enhance the position of certain groups and disadvantage or damage the position of others. Innovations can threaten the self-interests of participants by undermining established identities, by deskilling and therefore reducing job satisfaction. By introducing new working practices which replace established and cherished ways of working, they threaten individual self-concepts. Vested interests may also be under threat: innovations not infrequently involve the redistribution of resources, the restructuring of job allocations and redirection of lines of information flow. The career prospects of individuals or groups may be curtailed or fundamentally diverted.

(Ball 1987: 32)

Introducing design and technology

The introduction of D&T in 1990, as part of the National Curriculum for England and Wales, is a clear and particularly interesting example of top-down curriculum change. In designating D&T as a National Curriculum extended core subject, the UK government was attempting to alter the status of a school subject by government fiat. At the same time, the Working Group for Design and Technology, charged with defining the new curriculum, set out to introduce a radically new combination of processes and content for the new subject. It is hardly surprising that teachers, faced with the rapid implementation of far-reaching, compulsory changes, found themselves confused and unhappy (Hargreaves 1994). This chapter traces the history of this episode, from the initial conception of the new curriculum, through its attempted implementation in schools, to its gradual disintegration.

D&T is an important case to look at when considering power/knowledge issues in schools. First, the elevation of the subject (or its components) to being a central element of the compulsory curriculum constituted an explicit intervention in power/knowledge relations between teachers and between subject areas. Second, because of its open nature and because of its emphasis on the consideration of human purposes and values in carrying out D&T activities, the new subject had the potential to affect teacher–student relations in a radical way. Third, as a subject integrated throughout compulsory education, with its component areas subordinated to the 'relational idea' (Bernstein 1971) of design and technology capability, D&T threatened wider social structures. Hargreaves *et al.* note that:

> While the emergence of curriculum integration can be precipitated by wider social change, such integration can in turn pose challenges to the existing social order. This happens when curriculum integration extends beyond isolated experiments with the urban poor or with middle-class groups who embrace alternative lifestyles, to being a policy requirement for all children, of all backgrounds and abilities. Integration also poses challenges to the existing order when it is not confined to younger children but becomes a requirement for secondary school children, who are closer to the exit gates of school that lead to university and occupational selection. When it affects almost all children, including older children, curriculum integration begins to threaten society's 'basic classifications and frames', its structures of power and control, and the recognized forms of knowledge through which the powerful perpetuate their advantage.
>
> (1996: 101)

Fourth, the new subject's focus was not subject knowledge but 'design and technology capability', which 'emphasizes that technology is concerned with practical action, drawing on knowledge and understanding from a wide range of subjects' (National Curriculum Council 1990b: introductory pages). These four features, however, were also major factors in its downfall, presenting too great a challenge to the hegemonic order and being too much of a change for those not involved in its devising to take on board. In this section I am going set the scene for my analysis of subsequent developments by outlining the original version of the D&T curriculum in some detail. In doing this I hope to help the reader to understand both why the subject was so potentially exciting and why it ultimately became too much of a challenge to those forced to implement it.

In outlining the National Curriculum for D&T I intend in the main to confine myself to the official documents associated with its introduction, and commentaries on these. In particular, I shall be concerned with the original Order[1] for technology (Department of Education and Science/Welsh Office 1990), the accompanying non-statutory guidance (National Curriculum Council 1990b),[2] the reports of the Working Group that formulated them (National Curriculum Technology Working Group 1988; Department of Education and Science/Welsh Office 1989) and that of the National Curriculum Council (NCC),[3] who made alterations to the curriculum after national consultation (National Curriculum Council 1990b). Although the National Curriculum subject of technology originally also encompassed IT, this was a distinct and separately assessed component, and does not form part of my analysis. Of course, the nature and purpose of school technology had been a matter of debate at national level for some years (see, for example, Black and Harrison 1985; McCulloch *et al.* 1985; Chapman 1986; Cross and McCormick 1986; Sharon 1989; Green 1991; Donnelly 1992; Layton 1995). However, from the point of view of those having to deal with the subject in schools, it was the definition of D&T as part of the National Curriculum that was most salient. It is on this, therefore, that I shall focus.

D&T was unique among the National Curriculum subjects in that it was essentially new (Black 1990; Medway 1990). The other areas prescribed by the National Curriculum, with the possible exception of IT, were already being taught in schools, often in a form not dissimilar to the one they took prior to the regularization of this in law. D&T, however, partly because of the unresolved disputes about its nature, was essentially created by the National Curriculum Technology Working Group and the NCC (McCormick 1990), and much of the formal definition of the subject was to be found in the working group's interim and final reports (National Curriculum Technology Working Group 1988; Department of Education and Science/Welsh Office 1989), and in the non-statutory guidance published by the NCC (National Curriculum Council 1990a). This made the subject very unusual in curriculum history terms. Goodson (1983a, b) has pointed out that most new school subjects are established through a long and painful process during which they gain in status by consolidating their academic respectability, as subject associations are set up and A level and university courses developed. Although in the past there had been attempts (for example, Project Technology) to use these or similar methods to establish D&T (or something vaguely like it) in schools, they had largely been unsuccessful (McCulloch *et al.* 1985). With the National Curriculum, however, an attempt was made to establish the subject by government legislation, partly under pressure from a variety of interest and subject groups (Penfold 1988; McCormick 1990; Layton 1995) and from industry.[4] Its fundamental ideas were and are laid down by statute (and, indeed, disputed at this level, through changes to and attempts to change the Order) and its place and status in the curriculum were, in theory at least, decreed by its position as a National Curriculum foundation subject, required through all years of compulsory schooling.

Although the terms of reference for the working group required that their new curriculum reflect best practice in schools (National Curriculum Technology Working Group 1988), there were very few teachers who could be said already to be teaching D&T as described in the Order. In many ways this was seen as an asset; a chance to make fundamental changes in the nature of teaching and learning in schools:

> we must accept a new vision. The subject is radically new and unless those involved see it as radically new, they might in fact be missing the point. That is, anyone who says, 'We're doing this already, we already handle this in business studies very well, or in CDT very well, and it only needs a minor adaptation' will probably be missing the point.
>
> (Black 1990: 4)

At the same time, the introduction of a new subject into the curriculum cannot take place without a group of people to take responsibility for teaching it. From the outset, D&T was conceived of as cross-curricular in nature, incorporating a range of subjects and taught in an integrated way. Five already existing areas were seen as central:

> Design and technology is not an amalgam of existing subjects, but teachers of art & design, business education, craft design & technology, home economics, information technology/computer studies have vital contributions to make. In some cases most of their teaching will be design and technology; in others, they may be contributing to a number of subjects.
>
> (National Curriculum Council 1990a: B10)

These subjects were identified as 'those parts of the curriculum where substantial designing and making already takes place' (Department of Education and Science/Welsh Office 1989: 90). The new curriculum area was thus conceived of as being integrated through a group of specialists coming together to work through the new overarching concept of D&T.

The subject was not only seen as new, but as fundamentally different to the rest of the National Curriculum:

> Technology is the one subject in the National Curriculum that is directly concerned with generating ideas, making and doing. In emphasising the importance of practical capability, and providing opportunities for pupils to develop their powers to innovate, to make decisions, to create new solutions, it can play a unique role. Central to this role is the task of providing a balance in a curriculum based on academic subjects – a

balance in which the creative and practical capabilities of pupils can be fully developed and inter-related.

(National Curriculum Council 1989: 7)

Although some commentators felt that it was a rather tall order for one subject alone to provide balance in the curriculum (Barnett 1991), this difference was recognized and the move towards education for capability, referred to as emphasizing that technology 'is a subject concerned with practical action' (National Curriculum Council 1990a), was welcomed, despite previous debates about the nature and importance of this concept (Thompson 1984; Ashton 1986; Burgess 1986; Medway 1990). In particular, the Working Group saw knowledge as having a different function in D&T to that in other subjects. Knowledge and understanding were to be related at all times to D&T activities rather than studied in isolation:

> Within other subjects, however, the knowledge and skills have the function of advancing understanding and mastery of those particular subjects, and will be located at levels judged appropriate to this end. Their function in relation to design and technology is different, being to service the development of design and technological capability through their application and use in activities.
>
> (Department of Education and Science/Welsh Office 1989: 10)

Because of this both the attainment targets (ATs)[5] and the programmes of study (PoSs) were rather different from those of other subjects. The ATs described a 'design cycle', the process by which artefacts, systems and environments are identified as necessary, designed, planned and made, and evaluated against criteria of fitness for their intended use. In doing this, students were expected to take into account human purposes and values; the work was to be carried out in real contexts with their multiple constraints. Furthermore, the focus of the prescribed curriculum was on integrated practical activity, and there was a marked reluctance on the part of its authors to indicate specific content:

> Even if a definitive map [of the knowledge base] were a possibility, there is still a fundamental objection to the specification of knowledge-led attainment targets for design and technology. We believe that they could encourage the learning of knowledge as an activity separate from its application in design and technological tasks. Such a disjunction between theory and practice, with its implied sequential relationship between knowledge and action, is at odds with our view of the integrative nature of design and technology. Knowledge here is a resource inseparable from practical action, not a commodity to be stockpiled before action can begin.
>
> (National Curriculum Technology Working Group 1988: 25)

The emphasis on students carrying out holistic tasks negotiated on an individual or group basis with their teachers was a further unusual feature of the D&T curriculum. Although teachers were expected to ensure that students experience a balanced range of contexts over a year and a key stage, it was considered important that there should be enough flexibility for a considerable degree of self-direction. The documentation made clear that students should be able to choose to work with materials suitable to the identified task, and to move between resource areas, seeking specialist advice where necessary (National Curriculum Council 1990a). Because students would thus have a significant input into the choice of tasks, it might be expected that they would bring their non-school, or student-owned knowledge (Paechter 1998b) into the classroom, especially as these tasks were expected to be carried out within the constraints of the real situation. Common sense was thus potentially as important as theory; there is no point, for example, in devising a wonderful electronic system for detecting lowered body temperature if the elderly people for whom it is made find it uncomfortable to wear. This, in theory, gave student-owned knowledge a place in the legitimated world of the school, and provided a place where students could be given credit for using it. At the same time it was expected that the boundaries between subjects would also become blurred; D&T tasks were expected to call on knowledge from subjects outside the central curriculum area, particularly science and mathematics (National Curriculum Council 1990a; Wolf 1991).

The inclusion of real-world knowledge, through the consideration of human purposes and values, was particularly unusual in what was to be, at least in theory, a high status subject. As Layton (1972) points out, there has historically been a tendency for subjects progressively to lose their relevance to students' concerns (whatever these might be) as academic status is gained. D&T, however, did not have to fight for status in the traditional manner, but had it conferred upon it by its designation as a subject that was be studied throughout compulsory schooling. This broke into the traditional divide between academic and common-sense knowledge (Bernstein 1971; Young 1971; Layton 1991), legitimating, both in pedagogy and in assessment, areas of understanding that had until then been considered suitable only for 'less able' students (Keddie 1971; Young 1971; Medway 1989; Paechter 1993a).

What this meant was that students' common-sense judgements, based on contextualized, culturally based values, were given an explicit place in both teaching and assessment. The requirement that students should consider human purposes and values when carrying out D&T tasks cut across the distinction between school and student-owned knowledge, giving each importance in different ways. It represented an attempt to intervene in prevailing power/knowledge relations by including and legitimating something that students brought to school from the out-of-school world, and in particular to recognize and value variations and differences in their cultural backgrounds.

At the same time, the contextualized nature of the curriculum emphasized the provisional and permeable nature of knowledge. Technology is a cultural phenomenon that is always designed for particular purposes (Young 1991). Consequently, 'its solutions are not right or wrong, verifiable or falsifiable, but more or less effective from different points of view' (Medway 1989: 6). The teacher would thus no longer be the person who had all the answers. They might possess a number of skills in, or knowledge about, the use of various materials, but would not necessarily have any better ideas than the students about how, for example, to address the need of the local nursery school for equipment to help children learn shape discrimination. Students would thus be given access both to the contextualized and provisional nature of knowledge and to the constraints that are imposed upon it by the real world.

Contextualization and the consideration of human purposes and values were also important because they had the potential to focus students' attention on the purposes for which technology is used. As Percy (1991) points out, any criteria for judging the usefulness of technological products must take into account potential users. This is not explicit in the National Curriculum documentation, however, some of which was criticized for presenting technological development as unerringly progressive. Nevertheless, the requirement to consider a variety of values and cultures, however understated, remained, and could be taken up by teachers (Grant 1984; Barnett 1991), who were encouraged, for example, to consider questions such as:

What is a good atomic bomb? One which goes off or one which does not? Does it depend on whether you are dropping it or having it dropped upon you? Can it make sense to say 'This is a well designed bomb: it would have been better if it was badly designed'?

(Pitt 1991: 34)

Teachers are not necessarily constrained by the ideological purposes of official curriculum documents and they can and do interpret them in a number of ways (Bowe *et al.* 1992). It is unclear to what extent teachers in general were able to see the potential for social critique inherent in the D&T curriculum. Furthermore, given that those teaching CDT and HE, the main contributory areas, have been found to be among the most socially conservative in the staffroom (Kelly *et al.* 1987) they may well not have wished to take such opportunities forward. However, it remains the case that such potential was there, and was stressed by those promoting the new curriculum, such as Black, here speaking to a joint meeting of the Standing Conference on School Science and the Design and Technology Association:

Let's be clear about one feature of this area. To avoid the issues concerning beliefs and value is to decide to teach a powerful lesson. You teach the lesson that they are not important, that they are not manageable, they are personal opinion only. That I think is a very powerful, and powerfully bad, lesson which is taught simply by avoiding the issue of values and awareness in technology as a whole.

(Black 1990: 17)

The converse is also extremely powerful: by explicitly including value issues into D&T, teachers would be saying to students that these things are crucially important in making decisions about technology in the real world. Furthermore, in relating the work of the D&T classroom to students' concerns about the environment, about war and about the structure of society, space would be made for their knowledge as well as for that of the school.

It is thus clear that the D&T National Curriculum, as originally intended, had the potential to present a serious challenge to power/knowledge relations as traditionally found in classrooms and schools. Its interdisciplinary nature, its context-dependent, task based learning and its emphasis on human concerns made it a powerful arena for the introduction of student-owned knowledge into the legitimated school curriculum and for challenges to prevailing power/knowledge relations between teachers and students, teachers and their colleagues, and between school subjects. None of this, however, was to happen. The remainder of this chapter traces what happened in the first few years of the new subject, in an attempt to explain why this was the case.

The disintegration of design and technology[6]

There were two major factors in the disintegration of the supposedly integrated D&T curriculum between 1990 and 1995. Resistance from teachers came partly as a reaction to the threat posed by the new subject to the status quo and partly because of increasing difficulties with the implementation of its radical ideas in practice. At the same time, there was an increasingly voluble group, outside schools, opposed to the principles underlying National Curriculum D&T and agitating for it to be replaced by something different. This opposition centred around the Engineering Council and other groups promoting more explicitly vocational education, in particular the National Institute for Economic and Social Research (Layton 1995). As I shall explain, it was the interaction between teachers struggling in the classroom and the damning (if often very crude) critiques in the national press that led finally to a revision of the D&T curriculum in 1994 that removed some of its most radical and innovative features.

In describing the process of curriculum disintegration, I shall take the main factors more or less chronologically. Although it must be emphasized that some of these operated continuously throughout the period, each was more salient at some times than at others. Some key events, such as the introduction of the D&T Standard Assessment Tasks (SATs) or the initial curriculum review in late 1992, had a profound influence on events specifically because of their timing; others formed a more continuous challenge to the new subject's survival. I shall start in the period between the initial definition of D&T in 1988 and its introduction in 1990, when teachers and curriculum areas struggled with each other for perceived centrality in the new scheme of things. I then move on to look at how teachers dealt with the imposition of new structures, both of curriculum and of staff organization. At this point, I move into the public arena, and look briefly at what had been taking place in the educational press, focusing specifically on the events in the summer of 1992, when the new curriculum came under severe public criticism. This led to a series of curriculum changes, which I shall outline before going on to consider the effects and implications of the first D&T SATs in 1993. Finally, I describe how integration finally broke down.

The struggle for centrality

The new curriculum was designed to be interdisciplinary. School structures, however, do not fit well with cross-subject initiatives, and there was an early impetus, on the part of both teachers and school administrators, to identify a home base for the new subject. There was a drive to fit D&T into existing subject structures, to locate its central features in an already existing area. Although developments during the 1980s might have implied that D&T would be associated with science, the publication of the Working Group's interim report (National Curriculum Technology Working Group 1988) made it clear that the new subject, although involving some science, would be much more practical and located in the real world, and would have CDT and HE as its core components, focusing on work with resistant materials, and on food and textiles, respectively. Up until this time, however, these two subject areas had little to do with each other and almost no history of collaboration apart from one or two local initiatives such as school based Technical and Vocational Education Initiative (TVEI) projects.

During the period from the publication of the Working Group's interim report in 1988 until the implementation of the new curriculum in 1990, there was a period of intense struggle, particularly between CDT and HE, for ownership of the new curriculum. This struggle was, because of the histories, content and personnel of the two subjects, strongly gendered, and involved issues of power relations at all levels. There were two intersecting issues involved here. The first was to do with the status of individual teachers and how it was affected by the rise in status of the subject as a whole. At the same time, and intersecting with this, was the question of teacher confidence and the need to come to terms with being a teacher of a new subject that contained components of which one had no prior experience. Both of these involve an individual's sense of personal empowerment or powerfulness (Paechter and Head 1995). Furthermore, the two became more deeply intertwined as the school management's view of the centrality of one or other contributing area to D&T was reflected in differential opportunities for individuals to progress their careers within the new subject. It therefore became increasingly important for teachers to feel, and to communicate to others, that their subject of origin was at the core of the new interdisciplinary curriculum.

How this operated in practice can be best explained through a number of illustrative examples. First, a key issue in almost all schools was the appointment of a new head of D&T from among the staff of the contributing subjects. Because of the elevation of D&T to extended core status within the National Curriculum, many schools chose to appoint an overall subject leader at an enhanced salary on an equivalent level to the heads of English, mathematics and science. Whether someone was called 'head' or 'coordinator' of D&T also carried differential connotations, both to themselves and to others, with regard to both power and responsibility. At Turnhill School, the CDT staff felt that the slippage, from the title of 'coordinator' to that of 'head' of technology, occurring with the arrival of a new headteacher, constituted a cause for complaint as it implied loss of status for heads of the constituent departments. Meanwhile at Hanbridge School, the technology coordinator, also head of HE, told me that she had explicitly chosen this title as she did not want to be held responsible when (as she anticipated) things went wrong.

How this person was appointed, and who it was, conveyed very different messages to the departments concerned, as well as to others in the school, and could have long-term implications for the functioning of the new department. At Stitchers School, for example, the existing male head of CDT was called into the headteacher's office one day and informed that he was now promoted to the post of coordinator for D&T. This unilateral move on the part of the head surprised even the senior managers, one of whom commented, 'No notice asking people to apply appeared on the staff notice board. He didn't discuss it with the senior management team' (Graham Peacock, TVEI coordinator, Stitchers School: field notes). As well as being a clear signal that this headteacher saw CDT as the most important component of the new subject, this constituted a breach of normal appointment procedures. The female head of HE, who had intended to apply for the job when (as was expected) it was advertised, was understandably angry. She consulted the Equal Opportunities Commission, but, Graham Peacock told me, was persuaded by the headteacher to withdraw her case 'if she valued her future in the school' (field notes). Her feelings of disempowerment caused by this episode, coupled with the embarrassment of the new coordinator, who would have liked to have gained his job in open competition, made for enormous difficulties in negotiating the new curriculum the following year.

At Stonemasons School, it was the female head of HE who was given the coordinator's post, after internal interviews. The manner of her appointment, however, was also somewhat disempowering. She was made coordinator of technology initially for one year only, the temporary nature of the appointment being mainly due to budgetary constraints. For most of this period she believed that her promotion would not continue into a second year, partly because although the headteacher thought she was doing a good job, he was not in a position to renew her appointment until the summer term. This perceived lack of stability and continuity, coupled with a difficult and sometimes rebellious staff team, made her work particularly difficult.

Appointments as D&T coordinator were also used in some schools to give signals to staff from senior managers about both the subject and the personnel. In Turnhill School, for example, the post was given to the existing head of IT, by a headteacher reluctant to introduce D&T at all, because she was willing, already paid at an appropriate level and 'was aware of what was happening' (Sue Pennington, Head of Technology, Turnhill School). At the same time this signalled to the CDT and HE staff not only that they were not competent to lead the overall subject, but that the experience of teaching a practical subject, which they particularly valued, was not seen as important. Subsequently, whenever they disagreed with Sue Pennington about the implementation of the curriculum, they argued that she was unable to understand the constraints of teaching in workshops and kitchens. Similar signals indicating lack of management esteem for D&T staff were given out at Knype School, where, when the head of department's post was advertised, the heads of CDT and HE were not shortlisted. Unable to make an outside appointment, the headteacher gave them the head of department post jointly, with disastrous consequences as they competed for dominance of the area as a whole.

Changes in curriculum and staffing structures

Even when the appointment of the D&T coordinator went comparatively smoothly, there still might be knock-on effects. For each head of a contributing department appointed overall coordinator, there was at least one other person who no longer strictly had a department to lead. Although salaries were protected, status was not, and people could feel that they had been demoted. This affected actual, as well as symbolic power relations. For example, at Stonemasons, the budget formerly given to the HE department was gradually transferred to D&T as a whole, so that the former head of HE lost financial autonomy. At Turnhill, the former head of CDT, now in charge of D&T in Key Stage (KS) 3 (ages 11–14), felt that, as well as loss of status, a key issue was that he was no longer in a position to negotiate on behalf of his team:

> I've been a head of department and being on that status of middle management, that's been lost . . . The head actually said that I'm quite welcome to go to curriculum meetings but it's not the same, is it, as being a head of department where you make the decisions . . . Sometimes I feel a bit tied because there's certain things like finances . . . and workshops and space . . . and numbers in workshops, and I do get a bit annoyed about things like that, and I don't seem to have a lot of say. . . . I'm not at the front line, if you see what I mean. I can't, I don't feel that I should go into the head's office and say, look, I'm not happy about it, because I'm not the head of department any more.
>
> (Tom Harty, former Head of CDT, Turnhill School)

In some schools, teachers actively or passively resisted such changes in staffing structures. This might also involve resisting the new curriculum that accompanied them. At Turnhill School, while the head of department, an IT specialist, was enthusiastic about the new curriculum, the CDT and HE teachers were not. Tom Harty, for example described how he and another colleague from CDT:

> didn't like the changes very much. Now things have been sorted out, but we raised objections to a number of things, and the head did come and see me . . . She said, 'Are you refusing to do what Sue is telling you to do?' And I said 'No, it's just that what I've been asked to do is very difficult.' . . . So it was made clear to me that I had to do what I was told.
>
> (Tom Harty, former Head of CDT, Turnhill School)

Although conspicuous and active resistance did cease after this incident, both the CDT and HE staff in this school continued (partly subconsciously, I think) passively to resist the new curriculum. For example, I observed several planning meetings being taken up with the repeated airing of complaints rather than the devising of new curriculum materials. My fieldnotes of one, supposed to be given over to writing differentiated worksheets, record that:

> This meeting is an amazing example of how to let red herrings get in the way of getting down to the task at hand. Part of the problem is what looks like ambition to make the worksheets really good, so that they

need training, discussion, etc. to get them right. But in fact none of them are really convinced they need them at all, except to satisfy Sue and the senior management. . . . My main impression is of talking as a way of avoiding a task that's not believed in.

(fieldnotes, Turnhill School)

At the same time as teachers competed for senior posts within the new subject, they also struggled with its definition. In this they were not helped by successive versions of the curriculum documentation containing slightly different requirements, this being due in its turn to macropolitical struggles within and beyond the National Curriculum Technology Working Group and the NCC (Layton 1995). Within schools, presenting one's own subject as central to D&T not only made it more likely that one would be seen as the obvious candidate for the head of department post, but also made it easier to come to terms with the level of curriculum change that would be required. As Sparkes (1990, 1991b, 1993) points out, in approaching curriculum change, teachers weigh up the extent to which they will win or lose by the innovation. Potential winners are, of course, more likely to embrace change, and potential losers to reject it. In the case of D&T, the likelihood of one being a winner depended to a large extent on how much of one's current work might be, or be perceived by senior managers to be, central to the new subject. Teachers made claims for centrality either by attempting to demonstrate how much of their previous subject was 'really' D&T or by suggesting that while they would themselves, of course, have to make some changes, their counterparts in the other contributing subjects would have far more to do. So, for example, several CDT teachers either said or implied that D&T would involve the retraining of HE staff in resistant materials, while one former head of HE remarked that 'We have always done technology in Home Economics – the only new thing is the technology umbrella' (Rachel McBride, former Head of HE, Stitchers School). Meanwhile, her counterpart in CDT, now overall coordinator for D&T, did not feel that this was so obvious, and his view seemed to be shared by the local advisory team, all former CDT specialists:

There are certain other subjects that are trying very hard to attach themselves to every element within it, almost to prove their worth in the scheme of things, I think. . . . I think, when the first report came out, it was very obviously CDT, and we thought, well, we are home and dry. We have done all this. Other subjects, like home economics, really, were saying, what's in it for us, where are we? And I think to an extent they are still saying that. Certainly there are far more courses that are being put on for home economics teachers in order for them to look at their subject in terms of D&T.

(Kenton Clark, coordinator for D&T, Stitchers School)

To believe that one's subject expertise has little importance to the area in which one is expected to teach could of course have far-reaching consequences for one's morale and sense of worth as a teacher. One HE teacher, now coordinator for technology at Stonemason's, faced precisely this dilemma. She told me that 'You can cover all the ATs and programmes of study in one subject, in CDT. You're not supposed to say that, but you can. It's better with the integrated approach, but you can do it' (Janet Parker, Stonemason's School). Faced with this belief, with the job of coordinating a subject to which she felt her own contribution was peripheral, she maintained her feelings of self-worth by emphasizing and fighting for aspects of HE that she saw as intrinsically important. She was particularly concerned that the food aspect of the subject should remain because of what she saw as the poor eating habits of the students, commenting that 'It's more important for their general education than CDT, *I* think'. It is noteworthy, however, that this aspect of HE was not really taken seriously in the Technology Order itself, and was later explicitly undermined by the first D&T SATs.

In making sense of the new curriculum it was of course crucially important for teachers to assimilate and interpret the new curriculum texts (Paechter 1993b). It was not a straightforward matter for them to translate ATs and PoSs into actual lessons and projects. In a situation in which curriculum emphases could be crucial, anyone who had a coherent interpretation of the key texts had a clear advantage in power terms, both within the department and in representing it to others. As Bowe *et al.* point out, 'Like other innovations the National Curriculum can disrupt existing hierarchies, advantage some and disadvantage others. Information and understanding, "authoritative readings", are at a premium in the process of accommodation' (1992: 90).

Given the openness of the original Order for Technology, such 'authoritative readings' were many and various, and what actually took place in classrooms differed enormously from school to school. This was exacerbated by the process of curriculum revision, which started as early as 1992 (see below). By the time the 1992 draft revised version of the curriculum (Department for Education/Welsh Office 1992) reached schools, in January 1993, teachers' workload had increased to a level at which they found it difficult to make time to engage with the new curriculum proposals at all. When the original Order was in preparation, teachers were, generally, excited and interested in the process, and read each document as it appeared. The second time round, however, many remembered how much the original curriculum had changed with each successive publication. They felt (correctly, as it turned out) that it would not be helpful to get too familiar with a document that might be changed before implementation. It was difficult enough keeping the new D&T curriculum clear in their heads alongside and distinct from the old GCSEs in HE and CDT still being studied by Years 10 and 11 (ages 14–16), without trying to understand a further variant that they were not at the time required to teach. As a result they disengaged themselves from the policy process. Under more immediate pressures, such as the need to prepare for the first D&T SATs and the urgency of decisions regarding the first KS4[7] D&T syllabuses, many teachers did not bother to read the 1992 proposals at all, choosing to wait instead for the final Order. This left them dependent for information on the educational and other press, and on any individual in the department or school who did decide to read the documents. Such people thus had an advantage in the struggle to persuade the department to recognize and adopt any particular reading as its own. In some schools this had serious repercussions. For example, at Bursley, a united CDT department had all read at least some of the documentation. Starting from their position that construction would now be the basis of KS3 D&T, they successfully argued that it no longer mattered whether food remained part of D&T at all.

Different interpretations both of the original Order and of the subsequent revised version were used both by teachers and by senior managers to promote or impose particular curriculum models. At Knype, where the department was unable to agree on an interpretation of the KS4 proposals, the headteacher used their disarray to impose her preferred interpretation. She introduced yet more change and interdisciplinarity in the form of joint courses with music, art and BS, as well as options in food, graphic media and textiles, a move which united the department in somewhat belated (and unsuccessful) opposition.

At Hanbridge, the Non-Statutory Guidance for D&T (National Curriculum Council 1990a) was used as part of a strongly gendered power struggle over the ownership and direction of the D&T curriculum in the school. The D&T coordinator was the female head of HE, who had worked mainly with two other women; an art teacher and the deputy head (subsequently head) of CDT. They had designed a curriculum structure in which students came together in interdisciplinary base groups for some lessons but spent most of their time rotating between separate materials areas, in order to carry out specialist design work. After nearly three years of this the male CDT staff were finding it unsatisfactory, and mounted an attack on this system, arguing that it would be better for art to be taught separately from D&T and for CDT, HE and IT to be taught in a non-integrated way. As supporting evidence they photocopied a paragraph from the Non-Statutory Guidance for D&T:

Schools will need to develop models for teaching design and technology, and examples of models are given below. These are for illustration, and to promote discussion. There are many other ways of providing design and technology. The 'carousel' or 'circus' model, in which pupils work with one material for a period of time before moving on to work with another material, is not recommended. This cannot provide progression, and the range of products is constrained by the limited materials available.

(National Curriculum Council 1990a: B11)

This paragraph, with the sentence condemning carousels highlighted, was used to argue against the department's existing curriculum model in a number of ways. Particular emphasis was laid on the rejection of carousel-based timetabling, although the department did not in fact use such a simple rotational model. At the same time, it was argued, along the lines of the quoted paragraph, that student progression under the current system was difficult to achieve or to track. In taking this line the male CDT teachers gained the support of their head of department, who was concerned about progression while generally supportive of integrated D&T. Most interesting, however, was the way that official condemnation of what amounts to separate delivery (students working with one material at a time with no linking themes or common lessons) was used to move the department precisely in this direction. They went from having some general, integrated input, to a decision to have none in future in Years 8 and 9. The use of the quoted paragraph is particularly ironic in this context as it is immediately followed by exemplar curriculum models, one of which is not dissimilar to the one being challenged (National Curriculum Council 1990a: B13).

Working with the new curriculum

You have to say when you give up some of these cherished things that you have, and I've got many, you have to see something better there, so that you say, 'I know we're not doing this, but the overall thing is for the greater good of what we're trying to achieve, and that's what's important.' And if people have doubts, of course you start to lose the enthusiasm for what you're doing and people pay lip service to it, and then of course it fails and everybody says, I told you so.

(Paddy Carpenter, former Head of CDT, Stonemasons School)

Teachers found it difficult to work with the new curriculum from the very beginning. Although many approached the innovation with optimism, the rapid pace of change, limited time for in-service training and the need to grapple with an almost content-free subject made it difficult to implement in practice. Furthermore, despite support from many teachers, each new department seemed to contain at least one person totally opposed to the new curriculum, who not only worked against its implementation but undermined the morale of other members. This in turn made things particularly difficult for the newly appointed head of department who might have to take ultimate responsibility for any failure. Given the subcultural and interpersonal struggles that had begun from the publication of the first set of National Curriculum documents, it is not surprising that generally disunited departments found it difficult to work together to make the vision of the new curriculum a reality.

For many teachers, the need to work with the full design cycle was a particular problem. None of the contributing departments had, up to then, given equal emphasis to all aspects of the cycle, and the need to plan and evaluate, particularly in writing, posed problems for departments previously heavily committed to practical activity. In many schools, particularly in working-class areas, CDT and HE had been seen as important areas where 'less able' students could do well and be kept out of trouble; particularly after age 14, some students had been able to spend a considerable proportion of their school time in practical subjects (Attar 1990). This ability to deal with students disaffected by the rest of school life had given these academically low status departments a paradoxically high status in some schools. The increased 'academic' emphasis of the subject (derided by several teachers as 'paperwork'), coupled with the presence for the first time of significant numbers of 'more able' students at KS4, made the move to D&T not just a matter of altering the curriculum but of changing teaching styles, classroom management approaches and assessment foci. Most teachers found the new subject more difficult to teach, even if they continued to work through their former CDT and HE projects, and, although they might welcome the opportunity to teach a wider range of students, they regretted the loss of parts of the curriculum they held particularly dear. Even those who were supposed to be supporting teachers in implementing the new curriculum might feel this way. Peter Simpson, a senior inspector in the area in which Bursley School was located, put these concerns particularly clearly:

> There's been this over-intellectualization. So if you look at GCSE technology papers, for example, they are designed, like the rest of the curriculum, for the most able, academic kids. . . . and that was the last, if you like, redoubt of technology, where kids could go into workshops, make things, develop an understanding of materials, to take some pride in practical skills, to be able to develop practical skills and get accredited for it. Even that now has gone.
>
> (Peter Simpson, LEA inspector)

As time went on there was also concern about continuing to teach all students throughout KS4, instead of only having to deal with those who had chosen the subject. The trade-off between gaining the 'more able' students and the disadvantages of having them there under compulsion, coupled with losing the opportunity to go into one's own specialism in more depth caused some teachers to worry about the future:

> We'll have the bright kids as well, but . . . we're actually not going to have any options.[8] We'll end up going to be teaching just a core and we've got no options. . . . It'll be horrendous. Everybody's nightmare is the third year [Year 9, ages 13–14], isn't it? Everybody thinks, 'third year, oh, thank goodness the third year have gone. At least we'll get the kids who want to be down here'. But we're going to have that same thinking without being able to extend the kids at all. . . . It's just like getting the third year all over again. And . . . subject skills, your skill areas, your interest areas, it'll be nothing really.
>
> (Alan McDonald, CDT teacher, Knype School)

Some teachers, faced with the loss of their traditional constituency and role in the school, struggling to teach a curriculum they were not clear that they understood and seeing nothing but change for the next five years as the new curriculum worked its way up the school, began to look back nostalgically to their former lives as craft specialists (Paechter 1995a). For CDT teachers in particular, this might mean harking back to even earlier times, when they specialized in woodwork or metalwork and focused almost entirely on making skills. Paddy Carpenter, former Head of CDT at Stonemasons School, for example, while saying several times that he felt that CDT should be the basis for D&T, still spoke with regret about the loss of his original role as a craft teacher: 'I've had years of being a craft teacher, which I must admit I thoroughly enjoyed. I thought it was valid in its own right' (Paddy Carpenter, former Head of CDT, Stonemasons School). This 'subcultural retreat' (Paechter 1995a) emphasized the difficulties teachers were having with the new subject, as well as in some cases widening the gap between those, gradually coming into schools, who had been trained to teach D&T or who had embraced it wholeheartedly, and those who were still fighting its introduction. Furthermore, because it tended to be male CDT staff who took this particularly nostalgic stance, such splits emphasized the gendered nature of many departmental divisions. Male staff increasingly seemed less adaptable than female, partly because they appeared to locate their professional identities in their designing and making skills (now less often needed) rather than in their competence as teachers (Paechter and Head 1996b). As the picture increasingly polarized into a situation in which enthusiastic women were attempting to move ahead into the new curriculum, resisted by men who remained defensive of the status quo, it is not surprising that morale in most of the departments studied became increasingly low as time went on.

National developments

> In 1989 Margaret Parkes' Technology Working Party report enjoyed more accolades than all the others put together. Visionary, revolutionary and inspiring were some of the adjectives used. Three years later technology education seems in crisis and the adjectives most often heard are demoralised, unworkable and even disastrous.
>
> (Eggleston 1992b: 14)

Although initially the public response to D&T, such as it was, was largely enthusiastic, as time went on, particularly after implementation in the autumn of 1990, there were an increasing number of reports in the press arguing that technology was failing and teachers discontented. These were reinforced by a damning (and much criticized) report commissioned by the Engineering Council (Smithers and Robinson 1992), followed a week later by a critical report from Her Majesty's Inspectorate of Schools (HMI) in the summer of 1992 (Her Majesty's Inspectorate of Schools 1992). As a result, the Secretary of State ordered a review of D&T, to be carried out by HMI. This was published in December 1992, and, although never actually implemented as it was overtaken by revisions to the whole curriculum carried out by Dearing (Dearing 1994), had a significant influence on events in schools.

Meanwhile, in the education press, there was an ongoing debate about the nature of D&T, paralleling that taking place in schools. This was framed by assumptions regarding the purpose of its introduction, and particularly by debates about the importance of general capability as compared with specific vocational skills. The more skilled rhetoricians actually encompassed both, arguing that capability was primarily vocational and that a failure to address the immediate perceived needs of industry implied the failure of the curriculum to address its intended goal; human capability for practical action. Examples from industry were used on both sides of the argument, and there remained an underlying assumption on the part of many writers that the importance of the subject to future industrial performance was the key issue. This was complicated by a concurrent and sometimes intersecting debate about the importance of craft skills and the issue of whether technology should be primarily about making, exemplified in its theorized form in an article in the *Times Educational Supplement* (*TES*) by Medway, lecturer in the School of Education, University of Leeds (Medway 1990). While appearing to support the approach of starting from the activities of practitioners, he described the resulting conception of D&T as 'bizarre' in its inclusion of a wide range of activities under one conceptual umbrella. He went on to suggest that the new curriculum contained a 'bias towards the cerebral', emphasizing consciously formulated design in a way that was not consonant with the actual experience of such activities as cooking, which 'proceeds by improvisation and adaptation in an ongoing response to available materials and equipment, time pressures and emerging flavours' (Medway 1990: 7). This, he argued, was coupled with 'confusion between technological and practical capability' (p. 7). Practical capability, he suggested, encompasses a wide range of situations, such as nursing, counselling and breaking in a horse, which do not involve technology; the absence of any other home for the practical, however, had left D&T to carry the whole burden of practical education. He concluded that the result was an artificial activity that bore little relation to the world outside the school.

The debate about the vocational nature of the subject had opened as early as December 1988 with an article in the *TES* reporting that a survey of skilled workers and artists had established that they had generally not been trained for their work through the traditional craft curriculum, which was seen as too narrow. It was hoped that the emphasis in the working group report (National Curriculum Technology Working Group 1988) on a wide range of craft skills would help to address this deficiency (Nash 1988). Most commentators, however, had the opposite opinion. In February 1990, for example, the Engineering Employers Federation argued that the proposals for the D&T curriculum would 'trivialize the subject and will water down demands' (Nash 1990). Such concerns were echoed by the Fellowship of Engineering and the British Management Data Foundation, although in the short term they had little effect (Layton 1995).

At the start of the second year of implementation, the debate between capability and a narrow interpretation of the vocational was intensified by the publication in October 1991 of a report (Prais and Beadle 1991) comparing the D&T curriculum to more specifically pre-vocational training in Germany, the Netherlands and France, and describing the work done in this country as 'Blue Peter[9] activities', a description that was picked up by critics and used, with little consideration of its applicability, to attack D&T in schools. At the same time a group of academics forming a Channel 4 Commission on Education recommended two new post-14 technical and vocational tracks, focused on GCSEs such as woodwork and metalwork (Halsey *et al.* 1991). A *TES* leader article (1991), while pointing out that in the Prais and Beadle report 'there was little recognition . . . that work with scrap and salvage materials is all that some schools can afford' argued that, with the introduction of the option to take only a half course in D&T at KS4, it should also be possible to offer examination options that combined this with more specifically vocational work, making the curriculum more suitable for practically inclined students. The attack on the broader interpretation of D&T as concerned with capability rather than skills was now well under way, leading Eggleston to describe it as a flower fading in the 'cold blasts of a New Right winter' (Eggleston 1991).

These attacks ran alongside and at times intersected with the struggle, outside as well as inside schools, for pre-eminence between the component subject areas. In the press, the background of subcultural struggle within schools was generally referred to somewhat obliquely, perhaps with the intention of not exacerbating an already difficult situation. However, a letter to the *TES* from the honorary secretary of the Association of Advisers in Craft, Design and Technology, for example, notes that 'What should be regarded as an entitlement for children has been interpreted by some as an entitlement for subject areas' (Welch 1990). Culpin, president of the same association, was more specific when he noted that 'Many subject associations have spent too much time in recent years justifying their own component part of D&T and not enough time concentrating on the combination of features which originally secured it a place in [the] national curriculum' (Culpin 1991).

Such attempts to justify one's own place might be more easily understood given some of the other things that were being written during this period. Harrison, for example, must have worried a number of those caught up in an in-school struggle for survival with his assertion that:

> A misleading but inevitable part of the emergence of technology as a subject in the national curriculum has been the indication that its activities are currently found in five particular subjects in schools . . . I have seen excellent delivery of virtually everything needed for the national curriculum design and technology all from a CDT department; equally, in another school, it has emerged under the banner of art and design. Home economists have also been able to put it all together. What is common about all these approaches is that the host department has dropped the conventional, defensive approach to their subject.
>
> (Harrison 1990)

The problem for teachers with the idea that one department might be able to 'put it all together' is that it could mean redundancy for those working in any area now deemed unnecessary. This was a particular issue for teachers of HE and, to a lesser extent, BS. There was a persistent idea in some press articles, and stated most clearly in the highly critical Smithers and Robinson report (1992), that these subjects were only included in D&T because there was nowhere else for them to go.

It was this report that really brought the debate out into the open. Its publication in May 1992 in itself caused little remark, despite it being 'rich in sound-bites' (Layton 1995: 106). It described technology teaching as being in a mess and recommended a return to designing and making as central activities (Smithers and Robinson 1992). The immediate response was fairly muted, although the narrowness of the authors' data set was noted (Welch 1992). The following week, however, everything began to change. An HMI report on the first year of D&T (Her Majesty's Inspectorate of

Schools 1992) found that in secondary schools only 59 per cent of D&T lessons were 'satisfactory or better' and that many teachers had found the Order difficult to understand (Blackburne 1992a; Layton 1995). This led John Patten, the Education Secretary, to ask the Inspectorate to conduct an urgent review of the subject, to be published in the autumn and introduced for pupils up to age 14 in September 1994. In an article in the *TES*, Blackburne (1992a) highlighted three schools of thought regarding how the Order should be rewritten. The first advocated a return to woodwork and metalwork. The second, Smithers and Robinson's position (given more space than the other two), was that designing and making should be central, with food, textiles and BS being taken out of the subject. The third approach involved preserving the spirit of the original Order while making the document itself more accessible to teachers. This range of approaches was picked up in a leader in the same issue, which also suggested that the government was asking for a fundamental rethink of the subject.

The struggle for control of D&T was now out in the open. In a review of recent events published the following week, Eggleston (1992a), while acknowledging that 'some projects are, quite frankly, appalling', defended the existing Order and noted the speed with which both the School Examinations and Assessment Council (SEAC) (in increasing the weighting of AT3, the practical component) and the NCC had reacted to press coverage. He also pointed to what he saw as the real issues behind the changes, arguing that the Engineering Council and the press (the *Daily Mail* had blamed the failure of technology on teachers' distaste for the practical) had ignored the fact that professional designers themselves reflect the status quo in which academic subjects lead to high-flying careers, and do not generally have craft based qualifications.

Meanwhile, faced with Engineering Council calls for their exclusion, the home economists began to fight back, although from a position of subcultural retreat rather than support for D&T. During the summer of 1992, two *TES* articles and a letter argued that children were not learning basic food skills and that a marginalization of home economics would make it impossible to meet national healthy eating targets (O'Grady 1992; Rafferty 1992). Meanwhile, a *TES* news item on 26 June (Blackburne 1992c), reported the Secretary of State's brief to the HMI team as 'a victory for the traditionalists in the CDT lobby'. The reporter interpreted the instruction to put designing and making at the centre of the new curriculum as pointing to the end of the two year 'experiment' of D&T, suggesting that the rewrite would exclude HE and that teachers of these subjects would have to retrain as specialists in wood, metal and plastic. This led to a whole page of letters on 10 July, protesting at such proposals, including one from the chair of the NCC, emphasizing that their advice to the Secretary of State did not advocate a return to traditional CDT teaching (Pascall 1992), and another from

Baroness Blatch, the Minister of State for Education, assuring readers that 'it is not our intention to exclude food, textiles or design from national curriculum technology. The terms of reference for the review . . . state explicitly that the underpinning conceptual framework of the technology Order will be preserved' (Blatch 1992). A senior executive of the Engineering Council also wrote to distance his organization from 'traditionalists in the craft, design and technology lobby' (Williams 1992).

Press reports through the autumn of 1992 were characterized more by rumour than by hard news. On 30 October it was reported in the *TES* that the review team had proposed that the four attainment targets be reduced to two (Blackburne 1992b); this was described as being in line with the recommendations of the Smithers and Robinson report. The same edition carried a letter pointing out that school CDT accommodation would be insufficient for the whole of Year 10 to spend 5 per cent of their curriculum time on a course focused on construction materials. This was echoed in an article by a headteacher in December 1992 (Dunford 1992), who also pointed out that KS4 had to be planned for September 1993, using as yet unseen syllabuses that, while conforming to the current Order, were also supposed to take into account the revisions that had not as yet been published. He argued that, in the absence of approved syllabuses, he was unable to tell parents what would be on offer to their children in the next academic year, and that it would be better to postpone the introduction of KS4 for two years.

The effects of assessment

Meanwhile, teachers had been grappling with the problems not just of teaching the new curriculum, but of assessing it. These came to a head in the spring of 1993, when students were to take the first D&T KS3 SATs (Paechter 1995c). Although in the first two years of KS3 there was supposed to have been ongoing teacher based formative assessment, what had actually taken place had varied in both quality and quantity from school to school. Hanbridge, for example, had a complex system in place and more or less functioning (although Judas Sunshine, a particularly recalcitrant CDT teacher, had to be given a formal warning by the headteacher before he would complete the forms). On the other hand, the department at Longshaw Girls' School never really got their act together at all, and the staff at Bursley declared the task to be impossible at an early stage and instead of matching students' work to ATs were extrapolating from their experience of GCSE assessment. The spectre of external assessment in the form of the SAT, suddenly brought this issue to the fore in the Spring of 1993,[10] and formed the final nail in the coffin of open and integrated D&T teaching.

The D&T SAT was unusual in that it was an extended task, supposed to be carried out in 12 hours of D&T lesson time. Students were expected in this time to produce a portfolio of eight sides of A3 paper, as well as a finished artefact. In theory, CDT teachers in particular were used to carrying out extended practical assessments because of their experience with GCSE projects; in practice working with the SAT was very different. To start with, the model on which it was based was not that of continuous assessment but of examination. It was expected that the work 'should be done in a semi-formal manner' (Department for Education 1993: 6) and that students should 'work independently' for the first two hours, this latter stipulation being interpreted by teachers as meaning working in silence. Teachers also generally believed that because this was an examination, students could not be taught anything while working on the task. Many refused to answer students' questions, and became very frustrated, not only by the difference between this and their normal teaching but also by the loss of time to work on new material (see Torrance 1991).

Teachers were also frustrated by the nature and structure of the tasks set. There was a choice of three closely specified design briefs: a small clamp which had to work using a compression block; a warning beacon for use when camping; and an 'energy bar' to be eaten as a meal replacement on a hike. The specific materials to be worked with caused widespread alarm, particularly as the curriculum was by then under review. Many believed that the lack of a task based in textiles meant that it was about to be written out of the subject altogether. In all the schools except Knype, where some indication of the nature of the beacon task had been leaked to the staff by someone close to the SAT development team, the tasks came as a considerable shock. They differed considerably from the pilot SATs of previous years, and appeared to be more in accordance with the proposed revision of the D&T curriculum (Department for Education/Welsh Office 1992), the draft of which had only just been published. Teachers felt uncomfortable about what they saw as the poor relationship between the detailed knowledge required for the tasks set and the much more open curriculum that they had been following up until then. They felt that they had not been given the chance to prepare students properly for the examination, for example by giving them appropriate practice activities (Madaus 1988): 'We've been examined this year on an Order we haven't yet seen, because there's nowhere in [the current] Order that we're supposed to teach to the depth of electronics that they're asking kids to actually produce' (John Wallace, CDT teacher, Knype School). The tasks were also widely seen as lacklustre and prescriptive. Only one teacher in my study actually liked the activities; the others saw them as potentially limiting for their students: 'Emlyn says he's beginning to suggest to students that they become less adventurous, which he hates' (fieldnotes, Longshaw Girls' School). Home economists were particularly unhappy about the energy bar, which they saw as undermining the healthy eating based principles of their subject. Furthermore, this normal emphasis meant that their students had little or no previous experience of mixing sugar and syrup, or of working with chocolate, and it was considered necessary to prepare them specifically with work in this area before the SAT could be carried out.

Once the task got underway further problems were encountered. It rapidly became clear that it was not going to be possible for students to produce sufficient work in the 12 hours specified. Because the results of the tests were supposed to be being published, this put both teachers and students under a great deal of pressure. This was compounded by their five years of experience with GCSE coursework, with its emphasis on showing what students can do, rather than demonstrating their failures. Teachers felt unable simply to assess what was achieved in the limited time, and gradually began to look for ways around it. At Knype, for example, the 12-hour limit was interpreted strictly as 12 hours of work, with time spent getting out and packing up equipment excluded. This meant that the total lesson time allowed was nearer to 20 hours than 12. At Bursley, where, as in all the schools, there was a whole-school policy of requiring regular homework, the teachers simply came to the conclusion that it was more important for the students to be able to show their best work, by doing extra at home, than to adhere to the regulations. Although individually they had doubts about whether this was right, once they realized they were all doing the same, they were quite open about their stance:

> Yes, they're all breaking the rules. We all have. Funny how we didn't admit to it to start with. We were hiding that we were doing this, from each other, until that meeting when suddenly it all came out in the open. I think it was me that said, 'Well, to be honest with you I am not doing as we've been suggested to do'. And then someone else said something, then someone else.
>
> (Paula Tomson, HE teacher, Bursley School)

Once liberated by their solidarity in deciding that students were more important than official procedures, this department went on to apply this principle in other areas. One teacher regarded the stipulation that the clamp should have a sprung mechanism operated by downward pressure as so inappropriate that he ignored it and his students made clamps with screw threads. The head of department justified this modification of the design brief on pedagogic grounds, arguing that it was absurd to spend three years teaching students that there can be a variety of solutions, and then insist that the clamp be worked by pushing down. The department as a group, supported by the headteacher, then felt sufficiently emboldened by their solidarity in defiance of authority to decide that they would (in contravention of the Education Reform Act 1988) refuse to implement KS4 in D&T and in future only teach those parts of KS3 with which they were in agreement.

Although the experience of the SATs was ultimately empowering for this group, it had the reverse effect on others. For most, the conflict between the teacher and examiner role was a significant source of stress, which exacerbated that already experienced by those who had found it hard to come to terms with the D&T curriculum as a whole. For example, under the impact of the SATs (and particularly because of conflicts about how they should be assessed), the already riven D&T department at Knype split still further into mistrustful factions. On the other hand, given that the SATs, however boring, had a greater emphasis on making and craft skills than the Order itself, some teachers saw their practical nature as suggesting that the curriculum was more in line with their previous work than they had thought. This, particularly as it allowed them to argue that they did not need to make such radical changes as they had feared, partially resolved their former conflict, and made it easier for them to accept the Order and work within it. This was, however, at the expense of the ideal of integrated D&T. The detail of specific content in the SAT tasks also suggested to most teachers in my study that, if they had not done so already, they needed to move away from integrated provision and back to delivering separate parts of a loosely connected curriculum. As one teacher put it:

> I was a bit unhappy, but I didn't feel the system we had was unworkable, not until the SATs came up . . . and we realized that it would be better to keep the subject areas separate so that all pupils went to all subjects continually throughout the year and that their skills could be built from the most simple to the more complex to raise the levels of achievement.
>
> (Lila Patel, HE teacher, Hanbridge School)

The end of integration

The revised Draft Order (Department for Education/Welsh Office 1992) was finally published in mid-December of 1992 and reached schools in early 1993, ending six months of debate and speculation. After all the triumphalism and anxiety, it was not radically different from its predecessor. Events, however, had meanwhile overtaken this review, and it turned out that teachers had been justified in their lack of interest in the proposed revisions. In April 1993, the Secretary of State for Education asked Sir Ron Dearing, the new chair of both the NCC and SEAC (now to be combined to form the School Curriculum and Assessment Authority (SCAA)) to undertake a thorough review of the whole National Curriculum, with a view to making it less burdensome on teachers and schools. The revisions to D&T were necessarily postponed and did not appear until March 1994. Meanwhile, teachers were asked to continue working to the 1990 Order for KS1–KS3, although, as a result of the recommendations of the Dearing Committee (Dearing 1994), D&T was no longer to be compulsory in KS4 for the next two years, pending the introduction of a new curriculum for the subject.

When it did finally appear, the new Order for D&T (Department for Education/Welsh Office 1995) represented the final disintegration of the integrated subject. Particularly from KS3 onwards, it was dominated by resistant materials, work in only one of the two HE areas, compliant materials (textiles) and food, being compulsory.[11] BS had more or less disappeared from the Order. Furthermore, at KS4, students would be required to take a short course only, leaving open the possibility that D&T could be combined with a number of other subjects or vocational options at GCSE level. The curriculum was to be focused around designing and making skills, with the knowledge and understanding to be conveyed specified in the PoSs. The openness that had given the curriculum both its enormous potential and made its implementation so difficult had finally gone, and the requirement to consider human purposes and values played a much less important role. The detailed specification of the subject's base of knowledge and understanding in particular made it much more difficult for teachers to work in an integrated, interdisciplinary way, and made it more or less inevitable that departments that had not split their teaching back into subject areas would rapidly do so. By 1995, the innovation represented by the ideas in the original Working Group interim report (National Curriculum Technology Working Group 1988) and carried through in the first version of National Curriculum D&T (National Curriculum Council 1989) had all but disappeared.

Notes

1 The D&T Order has subsequently been changed, partly as a result of the events outlined in this chapter.
2 For each National Curriculum subject, non-statutory guidance was issued, to support teachers in implementing the new curriculum. In the case of D&T it included possible curriculum models and sample projects.
3 A quango set up to oversee the National Curriculum.
4 Industrial pressure had been in evidence in the past (McCulloch *et al.* 1985), but by necessity in the form of sponsorship of curriculum development projects, given that the actuality of a compulsory curriculum was a new feature.
5 These specify the criteria against which students are assessed. There were ten attainment levels (now eight, as education after age 14 is assessed by public examination), and the ATs are the same for all stages of schooling, so students would be expected to progress through the levels as they progress through school.
6 For details of the research on which this account is based, see Appendix.

7 Ages 14–16. The GCSE is taken at the end of this period.
8 Students in England and Wales had previously had a considerable degree of choice about what subjects they studied between ages 14 and 16. With the advent of the National Curriculum this was, particularly in the first few years, considerably restricted. Compulsory D&T meant that it was no longer possible for anyone to opt out of working with resistant materials or for schools to offer the traditional CDT and HE subjects such as Design and Realization, HE Food or Child Development.
9 *Blue Peter* is a popular and longstanding children's television programme in which artefacts are famously constructed from washing-up liquid bottles and egg boxes.
10 Although a national boycott of the SATs was begun at Easter 1993, the timing of the D&T task meant that most schools still carried it out, although it was assessed as normal schoolwork.
11 From 2000 students at KS3 are 'expected' to work with both areas in the majority of schools (Qualifications and Curriculum Authority 2000).

six

PHYSICAL EDUCATION, SPORT AND THE BODY

First of all one must set aside the widely held thesis that power, in our bourgeois, capitalist, societies has denied the reality of the body in favour of the soul, consciousness, ideality. In fact nothing is more material, physical, corporal than the exercise of power. What mode of investment of the body is necessary and adequate for the functioning of a capitalist society like ours? From the eighteenth to the early twentieth century I think it was believed that the investment of the body by power had to be heavy, ponderous, meticulous and constant. Hence those formidable disciplinary regimes in the schools, hospitals, barracks, factories, cities, lodgings, families.

(Foucault 1980: 58)

The school curriculum is, overtly at least, largely unconcerned with the body. The focus is mainly on the mind, attention to the physical being separated off into a low status subject and extra-curricular activities. In many ways, this reflects the mind–body dualism prevalent in Western society (Spelman 1982; Gatens 1991). Much writing about the curriculum, with the exception of that explicitly focused on PE or, to a lesser extent, manual crafts, treats students as if they were disembodied; it is their minds that are the focus of our attention. When, as in the hormonal disruptions of adolescence, the embodiment of students cannot be prevented from intruding on our consciousness, this is treated as a problem, a distraction. The experience of ourselves as bodies as well as minds is sidelined by the school (Nespor 1997). PE, as the only aspect of the curriculum explicitly and solely dealing with students' bodies, is expected to compensate for this disparity.

This is not to say, of course, that schooling ignores the body. On the contrary, much of school practice is concerned with disciplining the bodies of students (Foucault 1977). In most UK secondary schools, students' bodies are only permitted to be covered by specified, often restrictive and uncomfortable, gendered clothing (Shilling 1992, 1993). Students are expected to use their bodies in particular ways; they must stand up when teachers enter the room, but may not run in the corridors, sit on the tables or move about freely in most lessons (Gordon 1996; Gordon and Lahelma 1996). They are very aware of this and may even distinguish between school subjects mainly in terms of bodily freedoms: 'Well in drama you've got like freedom, haven't you, and what not. You're not sat behind a desk working – well, you are working, but not writing' (Year 10 student, Lacemakers School). Students are not allowed in some regions of the school, or may only enter them at certain times. The performance of basic bodily functions, such as eating and excreting, are restricted to particular periods (Nespor 1997). All of this is a part of the disciplining of students through school practices; their bodies are strictly and explicitly controlled in an attempt better to reach their minds as well as to prepare them for the further disciplinary structures of the workplace (Foucault 1978). Only in PE, however, is the body the explicit and only object of education. Even in those other subjects that involve work on the body, such as music, art, drama and D&T, bodily or manual training is seen as a means to a mental end. In PE, work on the body is carried out, at least within the overt discourses of the school, for its own sake. As we shall see, however, this is only the 'official', 'educational' line; because of the disciplinary role of bodily constraint, PE has always been, and remains, hostage to attempts to use it for the control of particular social groups (Evans and Penney 1995b).

The school curriculum is also largely organized around what was originally a masculine model; the dominant mode of organization remains that devised for ruling-class boys. High status areas, despite attempts (for example in the area of science in the early twentieth century (Manthorpe 1986)) to introduce more female-orientated forms, remain dominated by masculine values (Paechter 1998a). It is only in low status subjects that separate male and female forms have persisted; the raising of the status of D&T, for example, was accompanied by an attempt to forge a new, gender-neutral area out of the significantly gendered predecessor subjects of CDT and HE. All aspects of schooling are dominated by men and boys, and by masculine curricular forms. Even though most primary teachers are female, more headteachers are male, and this disparity continues in secondary schooling (Arnot *et al.* 1996). Schooling practices also become more masculine as students get older. Relationships with teachers become more formal and distant, and the emphasis on achievement and competition becomes stronger (Öhrn 1993). The secondary curriculum, in particular, is also dominated by masculine forms of knowledge based on reason, such as mathematics and science (Paechter 1998a).

In the UK, PE remains the only subject on the curriculum that retains two parallel, gendered forms, taught separately to boys and girls. Even so, male sports, in particular, are dominant, in terms of both finances and facilities, over female, while the majority of school PE departments are in the overall charge of men, with a lower status woman looking after girls' PE (Evans and Williams 1988; Scraton 1993). Moves to provide equity in PE provision have focused on the idea that both genders should be offered the same diet. This has meant in practice that both genders have followed a curriculum based on male PE (Scraton 1993), despite the continuation of a female PE tradition so strong that Fletcher (1984) claims that its successful formulation as a school subject was wholly due to women. This is not really surprising and reflects power/gender relations in the education system as a whole.

However, the position of PE with respect to the pre-eminently masculine curriculum is somewhat contradictory. While male PE, and particularly some male sports, is a significant arena for the reproduction of hegemonic masculinity (Connell 1995), at the same time, in Western culture, inescapable embodiment has been seen as a fundamental aspect of femininity. One of the long-standing arguments put forward in the nineteenth century against equal access to education or civil society was that woman was fundamentally embodied, unable to transcend her bodily impulses and operate in a higher realm of reason (Spelman 1982; Hekman 1990; Gatens 1991; French 1994). Counterposed to the male, disciplined, rational mind was the female, undisciplined, emotional body. Some of this counterposition is retained in the male and female forms of PE, and underlies the difficulties in bringing the two together. Wright (1996a), for example, notes that students see indoor activities as being for girls, and outdoor activities as of higher status and for boys; this reflects traditional Western notions of gendered private and public spheres. Furthermore, male PE can, at least in its origins, be seen as concerned with the disciplining and subduing of the body, with bringing it into bounds so that the mind and the moral sense can take command. Female PE, on the other hand, is more to do with exploration and expression, with letting the body speak rather than bringing it under control. This, of course, also reflects the historical conditions pertaining at the time of its origins, when pioneering educationists sought to free women's bodies from the confinement of convention and corsetry (Fletcher 1984).

Disciplining the docile body

PE has traditionally, because of its direct work on the body, been an important medium for disciplining gendered bodies, producing a gendered docility. Foucault argues that the idea of the docile body emerged during the eighteenth century, alongside the notion that the body could be analysed and understood: 'A body is docile which may be subjected, used, transformed and improved' (Foucault 1977: 136). The body is no longer just a given, it can be altered, specifically for the benefit of the state. This is particularly the case for the bodies of soldiers:

> By the late eighteenth century, the soldier has become something that can be made; out of a formless clay, an inapt body, the machine required can be constructed; posture is gradually corrected; a calculated constraint runs slowly through each part of the body, mastering it, making it pliable, ready at all times, turning silently into the automatism of habit.
>
> (Foucault 1977: 135)

For whose purposes this newly formed machine is constructed is of course a matter of class. Whereas the peasant might be transformed into a soldier, subject to an external discipline rather than what would have been seen as his animal instincts, the ruling-class male would become fit to lead or to govern, his body subjected to the dictates of his higher self. The purpose of the disciplining of the body in each case, however, is to render it docile, to reduce its power with respect in the former case to outside authority and in the latter, to the superior dictates of the mind. The production of docility was particularly important at this juncture, with the increased mechanization of industrial processes and the growing importance of particular forms of warfare: 'On almost every occasion, [disciplinary processes] were adopted in response to particular needs: an industrial innovation, a renewed outbreak of certain epidemic diseases, the invention of the rifle or the victories of Prussia' (Foucault 1977: 139). In particular there was a tendency to break processes down into their component parts, to separate actions but at the same time require that they be performed in synchrony with one another. Bodies had to be disciplined in such a way that they would respond to commands, move to a regular drumbeat, or conform to the repetitive processes of the factory. This disciplining, while making it possible for bodies to function as required in the setting in which it took place, had the further function of making them, and thus people, behave in a more generally docile manner. The habit of discipline, of response to command, instilled at an early age as part of the disciplinary mechanism of the school and continued into the arrangements of the factory, became ingrained into the bodies and hence the minds, of citizens, thus supporting the work of the state. As people became more able to conform to the organization of the new factories, they became at the same time, more subject to the disciplinary power of the state apparatus.

> Thus discipline produces subjected and practised bodies, 'docile' bodies. Discipline increases the forces of the body (in economic terms

of utility) and diminishes these same forces (in political terms of obedi-ence). In short, it dissociates power from the body; on the one hand, it turns it into an 'aptitude', a 'capacity', which it seeks to increase; on the other hand, it reverses the course of the energy, the power that might result from it, and turns it into a relation of strict subjection. If econ-omic exploitation separates the force and the product of labour, let us say that disciplinary coercion establishes in the body the constricting link between an increased aptitude and an increased domination.

(Foucault 1977: 138)

It is important that we do not see this disciplinary work on the body as a purely negative force. One of the reasons that it has been so readily accepted is that a fit, strong body feels good; it gives the individual a powerful sense of agency and purpose (McCormack 1999). The disciplined body is docile, at least in part, because this form of discipline brings with it undeniable pleasures.

The disciplinary tendency with respect to the body has developed during the twentieth century into a moral imperative on both males and females to be physically fit and healthy (Wright 1996a). Sparkes (1991a) argues, for example, that, within the health-related fitness movement, concepts of morality have been translated into questions of lifestyle, so that those who lead 'unhealthy' lives are seen as morally lax. Those who are overweight, in particular, are seen as lacking in self-discipline, needing the interventionist powers of the state to encourage and support them in conforming to bodily norms.

Male PE has played a particularly important and overt role in the pro-duction of docile bodies. While the rhetoric surrounding the introduction of female PE reflected the belief that physical exercise was the best training for motherhood (Fletcher 1984), the dominant discourse of its male counter-part, particularly as regards sport, was and remains, concerned with the need for a strong, yet well ordered, citizenry. A recent UK Minister for Sport, for example, argued that

The behavioural lessons of discipline, especially self-discipline, courage, team spirit, learning to play with others and learning to live within the rules are all vital. If sport had been better taught in schools over recent years, I am sure we would not have witnessed some of the recent out-breaks of ill-behaviour. That is why the Government start from the premise that sport in schools is important.

(*Hansard*, 7 June 1996, quoted in Davies *et al.* 1997: 261)

Davies *et al.* note the overt use of male PE in the promotion of Welsh nationalism, with students being encouraged to take up rugby, the 'national sport': 'Teachers convey the view that they and their pupils are guardians of the language, thus of Welsh heritage and tradition, of standards best expressed in sport and PE by playing and offering allegiance to the nation's major team games' (1997: 266). Rees (1997) argues that this is further developed in the USA into an emphasis not just on sport, but on sporting success, in building national character. He suggests that winning has become an American tradition which symbolizes both moral superiority to and dominance over other nations. There is some evidence (Campbell and Wintour 1999) of government sponsored moves in this direction in the UK, contrasting with the traditional (official) British attitude that it is participation rather than winning that develops the sound moral qualities desired.

The separate traditions of male and female PE

The traditions of male PE arise directly from this disciplinary tendency. Drill was introduced into elementary schools in the 1870s in order to improve the health of military recruits; although Swedish gymnastics was taught in London from the 1880s, in the rest of the country, boys in particular had drill as their main PE diet. Many elementary schools had insufficient space for games, which remained the preserve of the elite private boys' schools (Fletcher 1984). This distinction also reflects the purposes of PE for the two groups. For working-class children of both genders, health was conceived in terms of order, cleanliness and neatness; mass marching and drill were seen as encouraging social regulation. For middle-class and upper-middle-class males, health outcomes were seen as less salient; they played organized team games and sport to develop courage, loyalty and leadership. Until the 1930s, the male teachers who worked with both these groups were trained, not as teachers, but during military service, giving them a focus not on education but on order, rapid obedience to commands and sporting excellence (Wright 1996b).

Female PE, on the other hand, has directly educational roots. Women's PE colleges, set up in the UK in the late nineteenth and early twentieth century, trained women to teach gymnastics according to the Swedish Ling system, concentrating on movement, poise and physical remediation. These colleges were extremely influential; Wright (1996b) notes that they trained not only several important figures in the development of PE in Australia, but also most teachers in the Australian girls' private school system. Students in these colleges were taught theory of gymnastics, anatomy, physiology and games (Fletcher 1984). Like drill, Swedish gymnastics emphasized formal and command-led teaching, and was relaxed during the 1920s and 1930s to include more rhythmic work done to music. By the 1940s it had been displaced by a form of educational gymnastics associated with the work of Laban; this blurred the line between gymnastics and dance. Its view of every human being as a dancer gave it a close affinity with the child-centred, problem-solving discourses prevalent in education more generally at that time (Fletcher 1984; Wright 1996b). By this time, however, male PE colleges had opened and were also teaching gymnastics. In this case, however, it was the Olympic form, stressing not individual, non-directive problem solving but skill acquisition, strength and expert performance (Kirk 1990); in Australia this also spread into girls' PE, where artistic gymnastics was often taught at secondary level (Wright 1996b).

These separate traditions have brought with them entirely different subject cultures. Although PE teacher training is increasingly coeducational, PE staff still orientate themselves according to the two traditions, and partly still along gender lines. On the one side are those with a background in human movement science, who focus on success and concentrate their attention on maintaining a high level of physical skills in elite performers and in particular on promoting sporting excellence. On the other are those from movement education who see PE as child-centred, egalitarian and concerned with the personal and social development of all students via individual, self-paced activities such as educational gymnastics and swimming (Sparkes 1990; Wright 1996b). In the USA this split is further complicated by the distinction between physical educators, concerned with fitness for all, and high school sports coaches, who may not be trained in PE at all, and whose focus is entirely on training elite players to win in competitive arenas (Rees 1997).

Frank (1991) identifies four ideal types of bodily usage, which can be mapped on to the various forms of PE and sport/leisure pursuits. He suggests that in response to the four 'action problems' of control, desire, the body's relation to others and the self-relatedness of the body, there are four distinct ways in which the body is used:

> These ideal types are not meant to encompass all possible types of bodily usage but serve as heuristic guides through which bodily behaviour can be understood. For the *disciplined* body the medium is *regimentation*, the model of which is the rationalization of the monastic order. For the *mirroring* body the medium is *consumption*, the model of which is the department store. For the *dominating* body the medium is *force*, the model of which is war; and for the *communicative* body the medium is *recognition*, the model of which could be shared narratives, communal rituals and caring relationships.
>
> (Shilling 1993: 95, original emphasis)

We can map at least the first three of these forms on to uses of the body in sport and PE. The first, the disciplined body, is that found in the practice of drill both in military establishments and in elementary schools in the nineteenth and early twentieth centuries. Here, the body obeyed separate, precise commands, an individuation and division of a whole (the regiment, the movement) that reflects the regulation and separation of the monastic order. The mirroring body is to be found pre-eminently in body-building practices, where the look of the surface of the body is all important. The body of the body-builder is designed for visual consumption; what is seen is only partially reflective of the reality of physical development (male body-builders may remove body hair, females may have breast implants to replace those lost through diet and exercise) or the state of the body at rest. We might also see the appropriation of the female body within dance practices, which have at least an element of display, as coming under this heading (Frank 1991). The dominating body is, of course, to be found in competitive sports, particularly in those masculine arenas (male US high school teams, or at professional level) where winning is all important. It is important to note here that the dominating body, far from being empowered, is driven by fear, which is combated by being turned outward on to the destruction of others; others must be defeated in order for the dominating body to be able to live with itself. Frank suggests that the final form, the communicative body, 'is less a reality than a praxis' but that it might be found 'in the aesthetic practices of dance and performance and the caring practices of medicine. The essential quality of the communicative body is that it is a body *in process* of creating itself' (Frank 1991: 79, original emphasis). Given, however, that one feature of the communicating body is that it is comfortable with itself in relation to others, it might also be argued that it is an aspect of the ideal aimed at by those promoting group work within student-centred, problem-focused expressive movement.

These forms are, again, gendered. With the exception of the mirroring body, which seems to have separate masculine and feminine forms, they divide more or less on gender lines. Frank (1991), indeed, implies that the nature of masculinity makes it more or less impossible for able-bodied males to achieve a communicative body. The different traditions of male and female PE thus deal with and reflect very different ideas about and uses of the body. This becomes particularly significant when we consider the importance of PE as a site for the reproduction of gender relations.

PE and the reproduction of gender relations

PE is a particularly important arena in which stereotypical gender roles are played out and gendered power/knowledge relations displayed. By taking different stances towards different forms of PE, males and females can demonstrate or implicitly call into question their masculinity or femininity. This is because of the importance of embodiment to masculine or feminine stances, and of the way in which bodily display is used in different forms of PE.

Butler argues that the gendered body is performative. By this she means that 'It has no ontological status apart from the various acts that constitute its reality . . . acts and gestures, articulated and enacted desires create the illusion of an interior and organizing core' (1990: 136). To put it another way, we are all, in our daily lives, engaged in performing our gender, in demonstrating masculinity or femininity through our actions. Within PE and sport this is done in clear and distinct ways, by taking part in or abstaining from particular activities and by producing particular bodily forms, by conforming to or transgressing gender stereotypes.

Bryson (1987) points out that sport is a powerful institution through which masculine hegemony is constructed and reconstructed. She notes in particular the way in which a negative evaluation of women's capacities promotes male solidarity through exclusion (Nelson 1996). Brittan (1989) suggests that the most popular image of masculinity in everyday consciousness is as a hero, hunter, conqueror and competitor; it is these qualities that are celebrated in men's competitive sports. Nespor also points to the ways in which even talking about sports is used by prepubescent boys as a way to demonstrate an exclusive masculinity:

A public preoccupation with sports was an assertion that a boy was a member of an indisputably male domain, an assertion made plausible by the continuing dominance of men's sports in the popular media and by the boys' refusal to talk with girls about sports, even when girls knew demonstrably more about the subject than the boys did. Actual participation in organized team activity was much less important in establishing masculinity than constant talk about it, in part, perhaps, because girls were likely to be as active and proficient as boys in team sports such as basketball.

(1997: 147)

The precarious nature of adolescent identity (Head 1997) also means that extreme forms of masculinity are more prevalent in schools than in wider society; PE is often used as an arena for their expression. Parker (1996), for example, notes the importance of violence in the lives of many adolescent boys, and suggests that PE is a key site of its enactment. In the school he studied, violence was an accepted element of PE, with some groups taking advantage of the comparatively informal situation to use 'gladiatorial violence' to impose their own dominant form of masculinity while marginalizing others. Walker (1988) also describes the way in which a 'footballer culture' dominant in an Australian urban boys' high school imposed on other groups a particular definition of what it means to be a man, to which there seemed to be no clearly articulated alternative. In these cases, PE and sports, both inside and outside schools, are used to present and reinforce hegemonic masculinities that label male transgressors (those who dislike or perform badly at sport, or are good at forms of PE which offer fewer opportunities to display prowess (Sherlock 1987; Wright 1996a)) as non-masculine.

At the same time, adolescent girls may use their relationship to PE as a way of demonstrating or asserting their femininity. The use of the body as a strong, powerful instrument goes against dominant constructions of femininity and may be off-putting to adolescent girls struggling to establish a clear sense of what it is to be a woman. At the same time, the elements of bodily display involved, particularly in the relatively skimpy or body-hugging clothing often required by schools, may be acutely embarrassing to one whose body is undergoing rapid changes (Leaman 1984). Girls and young women may, therefore, use PE as a site for establishing their femininity through rejection; the feminine, inactive self is counterposed to those 'less feminine' young women who enjoy physical activity. In doing this they forgo the opportunity to develop 'physical capital' (health, fitness and physical expertise) (Shilling 1992) in the interests of a more secure feminine performance. On the other hand, some forms of PE actively construct a form of femininity that celebrates the body as an object to be displayed and viewed; central to this would be dance, although artistic gymnastics might also perform this function. The perception that dance is suitable for girls but not for boys (Talbot 1993) reinforces this idea.

For young Afro-Caribbean women, the situation is somewhat more complex. Racist stereotypes associated with images of female slaves as strong and hard-working (hooks 1982) mean that traditional models of femininity are less available to black girls. While limiting in some ways, this makes the projection and celebration of physical strength and a fit and healthy body less problematic for young Afro-Caribbean women than for other groups.[1] This has, however, had minimal effect on the white-orientated PE curriculum.

Moves towards the teaching of PE in mixed groups have reinforced, rather than undermined gender stereotyping. Scraton (1993) notes that coeducational PE tends to mean that both genders do what has been traditionally part of the male PE curriculum; even girls' games have less cultural status and so are rejected by boys. This leaves girls in a difficult position; because they have less prior experience of male-dominated sports they arrive at the lesson with fewer skills, reinforcing the stereotypical view that physical exercise is a male activity (Kenway *et al.* 1998). In coeducational situations, girls can also become caught up in displays of masculine dominance; both Flintoff and Scraton have observed that males (both child and adult) exclude females from mixed games by refusing to pass them the ball (Flintoff 1993; Scraton 1993). Scraton also notes that mixed swimming galas, where girls' bodies are very overtly on display, can be occasions for sexual harassment of girls by boys.

We can see the role of PE as a site for the reproduction of cultural stereotypes particularly clearly in cases where those stereotypes are transgressed. These point up what is seen as 'normal' and often require 'compensation' on the part of the transgressor. Flintoff (1993) notes, for example, that the male trainee PE teachers she studied were highly resistant to dance. In many ways, because this activity involves bodily display without overt demonstrations of strength or prowess (indeed, it should look effortless), it is the ultimate feminine activity, and thus highly challenging to the masculinity of male practitioners:

> Observation of dance classes showed how hard most male students worked to distance themselves from the activity, by laughing, 'fooling around' or exaggerating their lack of skill. Homophobic comments or gestures were common when men were asked to work together, since for men to touch one another in anything other than aggressive ways places their heterosexual 'masculinity' at risk.
>
> (Flintoff 1993: 195)

In this case, compensation is seen to be impossible; the only way that the male students can deal with the perceived threat to their masculinity is to reject the activity, to ensure that they perform badly. It is not even enough to say that one does not enjoy dancing; even competent performance must be avoided.

For female students who are good at PE, and sport in particular, there is a similar contradiction between competent or successful performance and femininity. This is especially so because their physical presentation as strong, fit and muscular is a stereotypically masculine embodiment (Connell 1995; Johnston 1996). Berger points out that 'A man's presence is dependent on the promise of power which he embodies. If the promise is large and credible, his presence is striking . . . A man's presence suggests what he is capable of doing to you or for you' (1972: 45). Girls and young women who are successful at sport and PE have a similar presence to the power-embodying male; their bodies promise action. They are embodied not as objects for display but as subjects, equipped for physical activity by the development of their muscles; this undercuts their attempts to present themselves as feminine (Dewar 1990; Coles 1994–95).

Here, however, there is the possibility of compensation, although it can put pressure on their male peers. Success at games, particularly those, such as basketball, which are not feminized forms of male sports, can pose a threat to a young woman's sense of her feminine self (Lenskyj 1987). The production of a strong and active body transgresses dominant notions of feminine passivity and display, and, while pleasurable in itself (Johnston 1996; Nelson 1996) can make the individual feel that femininity has to be demonstrated in other ways (Nelson 1996). Dewar (1990) found, for example, that, with few exceptions, female PE students saw being recognized as heterosexual, feminine and attractive as vitally important, and took some trouble (for example, wearing street rather than sports clothes to classes) to display 'appropriate' attributes. This allowed them to be accepted by their male peers: 'They would tolerate women who were aggressive, competitive and who 'played like men' as long as they displayed traditional forms of heterosexual femininity when they were not playing' (Dewar 1990: 91). Sherlock (1987) further argues that female PE students not only risk exclusion from the social group if their heterosexual femininity is not sufficiently displayed, but that success in sport can also threaten their sense of themselves as feminine. In order to undercut their powerful social presence as fit, strong women, they pressurize their male peers to exaggerate their own masculine identities; this allows them to feel small, weak and feminine by comparison.

Body-building (an activity of increasing interest to teenage boys) is another arena in which the construction of masculinity and femininity through sport is pointed up by elements of transgression. For male body-builders, the transgressive element is that of display. While having a lot of muscle is, of course, a masculine attribute, displaying rather than using it contains elements of the feminine; bodily display as an activity in itself is associated mainly with feminized sexuality. It is only the presence of the muscles that distinguishes the parades and posing of male body-building competitions from beauty contests; these preserve the sense of masculinity to such an extent that they negate such otherwise feminine behaviour. For female body-builders, on the other hand, it is the muscles themselves that are transgressive, and the practices of female body-building competition act directly to counter this:

> In the media, at women's bodybuilding championships, and in gyms, the 'How much is too much muscle?' debate again rages for women – but not for men. Even in sports magazines, female muscles are often hidden through 'soft' poses and occasionally even airbrushed away. A classic 1981 bodybuilding book by Joe Weider, the most influential man in the sport, offers this disclaimer: '. . . any muscle tissue a woman . . . might develop will show up on her body as feminine curves'.
>
> (Nelson 1996: 24)

Coles (1994–95) further notes that women are expected to compete in heavy makeup, with bouffant hair, and that competitions are often judged using conventional ideas of feminine attractiveness, not just muscle size. In the face of this, the loss of breast tissue through exercise presents sufficient problems for top female body-builders to feel the need to have breast implants (Johnston 1996).

Negotiating PE in the National Curriculum

The National Curriculum in PE for England and Wales was negotiated within this wider context of gendered discourses about the body. It also took place within, and as an extension of, a moral panic about the perceived reduction of competitive sport in schools and claims that this would be a threat to the health of the next generation (Evans 1990b; Evans and Penney 1995a; Roberts 1996). Even before the formulation of the new curriculum, there were attacks in the media on what was termed the 'new PE'. This was not, in fact, the single movement presented in the press, but was more a set of initiatives involving non-competitive, coeducational games, and an emphasis on PE for all students. It was attacked by sections of the print and broadcast media, which portrayed a situation in which young, liberal PE teachers were displacing a former tradition of competitive sport and thereby endangering the nation's strength and competitiveness (Evans 1990b; Thomas 1991). It is notable that, while the 'new PE' did not stem directly from either the male or the female tradition, the public critique counterposed it to a nostalgic view of school PE that privileged the male form of the subject and completely ignored the female.

It was clear that, as part of its generally 'restorationist' agenda, the then Conservative government hoped that the new curriculum would settle this issue by putting a strong emphasis on competitive games (Evans and Penney 1995b). The National Curriculum Working Group for PE, however, despite being chaired by the headteacher of a private school with a strong sporting tradition, and having as members a leading footballer and an Olympic athlete, was strongly influenced by a document prepared in advance by the British Council for PE, which advocated a progressive educationist discourse that linked PE with health education goals. While competitive sport was seen as important, so were outdoor education, dance and swimming. Three ATs were recommended: participating and performing, planning and composing, and appreciating and evaluating (Evans and Penney 1995b). This vision, however, was challenged by the Secretary of State for Education and the Minister for Sport. They insisted (partly because of subsequently justified fears of curriculum overload) that the three ATs be reduced to one, which would focus on the practical nature of PE, and attacked the provision for non sport-focused activity. Evans and Penney (1995b) argue that this division between the politicians and the working group reflected completely different visions of what PE is all about:

> For the group, the three attainment targets expressed a particular conception of PE. Together they announced the inseparability of body and mind and the equal status of the cognitive (planning and composing,

appreciating and evaluating) and the corporal/active (participation and performing physical activity) elements of PE. The Secretary of State's emphasis on *only* the active elements, on performance and practical activity in PE, was not just a request for a particular emphasis within the subject. It signalled a counterfactual, an alternative conception of PE and how the body within it was to be schooled.

(Evans and Penney 1995b: 37, original emphasis)

After some discussion, contestation and compromise, the Working Group did manage to accommodate at least the reduction to a single AT. The final Order, however, reduced the curriculum considerably. In response to the group's recommendation that all students at KS3 should experience four areas of activity, one of which must be games and another either gymnastics or dance, the NCC made only games compulsory throughout this key stage.[2] Evans and Penney comment that:

Thus the NCC recommendations for KS3 cleverly resolved both the economic and the ideological concerns of the Secretary of State and others, offering schools the scope for reducing the level of provision of PE in the secondary sector and ensuring that men and boys would not have to engage in activities 'inappropriate' for their sex. The regulative principles of patriarchy and restoration were sustained.

(1995b: 40)

The Conservative government's intervention into debates about the nature of school PE thus not only sought to promote a form of the subject most suited to the production of docile bodies through disciplined or dominating usage, but at the same time effectively sidelined from the debate forms of female PE that allow the body to become more aware of itself, such as problem-solving movement or improvised dance.

The privileging of the masculine sporting model of PE, even while revisions were being made to the curriculum during 1994, further exacerbated the difficulties for teachers of teaching the subject in mixed groups. As traditional games skills have become more important, girls who do not play sports outside school are seen as deficient within the discourses of PE (Scraton 1986; Carroll 1995; Wright 1996a), whereas boys' reluctance to compromise their perceived masculinity by taking part in dance is justified by the argument that such activities are 'inappropriate'. Teachers, faced with the realities of classroom life, and unwilling to take risks when they see their control as precarious, are unlikely to challenge or resist this (Sparkes 1991b). Such challenges are particularly unlikely to come from male PE teachers, who may themselves have little experience of educational gymnastics or dance (Curtner-Smith 1999). National Curriculum PE has thus, at the very least, further exacerbated the role of the subject in disciplining bodies, through the stereotypes both of masculine participation and of feminine resistance, into a gendered docility.

PE, the body and society

It seems to me that the ongoing debates about the nature of PE cluster around a series of gendered dichotomies. The first concerns masculinity versus femininity. Although it has shed most of these connotations now, the female PE tradition has its origins in ideas of stereotypical femininity; it was concerned for the health of women as mothers, focused on such attributes as grace and deportment, and emphasized neatness in appearance and dress (Scraton 1986; Sherlock 1987; Wright 1996b). It retains a focus on dance and educational gymnastics, both still strongly labelled as feminine, and many of its sports are foreshortened versions of those played by males. Male PE, by contrast, has always been concerned with the promotion of masculine attributes such as courage, physical strength and domination, and continuing to play despite risk of (or actual) injury (Nelson 1996).

Parallel to this dichotomy is another, often associated with masculine/feminine distinctions. Male sport, and to a lesser extent PE, is largely focused on group activity. It revolves around playing games, in public spaces, with other males. The focus is less on personal success than on that of the team. Female PE (particularly educational gymnastics) and the adult use of sports/leisure facilities, is more personal and private, focused on the individual body. This leads us to the third dichotomy, that concerned with the purposes of PE and sport. On the one hand is the argument, relating closely to the origins of male PE, that sport, in particular, is an important factor in forging a sense of collective identity and a strong, competitive nation (Davies *et al.* 1997; Rees 1997). The purpose of PE, in this formulation, is the good health (physical, mental, economic) of the group. On the other hand is the focus, given much more emphasis in the female PE tradition, but also enshrined in the Australian Health and Physical Education Profile (Kirk *et al.* 1997), of PE as a major factor in individual health. That this difference is gendered is reflected in the leisure pursuits of adults; while men may still be found playing team games such as football at weekends, women are more likely to pursue individually focused fitness activities, such as swimming, keep-fit or aerobics. This distinction is further connected to the fourth dichotomy, concerning the value of the activity to the individual taking part. Although it remains the case that students taking part in team games (at least in the UK) have as their main motivation the experience of playing as a team and for fun (Penney and Evans 1994), it is undeniable that the overt purpose of competitive sport is precisely that, competition. Other activities, particularly educational gymnastics, and, for adults, aerobics and other forms of fitness training, are focused on the 'improvement' or remodelling of the individual body (McCormack 1999). In this case, even when taking part in a class, everyone works separately, and one competes only against oneself.

Setting these dichotomies against each other, we come to the public/private distinction so prevalent in the construction of masculinity and femininity in Western culture. The male PE tradition concerns itself with masculine ideals and treats fitness as a public virtue. Team games, emphasized in this form of PE, are a public, group activity that parallels men's traditional participation in the state and public affairs. In them, the individual is subsumed in the whole, his or her interests are subordinated to those of the group. The female PE tradition, by contrast, is focused on the improvement of the female body, on personal health, aimed (originally at least) at the improvement of the private sphere of the family. The debate about the nature of PE is thus symbolic of a wider struggle about how an embodied person should be, where and how they should act, and their relationship to others and to the state.

It may be that the female tradition in PE was bound to lose out in the struggle for domination of the subject, not simply because it is female, but because its role in the disciplining of docile bodies is less overt. In some ways, female PE is empowering. Its origins lie in challenges to the restricting myth of woman as invalid, unfit either for physical activity or for education (Scraton 1986). Its early practitioners struggled to free girls from restrictive corsetry, thus directly liberating their bodies (Fletcher 1984). Physical fitness and participation even in 'women's' sports, allow girls and women to feel strong and powerful; the body is rendered fit for, and as part of, the empowering aspect of transgression.

> As athletes, we repossess our bodies. Told that we're weak, we develop our strengths. Told that certain sports are wrong for women, we decide what feels right. Told that our bodies are too dark, big, old, flabby, or wrinkly to be attractive to men, we look at naked women in locker rooms and discover for ourselves the beauty of actual women's bodies in all their colors, shapes, and sizes. Told that certain sports make women look 'like men', we notice the truth: working out doesn't make us look like men, it makes us look happy. It makes us smile. More important, it makes us healthy and powerful. It makes us feel good.
>
> (Nelson 1996: 33)

This aspect of female PE is threatening to hegemonic masculinity. It encroaches on one of the few remaining bastions of male exclusivity. While the transgressive nature of the athletic female can make her feel she has to prove her femininity, there is no doubt that it also gives her feelings of power and strength. It is not surprising that conservative forces are more supportive of the explicitly disciplinary, controlled nature of masculine competitive team sports.

At the same time, however, female PE is also implicated in the disciplining of the body, through discourses of docile femininity. Women and girls remain excluded from some sports, particularly those, such as rugby and American and Australian Rules football, that are inherently violent; instead they play foreshortened or adapted versions such as 'touch rugby' or netball. Much of female PE is concerned with the improvement of the look of the body in order to be the object of an implicit or explicit gaze; this is particularly the case in areas such as dance. Finally, the individuation inherent in the self-improvement philosophy underpinning health-related fitness is a key part of the disciplinary process. It focuses responsibility for physical fitness on to the individual, irrespective of their social positioning (Shilling 1993).

An androgynous and truly empowering PE will need to break away from and be transgressive of both the male and the female PE traditions. It will need to celebrate both the fit body and group collaborative activity and struggle against models of masculinity and femininity that deny aspects of the physical to either gender. While PE can probably never break free of its disciplinary function, at the same time, there is space for resistance, for active transgression, for the breaking down of boundaries and the development of new forms. Central to this is surely a focus on the communicative aspect of movement, on the relationship with others of an integrated, embodied self.

Notes

1 I am grateful to Maud Blair for making me aware of this difference.
2 From 2000, students study four areas: while games remains a compulsory part of the KS3 curriculum, it no longer has to be taught every year. Students still have to study gymnastics and/or dance, as well as outdoor activities and/or athletic activities and/or swimming. From 2001, games will no longer be compulsory at KS4 (Qualifications and Curriculum Authority 2000).

part 3

STUDENTS, SUBJECTS
AND EXAMINATIONS

STUDENTS AND SUBJECTS: POWER/KNOWLEDGE AND INTEGRATED CURRICULA

Any innovation that requires new activities on the part of students will succeed or fail according to whether students actually participate in these activities. Students will participate to the extent that they understand and are motivated to try what is expected. We have every reason to believe that, whatever the causes, students' experiences with innovations are not conducive to increasing their understanding and motivation. Nor could we expect it to be otherwise, if teachers, principals, and other administrators are having similar problems.

(Fullan 1991: 183)

In most of this book I have focused on how teachers deal with the changing nature of school subjects. But how do students react to changes in the curriculum? As curriculum innovations take place, students may see school subjects altering before their eyes. What their older siblings studied as CDT and HE may be presented to them as integrated D&T and include far less of the construction and cooking they expect; what last year was reading and story writing may this year have become 'the literacy hour' and be carried out in a very different way. Parents and elder siblings may have led them to expect one thing of school, or of particular subjects within it, but the reality confounds these expectations. How do students react to rapid changes? How do they adjust their responses as the curriculum evolves, develops or suddenly shifts? What scope is there for them to resist innovation?

It might be assumed that, because students go through school sequentially and only once, they would not be as aware of change as are teachers, whose approach is necessarily more cyclic in nature. However, students do not come to school as blank slates; they bring with them the experiences of their siblings and even their parents: 'My dad came to this school and he did drama and he said he loved it' (Year 10 student, Lacemakers School). Older students may support younger ones by sharing their experiences; Mac an Ghaill (1992) notes that change undercuts their ability to do this, causing student confusion. Subjects may also change in nature or orientation as students get older; if this is not made explicit they may continue to try to work within the framework of the version of the subject they were taught before, or they may make curriculum choices that they later come to regret. This is particularly likely to happen after age 14 when, in England and Wales, students for the first time have some (limited) choice about what they study, at the same time as some aspects of the curriculum become more formal in preparation for examinations.

Power/knowledge relations in school become particularly exposed when attempts are made to integrate aspects of the curriculum. Bernstein argues that a move to more integrated curricula, in which 'the various contents are subordinate to some idea which reduces their isolation from each other' (1971: 60) would result in changes both in pedagogy and in student understanding. He suggests that:

> Integrated codes will make available from the beginning of the pupils' educational career, clearly in a way appropriate to a given age level, the deep structure of the knowledge, i.e. the principles for generating new knowledge . . . The underlying theory of learning of integrated codes may well be more group or self-regulated.
>
> (1971: 60–61)

A move from collection to integrated codes, he argues, has the potential to:

> bring about a disturbance in the structure and distribution of power, in property relationships and in existing educational identities. This change of educational code involves a fundamental change in the nature and strength of boundaries. It involves a change in what counts as having knowledge, in what counts as a valid transmission of knowledge, and a change in the organizational context . . . This change of code involves fundamental changes in the structure and distribution of power and in principles of control.
>
> (1971: 63)

Inspired by these suggestions, and by the work of critical educators such as Giroux, there were a number of attempts during the 1980s to bring about more integrated curricula. It was argued that the increased participation of students in the learning process, the greater contextualization of the knowledge, and, most importantly, the involvement of student-owned knowledge in school curricula would produce more empowered learners (Black and Harrison 1985; Timpson 1988; Taylor 1989) and make it possible to use the curriculum to challenge the prevailing social order (Hargreaves *et al.* 1996). Because of the integrated nature of knowledge in the world outside school, it might be expected that interdisciplinary work would not only alter the power/knowledge relations of the classroom but also lead to more meaningful and transferable learning (National Curriculum Technology Working Group 1988; Barnett 1991). Hargreaves *et al.* (1996) point out, however, that in many of these curricular experiments the meaning of 'integration' is imprecise and poorly understood by those participating in the innovation; this, they argue, can be a strong barrier to success. Furthermore, curriculum planning does not always take into account the complex nature of power/knowledge relations or students' multiple strategies of resistance. Ruddock, for example, notes that when introducing a new, more 'open' humanities curriculum:

> The teachers used the 'new' relationship to find ways of retaining a comfortable feeling of social control and the pupils reacted by finding out, with an unerring sense of direction, the weaknesses in the situation and so were able to develop counter-strategies that gave them opportunities to find levels of work that suited them. So, while the situation *looked* different, the power relationships and the attitudes that those relationships habitually support remained essentially the same.
>
> (1991: 60, original emphasis)

The breaking down of disciplinary boundaries also brings to the fore some of the assumptions that lie behind the practices of the different subject areas and exposes some of the power struggles between the teachers involved. Students, meanwhile, are caught in the middle, trying to make sense of what is often an experimental curriculum, the implications of which may not have been fully thought through by the staff working with them (Paechter 1995b). If they feel uncomfortable, their only option is resistance: 'Since the student is at the bottom of the heap, he or she has only limited power to bring about positive changes (students can, as we have seen, exercise great negative power to reject what is being imposed)' (Fullan 1991: 189). In this chapter I am going to consider in detail two such integrated experiments, looking at them from the point of view of the students, for whom the work contributed to the high stakes assessment of GCSE.

By the time they reach the upper years of the secondary school, students have spent years getting used to the idea that school has significant differences from ordinary life, and that, in particular, these differences may vary between subjects. Students are expected automatically to foreground different aspects of their experience and their school learning in different subject contexts, which may be cued in a variety of ways. This can cause problems for students if they 'misread' the cues and give precedence to areas of experience that are not being emphasized in the classroom at that juncture.

Students are especially likely to run into difficulties if work is presented in a context, some of whose features have to be discounted for their work to be acceptable. In particular, school tasks presented to students embedded in real-life contexts do not usually require students to take into account all the features of those contexts (Gipps and Murphy 1994). Hence, students have to learn, very early in their school careers, that generally in school, contextualization is a form of surface decoration; it is not to be taken seriously. Walkerdine (1988), for example, describes a group of six- and seven-year-old children asked by their teacher to play a 'shopping game':

> The children are given a pack of cards on which are pictured items to be bought accompanied by a price in pence, below ten pence (e.g. 2p) The children are to take turns to pick a card. They each have ten 1p pieces in plastic money and they are to work out the subtraction operation with the coins and then record the change from 10p in the form of a subtraction sum on their paper.
>
> (Walkerdine 1988: 145)

Walkerdine points out that it is immediately obvious to the children that this game is not really like shopping at all, particularly because of the small amounts of money involved. They understand enough of the context of real shopping to be well aware that, as one of them puts it, 'Two pence's not rich. It's not enough to buy a bubble gum and a bazooka' (Walkerdine 1988: 158). Because the children realize that the 'shopping game' bears very little relation to actual shopping, they treat it as a fantasy and have a lot of fun with it. But this understanding depends on realizing that, in the primary classroom, and particularly in primary mathematics, the contexts in which tasks are obstensibly set have to be interrogated for their relevance to what is actually being asked. In order successfully to negotiate what is required of them in this task, the children have consciously to sideline some aspects of the presented context:

> It is the insertion [of the school mathematics] into the giving of change in shopping which is supposed to make the exercise meaningful for the children, and also render it of practical value. Yet it is precisely this which makes it unlike shopping . . . When people calculate their change in shopping not only do they work with larger amounts of money, they also rarely if ever use pencil and paper: they do not write subtraction sums. They are most likely to engage in quick mental arithmetic or approximation and estimation of amounts. The problems here do not resemble practical problems either in their content or in their methods of solution. In this sense they are 'fake' practical problems and most of the children seem to recognize this.
>
> (Walkerdine 1988: 146)

For children who are not fully aware that a presented real-life context may not always be fully relevant in the classroom, it may be difficult to carry out the required task. Murphy and Ellwood (1997), for example, discuss a student for whom taking seriously the presented context of a science task meant that she perceived it completely differently both to her teacher and to her peers, with a consequent breakdown of discussion about how the task should proceed. Gipps and Murphy (1994) note that girls are particularly likely to pay attention to the presented context of science tasks, and that their responses may as a result be seen by examiners and assessors as evidence of their lack of scientific understanding. Gordon, one of the children studied by Walkerdine, also takes certain aspects of the context literally, and, operating with the contextual constraints of real shopping, spends all his money. He is able to do the relevant sums, but he does not carry out the task as expected because he is not sufficiently aware that one of the implicit rules of the classroom is that presented contexts are not always to be taken literally. His teacher has explicitly to point out that in the game the rules are different:

G: I've just got one pence.
L [another child]: No you haven't, you've got all them.
G: That's over there. I spent that.
T: Oh, I see what you're doing, no, it's all right you . . . each time you get another ten pence to go shopping with.

(Walkerdine 1988: 156)

By the time they reach secondary school, most students have got used to this particular feature of school life and also begun to distinguish between different ways of working in different curriculum areas, although the extent to which they are able to do the latter will depend on the curriculum presentation of their particular primary school. As they go through secondary education, students are explicitly encouraged to understand not only that school is different from the world outside, but that in each subject there is a different set of expectations both of how students are to behave and of what sort of work they are to produce. This emphasis on difference may be particularly strong in high status subjects (Whitty *et al.* 1994). Young, for example, quotes a science teacher introducing the special arena of the laboratory to a group of students who have just entered secondary school:

It may well be the first time you've done science and there are a whole lot of different things about working in a lab than there are in all the other classrooms in the school . . . you have to work with certain kinds of rules which are different . . . later we'll give you a list of them which you can put in your folder . . . there are things that are potentially dangerous . . . we've got gas taps here . . . those of you who've been in a kitchen do not need to be told this (so abstracted from the real world is the teacher that he can even imagine that *some* kids may never have been in a kitchen!).

(Young 1976: 53–4, original emphasis)

Students engaging in interdisciplinary work bring all this subject based baggage with them. Furthermore, it is necessary for them to do so, if their work is to be assessed for separate GCSE subjects, as in the cases described below. When students carry out integrated projects within a context of high stakes assessment, disciplinary boundaries and distinctions have always to be borne in mind, ensuring that students remain aware of splits and differences between subject approaches. Furthermore, because the work is to be assessed, often by the teachers themselves, what counts as achievement is at best only partially negotiable. In the rest of this chapter I will examine how this can happen in practice, using two very different examples: the field study course at Stitchers School and combined arts at Lacemakers.

Status struggles: the Stitchers field study course

The integrated field study course at Stitchers School involved two high status subjects, mathematics and science, working with a traditionally academic but lower status area, geography. The purpose of the integration was, ostensibly at least, to provide a realistic context for coursework in mathematics and science, by taking the opportunity to join the geography department on a week-long GCSE field-study course in which students carried out stream and coastal studies in the summer term of Year 10. While much of the planning of the course was carried out exclusively by the geography department, mathematics and science teachers joined the group and supported students in carrying out work that could be used as coursework in their subject as well as in geography. I have described elsewhere (Paechter 1995b) what happened from the point of view of the teachers; here I am going to focus more closely on the student experience.

Both in the preparation for the field trip and while it took place, the students continually had to deal with the competing agendas and priorities of the teachers involved. Although all the teachers clearly believed they respected the values and purposes of each other's subjects, their competing agendas meant that each inevitably interfered in the work of the others both before and during the course. Both mathematics and science, the higher status subjects, were concerned that their rational and experimental approaches might be 'polluted' (Whitty *et al.* 1994) by the lower status geography, which they considered to be less 'rigorous' than their own areas (fieldnotes). Meanwhile, the geography department, which had an enviable record of examination success, were concerned to protect what for them was an important source of status. They had traditionally run the field trip in a rather controlled style, telling students exactly what to do at each stage. The more open experimental approach required by the science assessment scheme threatened the accuracy of their measurements, and, they believed, their Grade As. Consequently, the geographers were constantly pushing the students to use particular prescribed methods, while the science department wanted them to devise the methods themselves. The students had to negotiate a path between these two extremes which ensured that they satisfied the requirements of both subjects and of mathematics. They were well aware that different school subjects had different approaches, and that coursework carried out according to the demands of one subject might be unacceptable for the other. As this was part of their GCSE assessment, students felt it was important to be able to recognize which subject was which within the integrated whole, and they tried to do this throughout the week-long course: 'I think it got a bit confusing at times, you were wondering which one you were doing as they were very close knit' (Stitchers Year 11 student).

Students' perceived need to be aware of which subject's rules they should be following at any one time ran counter to the intentions of some of the staff involved. They were concerned to develop practical reasoning that might be transferred across contexts, and deliberately blurred the boundaries between the subjects. One teacher, for example, described an exchange about how to record results from a coastal study:

> We didn't say anything about a recording system. One of them had said, 'Shall we do it like a geographer would?', and I said, 'What do you mean, like a geographer would? You're supposed to be doing this like a thinking person, is a thinking person instantly, a geographer, a mathematician or a scientist?
>
> (Sarah Cordingley, mathematics teacher, Stitchers School)

In practice, however, the expectations of the teachers of the different subjects meant that students did explicitly have to behave like mathematicians, scientists or geographers. They were aware in particular that some of the ways of working required by geography (who needed accurate results) were considered unacceptable by science (where there was an emphasis on students devising and evaluating their own experiments). Students were particularly conscious that following the science requirements could have dire consequences for geography:

> S: If you did it the way you planned it and it didn't come out right then you didn't have enough time to do it the right way.

CP: And does that affect your geography?

S: Well, it would do, yeah, because you wouldn't have enough results.

(Stitchers Year 10 student)

In order to maximize their chances of success in each subject, students resorted to partial subterfuge, supported to some extent by at least one of the geography teachers. Here they are explaining to me what the differences were between carrying out experiments for geography and for science:

S1: You have to just change them slightly for science – trying to find out. With geography they always told you, you knew how to do it.

CP: But with science?

S1: You had to decide what experiment you were going to do instead of being told you had to do *that* experiment, you had to figure it out for yourself, kind of thing.

CP: Did you find that the geography teacher sort of got in the way of that by telling you what experiment to do?

S1: Yes. Before we went, Mr Paxton [the geography teacher] told us what we was doing, but he said don't tell Mr Simons [the science teacher] that he'd told us. Yes, because he wanted to make it as simple as possible but Mr Simons just sort of said, right, you make a test and see if it's true, and we were a bit confused about that because we didn't know how to go about it.

S2: But we sort of knew what to do because Mr Paxton had explained it before we went.

CP: So Mr Simons told you to make a test but you'd been told what test to do already?

S2: (laughing) Yeah, he said, don't say anything otherwise I'll get done.

(Stitchers Year 11 students)

For the students, the differences between geography and science in this context revolved around the amount of help they got in setting up and carrying out their experiments. However, this distinction was of little help to them in dealing with other aspects of the three subjects, for example when they came to write up their work. In deciding the best way to present work for different subjects, students are of course influenced by explicit or implicit instructions from teachers. On this occasion the teachers did not fully understand each other's requirements and gave conflicting messages to the students about what was expected, making the situation very difficult for students trying to satisfy both sets of demands. The mathematics teacher involved explained what happened from her point of view:

SC: [The geography teacher] didn't totally understand how it should be written up for science, because . . . he told them to write two sentences about, we did this measurement on the dune, and here's

the results, and the first thing I did was rip up one of the children's
bits of work and say, this is actually pure and total junk.

CP: And that's what he'd told them to do?

SC: I said, 'Well, you're writing this up as though it was a science
experiment; quite frankly if you showed that to me as a scientist,
the first thing I'd do was say, fine, you went and sat on the beach
and these results appeared out of thin air. This doesn't work.' That
was a problem with these children understanding that when you
write things up you've got to write them up in the right sort of way.
(Sarah Cordingley, mathematics teacher, Stitchers School)

In this situation the students are caught between conflicting views of what
constitutes appropriate practice, played out within asymmetrical power/
knowledge relations between teachers of different subjects. As head of a high
status department, Sarah Cordingley had no qualms about undercutting the
instructions of a member of a lower status area; the primacy of mathematics and science was clearly demonstrated to the students. Power plays such
as this, however, explicitly undermine any attempts to present or carry out
coursework in a more integrated fashion, because they emphasize to
students that, whatever the rhetoric of contextualized learning, what matters in this situation is that they remain aware of, and satisfy, separate
examination requirements.

Interdisciplinary teaching, therefore, requires students to negotiate complex and sometimes conflicting understandings of what is necessary for each
subject involved. In order to make this easier, they may have to separate out
the subjects they are studying, to make the situation feel to them more like
the clearly demarcated subjects of the usual collection curriculum (Bernstein
1971) found in secondary schools and foregrounded by most assessment
systems. At Stitchers this resulted in work that was parallel rather more than
integrated, and students saw integration simply in terms of the advantages
of being able to produce three pieces of GCSE coursework during one field
study course; in other respects the subjects remained for them unrelated.

Empowerment and resistance: combined arts at
Lacemakers School

While the aims of interdisciplinary work at Stitchers were to provide a realistic context for mathematics and science and to encourage students to transfer learned skills across subjects, at Lacemakers the teachers were more
concerned with student empowerment and with changing the nature of
schooling. The staff working with the combined arts course explicitly fostered more relaxed relationships with students than are usual in secondary

schools, and gave the students a lot of freedom, regarding both how they comported themselves in class and how they approached their work. What was not negotiable, however, was the interdisciplinary nature of the course. Nevertheless, partly because of the way that the balance of teacher–student power/knowledge relations was tipped further in the direction of the students than is usual, this insistence that two subjects were constantly combined in the course both enabled and led to resistance on the part of some students.

The combined arts course at Lacemakers was an interdisciplinary course leading to two GCSE examinations, drama and art (theatre design), and by the time of my research had been running successfully for several years. It had originally been introduced because the school wanted to provide a GCSE in drama, but had not had the time available on the timetable. In order to fit it in, it was decided that there would be an integrated combined arts course incorporating the theatre design option from the art syllabus, and a complete drama course. Two teachers, one from each contributing subject, took a double-sized class of students but only (at least at first) within the time allocation that would normally be given to one subject area. Thus by opting for this course and by organizing their coursework so that it would fit both examinations, students could gain two GCSEs in the time they would normally have spent on one. On the other hand, it meant that if they wanted to study drama, they had no choice but to study art with it. Students who wanted to take art but not drama could opt for a more conventional art course that took place separately.

The course was intended to be innovative in a number of respects. Within combined arts it was intended that the work of the two contributing subjects be fully integrated. Although this did not always happen in practice, all work was planned jointly by the two teachers and they were both present in all the lessons:

> We invariably start with the drama activities – although there have been occasions, odd occasions – but mostly it is a drama activity you start with. And what happens in there is that I often sit and absorb what is going on and then once the drama gets under way Sheila and I will start to discuss and start to talk about the possibilities that are coming out of the drama, because we just spark ideas off each other . . . and when we feel that it is appropriate, they do some theatre design work. Now sometimes the theatre design work will be small, such as a set, but on other occasions it may be something that the kids are actually going to use in a piece of drama work.
>
> (Martin Morton, art teacher, Lacemakers School)

While the two subjects were at least partially integrated within the course, there were strong disciplinary boundaries between combined arts and the rest of the school curriculum. The teachers quite explicitly set out to make the students' experience of the course unique within the school. This was achieved by using a special space in which all the joint teaching took place; a former school hall with a stage at one end. In the middle of the hall was a circle of benches, and at the other end was a (rather makeshift) art area. The atmosphere of the room was completely different from that of a normal classroom: 'It's the biggest and holiest room in the school, echoing slightly, the noise that you get . . . , actually, you know, when you go into a theatre, there's a sort of bigness of it all, they act in anticipation' (Malcolm Standish, art teacher, Lacemakers School). Furthermore, the teachers explicitly stressed to students that, unlike other, predictable subjects, this was a special space in which anything might happen:

> When they walk in they don't know what to expect, they know anything can happen, they know that there could be a role play situation going on and even if they walk in through the door they have to join in with it then and there. So we have told them, whatever is happening in that room we have always got to have this sense of anything goes, they've got to join in, and they do.
>
> (Sheila Langden, drama teacher, Lacemakers School)

Whitty *et al.* (1994) argue that strong boundaries between curriculum areas with an open, real-world based approach and the rest of the school is what makes such openness possible in some low status subjects. Teachers of higher status areas, anxious to avoid 'pollution' by non-academic concerns, enforce these boundaries as a condition for the existence of more open approaches elsewhere. However, Martin Morton, one of the Lacemakers art teachers, believed that in the long term this boundary needed to be broken down. He saw the combined arts course as providing a model for how school life should be more generally:

> In a sense to sort of say you're creating something different from the rest of the school is really a red herring. I mean, it's really the other way round, I think what we're trying to do is influence the rest of the school.
>
> (Martin Morton, art teacher, Lacemakers School)

Of course, the low status of the constituent subjects of Combined Arts made it unlikely that his aspiration would be realized in practice, despite his personal high status in the school (he was assistant deputy head) and the explicit support for this approach from the rest of the senior management. An attempt to implement D&T on a similar basis was resisted by a significant proportion of the school staff.

Before I discuss how students reacted to and dealt with these changes in power/knowledge relations, I should point out that there is insufficient evidence in this particular study to be clear whether these reactions are gendered.

Of approximately 40 Year 10 students who were the main focus of the research, only seven were male. Two of these were, at the time the interviews took place, the most resistant of all the students to parts of the curriculum they disliked. In Year 11 the genders were more balanced, but I was not able to interview all those participating in the course. Again, however, of those I interviewed it was males who were more selective about which aspects of the course they willingly took part in. It was also difficult to tell whether these students were resisting particular activities, the art teachers or the integrated aspect of the course as a whole. Their discontent tended to range over all three, but it was unclear which, if any, was most salient and to what extent any one was a rationalization of feelings of discomfort related to others. Certainly several of the students believed that drama, particularly the public display aspects of the subject, was easier for girls to deal with, and that it might take a special kind of boy to cope in the lessons: 'Some boys are afraid to stand up on a stage in front of everyone else and say words and things like that, because it takes a lot of guts, you've got to have some guts to stand up there, because when you're doing it by yourself, that's even worse' (male Lacemakers Year 10 student). This student, and the male friend with whom he was interviewed, also believed that the boys were more supportive of each other than were the girls, perhaps indicating that they also saw themselves as being in need of support in the self-disclosive atmosphere of combined arts. Another student commented on the participation of one of the more macho students, noting with surprise that, having calmed down as a result of the supportive atmosphere, he did seem to cope quite well: 'There's all those girls there, and then Luke walked in. I thought he was in the wrong lesson. He's doing quite well actually. He's doing just as well as we are' (Lacemakers Year 10 student).

Despite the relaxed and supportive atmosphere, the rules and norms of the integrated subject were not as clear, from the students' point of view, as they were for the staff. They certainly saw the combined arts lesson as a unique space and event, a situation in which they had far more freedom and control than in the rest of the school, in which they could express themselves and try out different personalities, and in which they could have a radically different relationship with teachers:

> Well it's different. I mean it's a lesson where you can actually express yourself more and you can have more of a say, and the teacher is more with you, and understands what you're saying rather than just standing there giving lectures like other teachers do.
>
> (Lacemakers Year 10 student)

> And you just sort of get to be other people, if you know what I mean. Acting other people, so you don't have to be yourself all the time.
>
> (Lacemakers Year 10 student)

When you walk into the room you can feel you can do whatever you want, say whatever you want . . . I just like it. I'd like to do it all day actually.

> (Lacemakers Year 10 student)

You feel more human in that lesson. You don't tend to feel like you're in a school.

> (Lacemakers Year 11 student)

It's just the atmosphere, there's something about the room, isn't there?

> (Lacemakers Year 11 student)

I think it's the atmosphere, and the people, well, they're working together more and talking instead of sitting there, you know, not supposed to talk . . . you don't copy out of books or anything, you're not just sitting there with your head in your book.

> (Lacemakers Year 10 student)

And [the teachers] don't have to act in a certain way. I mean, you expect teachers to act in a certain way, but when they're in drama they can act on a level basis with you themselves.

> (Lacemakers Year 10 student)

In contrast with the teachers, who saw the way they approached combined arts as a sort of Trojan horse that might eventually lead to more open learning situations and relationships throughout the school, the students generally felt that it would be impossible for other subjects to be taught in the same way. They believed that the school's disciplinary forces, particularly on their bodies, were not susceptible to fundamental change, though they did of course resist them. While some clearly thought that it would be wonderful if the whole school were like combined arts, and a few even believed that being treated as more responsible elsewhere would result in them working harder, others felt that the more open atmosphere would be counterproductive in some subjects. Students contrasted the low status combined arts course explicitly with more powerful areas of the curriculum. Here the 'facts' of mathematics are set against the 'just feelings' of drama; there is a sense that mental and physical discipline are seen as inherent to high status subjects such as mathematics and science:

> I don't know because drama's completely different to maths, physics, chemistry or whatever. They're all facts, aren't they, maths and all the lessons like that, they're just facts that you write down and you learn, whereas drama, you know, it's just feelings, drama, it's not right or wrong. So I don't know. Maybe you need a different atmosphere in class and you need more different kinds of teachers, because maybe if Ms Langden went into a maths lesson, she wouldn't get the best out of the pupils.
>
> (Lacemakers Year 11 student)

At the same time a few students actively relished the differences between combined arts and the rest of their school experiences. They felt that if the rest of the school were similar it would detract from the specialness of combined arts: 'I'm glad all the lessons aren't like that because then I wouldn't look forward to it. It's something to look forward to' (Lacemakers Year 11 student).

The distinctions between combined arts and the rest of their school experience were seen by students mainly in terms of two main features. First, they were very aware that they had closer and more informal relationships with the staff, more control over the pacing and to some extent the selection of the work they did, and that the lessons had explicit relevance to their lives outside school. Combined arts was seen as a place where mistakes were tolerated and where students felt confident, supported by their peers and empowered both in and out of the specific context of the lesson.

> If you make a mistake now everybody laughs. Everybody laughs and jokes about it, Ms Langden jokes about it. If you make a mistake you're not bothered. You don't feel like if you've made a bad mistake in maths.
> (Lacemakers Year 11 student)

> It sort of brings your confidence out there because you can feel you can sort of speak your mind in the drama lesson and speak your mind anywhere else, and if someone shouts you down, you think, 'What's their problem?'
> (Lacemakers Year 11 student)

Second, student perceptions of the specialness of combined arts were closely bound up with the physical sensations of being in a lesson that involved little or no writing and in which normal disciplinary rules (like having to remove one's coat or being forbidden to eat sweets or chew gum) were relaxed or ignored:

> S1: It's not like being in a classroom where you've got to write and sit at a desk and they say, Take your coat off and start writing', and if you talk you are told to shut up.
> S2: It's a chance for your mouth to move a bit. You don't have to sit there quietly like in other lessons.
> (Lacemakers Year 10 students)

From the students' point of view the most important distinction between combined arts and the rest of the school was summed up in the word 'relaxed'. In 16 interviews with 43 students, the words 'relax' or 'relaxed' were spontaneously mentioned 18 times, along with other similar terms such as 'relief'. They also talked a lot about freedom (mentioned seven times), particularly the freedom to express ideas, thoughts and emotions, and being allowed to get on (or not) at one's own pace. Again, much of this discussion centred on physical as well as mental freedoms, particularly on freedom from the restraints of the normal classroom and the discipline of sitting still and writing.

All these factors made for a very clear disciplinary boundary between the combined arts lesson and the rest of the school. Within the lesson, however, the two subjects involved were supposed to be integrated. The students, however, particularly those in Year 10 who had only had a relatively short experience with the course, found it difficult to come to terms with this integration. In particular, many of them experienced the course as a drama lesson and were unclear about what the art teachers were doing there at all. This was exacerbated by two things, one integral to the whole conception of the course, the other contingent to the time of the interviews. The first was the fact that it was only possible to study drama after age 14 if one took it as part of the combined arts course. While some students welcomed the opportunity to study two subjects they enjoyed, a significant number saw themselves as having chosen not combined arts, but drama. One or two seemed to have been very poorly advised about the nature of the course; others appeared to have simply ignored what they did not want to hear. Having failed to recognize the integrated nature of the course when they had originally chosen to take it, students were surprised and sometimes resentful that they were expected to take both aspects seriously. Furthermore, at the time of the interviews the Year 10 group had for some weeks been taught by a drama student on teaching practice, and the integrated aspect of the course had been suspended during this period. While the art teachers continued to attend the lessons, they did not do any actual teaching. This exacerbated the confusion of students who had not opted to do art in the first place:

> CP: What about the other teachers? What about Mr Morton and Mr Standish?
> S1: Who come into the lessons?
> CP: Yes, that are part of the combined arts course.
> S1: To be honest, I don't know what they're doing there.
> S2: I don't, because they don't really help us.
> S1: They don't really help us.
> S2: They come to just watch, they walk around, they don't really say anything. They go, 'Are you working all right?' and you go, 'Yes', and they walk off. I just wonder what they're doing there. Ms Langden motivates us. *She* makes us want to work.
> (Lacemakers Year 10 students)

This inability of some students to get to grips with the relationship between the two components of the combined arts course as a whole seemed to have caused problems for some time and resulted in particular in students failing to complete their theatre design coursework. In order to alleviate this problem, Year 10 students were also, commencing in the year of the research, expected to carry out a 12-week module of theatre design alone. While having a number of advantages, not least being taught in a proper art room with running water and the full range of equipment, this exacerbated the split between art and drama in the minds of the students. Although theatre design work continued as part of the combined arts lessons, the latter were seen by the students even more as basically concerned with drama. Furthermore, for those students who had not wanted to take art in the first place, a compulsory 12-week module added insult to injury.

> I'm like in an art lesson now, because I've just started this new module thing, and they told us to build a stage set, and I said, we've done that in drama. . . . But, you know, sounds funny. Once you've done it once, you don't feel like doing it again.
>
> (Lacemakers Year 10 student)

Although providing the extra theatre design module was a strategy to deal with resistance to art in the form of reluctance or refusal to take full part in that aspect of the course, in some ways it made such resistance much easier. Students who saw themselves as disliking or incompetent at art found theatre design tasks easier to identify and refuse in the module than when they were more fully integrated with the drama work, and were less likely to be drawn in over time.

The differences and barriers between the two aspects of the combined arts course were clearest when it came to students' willingness and ability to complete coursework. Generally they saw the requirements for each subject as separate and distinct, although those in Year 11 had found ways (as they were expected to) of making the same piece of work fit the formal assessment framework for each subject. Some students made it clear that they felt able to respond to the requirements of one subject but not to those of the other. Because the drama aspect of the course was so open and clearly related to their own lives, students seemed to have no problems with seeing what they had to do to carry out drama tasks appropriately. They might find them emotionally challenging, but they expected to be able to do all the work. Art, on the other hand, was seen as something only some people could be good at. This meant that constructive criticism from each teacher was seen in a totally different light.

> S1: I just don't like the art side of it.
> S2: He doesn't like the art side of it, because he's into drama.
> S1: I'm not very good at art. I can't do the art; I'm just useless at that sort of thing.

S2: Whereas I like doing the art because that's more relaxed.

S3: If I wanted to do art, I would have took art. I didn't expect it.

S1: It's partly to do with the fact that Mr Morton can't imagine anybody not being good at art, or he assumes that everybody can do it.

S3: Yeah, he assumes that everybody has a good ability.

S1: And if they don't do something, then he says, right, he gets annoyed and moody.

CP: But Ms Langden expects everyone to be good at drama, doesn't she?

S1: Yeah, but if you're not she's not bothered. She points it out to you. She says that you can do this in your play, you can speak up, look at the audience.

(Lacemakers Year 11 students)

This feeling that art was only for those 'naturally' good at it, combined with resentment at having to study a subject that they had not chosen, led some students to resist the theatre design aspect of the course. Two male Year 10 students were particularly vociferous in their rejection of art:

S2: What's art learn you? It should be an art lesson if you want to do art, not some stupid idiot coming in and doing art with you when you're supposed to be doing drama. . . . Personally I hate art.

S1: I do, yeah.

S2: I really hate it.

S1: It's crap.

S2: When it comes to practical work I just feel like sitting down and doing nothing.

S1: You just feel like going into a corner and just sitting there talking.

(Lacemakers Year 10 students)

By the time students reached Year 11 most seemed to have made more sense of the integration of the two aspects of combined arts, organizing their coursework projects so that they met the criteria for both subjects. In doing so they showed that they had managed to understand and come to terms with both the demands of the two subjects and with the integrated nature of the course as a whole: 'Certain things you can put in, like in the drama exam there's an extended study that you have to do, and you can use work from that to go in your art exam, or you can swap them round' (Lacemakers Year 11 student).

S1: Now we've got the detailed investigation which is picking one play or subject, making sets, costumes and things like that.

CP: Is that for the art or for the drama?

S1: Drama.

for drama, but we can use it for art.
(Lacemakers Year 11 students)

For a few students, however, coming up hard against the requirements for the art examination stiffened their resistance to the integrated nature of the course as a whole. Students who found art uncongenial or difficult were, by Year 11, failing to complete the coursework for that subject, thus in some senses achieving their original aim of opting only for GCSE drama.

Encouraging more open classroom relations may empower some students, but others may find it extremely threatening. One or two students, for example, found the combination of freedom and self-expression in combined arts too much to deal with, and withdrew from the experience, if not from the physical space of the lesson. Changing power/knowledge relations in a curriculum area may also make it easier for students to resist the aspects of the course they dislike, and this can, as it did at Lacemakers, run directly counter to teacher intentions. At Lacemakers, the openness of combined arts as a whole, stemming in part from the integrated nature of the course, actually made it easier for students to resist that integration and strengthen the boundary between theatre design and drama. It was unclear whether this would in turn lead to attempts by the teachers to reassert their institutional power to try to stop some students opting out of the theatre design element. Certainly it appeared that some, mainly male, students had succeeded in resisting the total integration of the course. Their reluctance to do theatre design in what they saw as a drama lesson led the school to introduce the supplementary art module, weakening the integration of the two components.

Conclusion

Because students enter subject areas with at least partially conceived ideas about what is expected of them there, changing the curriculum can impact on them in a significant way. Even in the relatively straightforward situation of the joint field course, the Stitchers students had to recognize and take into account different approaches from what might seem on the face of it to be the same task. Where, as in combined arts at Lacemakers, power/knowledge relations between teachers and students are altered in the students' favour, so that students have greater control over what counts as knowledge or as appropriate performance within a given classroom situation, this can still make for difficulties for them. Although the classroom may be superficially more open, students can find it difficult to work out what is implicitly expected, in terms both of behaviour and of subject performance (Ruddock 1991). Some of the combined arts students, for example, found it took a while to be sure about some of the more implicit ground rules of drama: 'We didn't know what the limit was. We didn't know what she'd definitely say no to, if she only wanted serious things, or she only wanted funny things' (Lacemakers Year 11 student). Similarly, the students at Stitchers found they had to focus even more than usual on the explicit and implicit rules of the component subjects. Instead of helping them to relate and integrate their knowledge and understanding across different subjects, and to see commonalities between them, the teachers' differences over how to approach the work meant that students were forced to make explicit to themselves what made mathematics, science and geography different from each other.

It is important to realize that, for many students, enjoyment of their learning is comparatively rare and unexpected (Fullan 1991). Most of the time they are focused on gaining the credentials they believe will help them in the future and they are therefore likely to give priority to conforming to the requirements of higher status subjects where these clash with the expectations of those considered less important. At Lacemakers, attempts in other areas to bring subjects together were far less successful than was combined arts, as students increasingly prioritized coursework for mathematics and science over subjects like environment; the students at Stitchers similarly had to take seriously the demands of science and mathematics even though they felt these impinged on what they saw primarily as a geography field course. Furthermore, as we shall see in Chapter 8, power/knowledge relations discipline teachers as well as students. It is not possible simply to relax the rules of the classroom; one is still bound by, for example, the disciplinary force of the external examination.

How students perceive different manifestations of the various school subjects is a complex matter that has been little researched. In particular, insufficient is known about whether there are any gender differences in how students understand what is expected of them in different subjects. While the Lacemakers study has been useful for considering student response to an innovative course, the proportion of male respondents was simply too low for much to be concluded about gender in this particular setting. More work also needs to be done about student reactions to more conventional courses, both in times of change and in periods of stability. In all this, we have to appreciate that students do not passively receive the curriculum. They are active both in its construction and its resistance.

eight

DISCIPLINE AS EXAMINATION/EXAMINATION AS DISCIPLINE: THE EFFECTS OF CURRICULUM CODIFICATION ON TEACHERS, STUDENTS AND SUBJECTS

The success of disciplinary power derives no doubt from the use of simple instruments; hierarchical observation, normalizing judgement and their combination in a procedure that is specific to it, the examination.

(Foucault 1977: 170)

Teachers, students and subjects

As I outlined in Chapter 1, in a traditional subject based secondary school curriculum the division of knowledge into subject areas is bound up with the initiation and socialization of teachers into subject subcultural groupings. Within these, there is a further division into competing ideological segments (such as those favouring investigationally based mathematics or a PE curriculum centred on team sports) (Ball and Lacey 1980; St John-Brooks 1983; Cooper 1985; Goodson 1985; Evans and Penney 1995a, b). Such subcultures construct contested but more-or-less consensus views about such things as the nature of the subject, the way it should be taught, the role of the teacher and what might be expected of the student. These subcultural givens allow subject teachers or segmental groupings of subject teachers to participate in a common understanding of the nature of teaching and learning and hence to communicate with each other using a shared language of that subject subculture that reflects these underlying assumptions. The subject subcultural group thus acts as a unifying focus for teachers, out of which can be developed ideas about pedagogy and assessment and within which an individual can locate her or himself with a reasonable degree of reliability. This unifying focus also acts as a pressure on the individual to conform to subcultural norms, as access to promotion can depend on one's ability to present oneself as a fully initiated and conforming member of the subject group (Sparkes 1987).

In primary schools in the UK, such subject based subcultures do not pertain; instead a more general and integrated 'primary teacher culture' predominates. This culture is relatively unconcerned with subject knowledge, focusing itself instead on issues of pedagogy and teacher–student relations (Alexander 1990; Pollard *et al.* 1994). Nevertheless, segmental disputes still feature, although they are more likely to be concerned with pedagogic issues (such as how to teach reading) than about the nature or emphasis of the subjects being studied. Despite these differences, however, both the primary and the various secondary subcultures have been, in the past decade, cut across by the increasing codification of the curriculum, in particular with the introduction into England and Wales, from 1989, of the National Curriculum.

Even before this, the fluid and contested nature of the subject subculture in the secondary school was increasingly influenced by the content of examination syllabuses and their accompanying assessment processes. Barnes and Seed point out that 'Examination papers . . . offer to teacher and taught the most persuasive arguments about what model of the subject is appropriate, what should go on in lessons, what knowledge, skills and activities should be emphasised and what can safely be ignored' (1984: 263). The effect of this is, as Reid points out, that 'school programmes tend towards topical uniformity within politically united or culturally homogeneous territories . . . [especially] . . . where national systems of assessment or accreditation result in *de facto* limitations on acceptable practice' (1984: 72).

With the introduction of the National Curriculum for England and Wales and the accompanying explosion in assessment practices, these effects began to become important in the earlier years of schooling. No longer were high stakes public examinations restricted to older students; the requirement that students be assessed at ages 7, 11, 14 and 16 meant that the influence of assessment instruments, and the curriculum that they were designed to represent, began to pervade the entire schooling system. The codification of the curriculum with the introduction of Orders specifying what was to be taught for each of ten National Curriculum subjects, and the dominance of assessment in those Orders, presented teachers with an exposition of the model of the subject deemed appropriate by the government, and, furthermore, made it inescapable that they should use that model in making judgements about students' work. In primary schools in England and Wales, some aspects of pedagogy have also come under the formal codification of the state: the 'strong encouragement' (enforced through inspection) for schools to provide a daily 'literacy hour' and 'numeracy hour', whose form and outline content are closely specified, represent a further disciplining of teachers and students, in addition to the influence of assessment.

These trends have been further exacerbated by the requirement that students be assessed not only through externally determined and moderated tests, but also continuously, through teacher assessment. This has meant that teachers have had to internalize the nationally mandated version of the curriculum to a much greater extent than before. Because teachers now have to note when a student achieves specific learning outcomes and, often, to provide evidence for this, the assessment has to pervade both how their teaching is carried out and how it is planned (Pollard *et al.* 1994; Spours 1997; Wolf 1999). Pollard *et al.* (1994), for example, quote a teacher's description of how this internalization has to be operationalized in the classroom on a day-to-day basis:

> If they're doing specific activities as part of the National Curriculum work, if I've perhaps asked them, for example, to write a story about something to do some sequencing work in story form, then I'd obviously be trying to assess whether they're achieving writing simple words on their own or whether they are beginning to write sentences, or sequencing their story in a logical way, so I'm making those sort of assessments as we go along.
>
> (1994: 193)

Gipps *et al.* (1996) note that for some early years teachers in particular, this cuts across their ideological commitment to child-centred learning and can mean that they have to 'translate' their intuitive assessments into National Curriculum levels. Pollard *et al.* suggest, for example, that:

> The dislike of many teachers for this requirement [to undertake summative and evaluative assessment] was not simply because it meant an increase in their workload or required skills that they did not feel they had. Rather their resistance was rooted in an objection to the use of the coercive power of the law to impose on teachers the obligation to operationalize a different set of understandings concerning the role of assessment in primary schooling. This conflict of understanding in turn reflected a fundamental challenge to the values typically held by primary school teachers concerning how children can best be helped to learn, and the particular role of assessment in this respect.
>
> (1994: 204)

Codification of the curriculum, coupled with high stakes assessment (a school's results for students aged 11 and 16 are published and used to form league tables of schools and local education authorities) has meant that assessment schemes have increased their importance to teacher cultures, both in their secondary subject based and primary pedagogy based forms. It has also meant that primary teachers, while retaining a focus on primary-culture methods and practices, have had to conform to the subject based thinking inherent in National Curriculum documentation. Given the masculinized nature of secondary education (Öhrn 1993), it is likely that this change of focus represents an increased masculine influence on the largely feminized world of the primary classroom.

This need to conform to centralized dominant subject culture comes about particularly because of the introduction of continuous teacher assessment as part of a summative as well as a formative process. In order to ensure that the work produced by students can be assessed at all, teachers have to develop and adopt internalized subcultural stances, aligned with the requirements of the assessment scheme being used, so that they can ensure that students' work is conformable with these. The assessment criteria have to, in a sense, enter the teacher's 'thinking as usual' (Schutz 1964) so that they are, at least on a day-to-day level, uncontested (Scarth 1983). Internalizing curriculum and assessment requirements in this way will involve different degrees of compromise for different people (Gipps *et al.* 1996), but remains necessary for all teachers because of the need to make rapid decisions about assessability within the teaching situation. Thus a teacher will be dealing simultaneously both with a view of the subject expressed through their own pedagogic aims, and the internalized, but possibly alternative, subject based requirements of assessment for the National Curriculum, or, after age 14, of a particular examination syllabus.

Internalized notions of assessability are developed from the teacher's reading of the constraints of the assessment scheme (Bowe *et al.* 1992). Such schemes may themselves contain implicit assumptions about what sort of work is assessable, as well as about the nature of assessment. Where the teacher's preferred ways of working do not align well with those assumed by the associated scheme, this may require teachers to change their classroom practices in order to make clearer the level of achievement involved in a particular piece of work. For example, a secondary English teacher working on a project in which students were writing books for 5-year-olds decided that they would have to keep a 'learning log' to show the level of their thinking:

> It's really special for this project because normally, like the other pieces of work they're doing, the learning obviously would be evident in the way that they had written it, the input, that would be evident by the way they've finished the piece of work, whereas with the children's project, to my mind just the pictures and the very short bits of text, they

need some more evidence that they have actually thought about it . . . I wanted it to be evidence of them thinking, evidence of them negotiating, reflecting on what they've done, reflecting on audience, talking to the kids, all of those things.

(Meagan Scanlan, English teacher, Shipbuilders School)

The increasing use of continuous assessment, while externally imposed, does bring a number of benefits. It offers students the chance to show what they can do given time and support and allows the inclusion of longer and more holistic projects into the assessment arena. Furthermore, it has the potential to bring about a change of the balance of power between teachers and the legitimating authorities:

The current trend away from narrow, academic, externally imposed certification procedures towards broader, more continuous, teacher-based certification procedures . . . means that the criteria of successful performance are increasingly being left to teachers to decide. Even where the criteria for such assessment are externally agreed, the breadth of such assessments can make any effective moderation of the *application* of the criteria almost impossible . . . leaving teachers very significant power in determining life chances.

(Broadfoot 1999: 79, original emphasis)

Of course, teachers may not use that increased power in an equitable way, and it could be argued that such shifts in power/knowledge relations are likely to result in detrimental outcomes for specific groups of students (Walkerdine 1988; Walkerdine and The Girls and Mathematics Unit 1989; Gillborn 1990; Murphy 1990; Mirza 1992; Murphy and Elwood 1997).

In the rest of this chapter I am going to explore how the increased codification of curriculum and the rise of continuous assessment throughout schooling affect the gendered power/knowledge relations of classrooms and schools. Specifically, I want to discuss how these changes point up the contradictions between open, student-centred learning as exemplified in the traditions of liberal and emancipatory education and the Panoptic nature of continuous assessment of students' work. I want to look at the way that the assessment-focused subject culture supports and is supported by the disciplinary force of continuous assessment, and at how this impacts on attempts to include and value student-owned knowledge (Paechter 1998b) in classroom practices.

Discipline/examination

In the last decades of the twentieth century there were a number of attempts to develop student-centred, open work as a means to student empowerment through the incorporation of students' owned knowledge into high status classroom activities (Rogers 1983; Resnick 1987; Giroux 1988; Timpson 1988; Taylor 1989). Because, in the wider society, power/knowledge relations are bound up with the possession of credentials, such high status activities inevitably involve assessment and examination. In dealing with student-owned knowledge, therefore, teachers have to keep continuously in mind what is the ultimate form of school knowledge, that legitimated by the assessment scheme. Attempts to 'open up' the classroom to student-centred activities are undercut by the relationship between the double meanings of 'discipline' and 'examination'. I am now going to move on to uncover some of the ramifications of these doubled meanings, and consider their importance in the relationship between knowledge and power and the resulting implications for the incorporation of students' 'owned knowledge' into assessed work.

Hoskin argues that discipline and examination are pivotal in the relationship between knowledge and power.

> Power and knowledge do not in any simple way imply each other; they do so only in certain specific and specifiable respects, through the operation of a third term, which is not the same as, or reducible to, either one of them. Discipline is one candidate for such a third term, as is examination; examination after all was the term which for Foucault embodied 'the superimposition of the power relations and the knowledge relations'.
>
> (1990: 51)

In mediating between knowledge and power, discipline and examination act together and through the relationship between all four of their meanings: between discipline as subject and as control, examination as judgement and as gaze. These meanings illustrate not only this interrelationship but both how it comes about and is used. Discipline, as Hoskin describes it, 'manifests the two sides of a power–knowledge equation. For it concerns *ab initio* the dual process: the discipline that is presenting certain knowledge to the learner, and the discipline of keeping the learner present before the knowledge' (1990: 30). Examination, similarly, is concerned not only with judging and labelling students, but also with the process by which such judgements are formed, with examination as scrutiny. It is through this duality of process and product, central to the operation of both discipline and examination, that knowledge is able to enter into a dynamic relationship with power, within the educational context.

In the enacting of this power/knowledge relation, examination has a key role. Through the influence of assessment, especially of coursework, on the activity of the classroom, it defines the knowledge that is legitimated there (Paechter 1992b). In doing this it regulates it into the form of a discipline;

school knowledge thus becomes disciplinary knowledge. This controls the work of the teacher, who is constrained by the pressure for examination success to remain within the boundaries of the examination-defined subject. Although one feature of the subject subculture has always been to develop a unified or at least dominant view of the nature of each subject, this has hitherto been moderated by dissent, debate and contestation. The increasing encroachment of assessment, however, has meant that any disagreement with this dominant view has to be subordinated to the requirement to ensure that students succeed. Assessment schemes, superficially at least, provide a unifying focus for any subject subcultural grouping, because they lay down a view of what product will result from teachers' and students' classroom work, whatever those teachers' personal stances regarding the nature of the subject (Bloomer 1998). The need to assess means that the teacher has to internalize a view of what counts as, for example, a 'level three piece of mathematics' which is particular to the definitions laid down in the assessment scheme, whatever their personally developed views might be. Similarly, teachers from a range of subjects negotiating their approach to the new area of D&T found that these negotiations were essentially overridden by the emphasis, in the first formal assessments, of a particular model of D&T that emphasized the construction of artefacts and effectively sidelined the contextualizing force of human purposes and values. Given that girls have been found to take context more seriously than boys in approaching assessment tasks (Gipps and Murphy 1994), this represented a masculinization of what was supposed to be a gender-neutral subject. At the same time as this disciplining of the teacher, a disciplinary force is also exerted on the learners, who are encouraged to persevere with the study of subject-matter even if it has been rendered uninteresting and irrelevant to their lives (McNeil 1986). The examination has the disciplinary function of retaining the attention of the vast majority of students, of keeping them, without force, quiescent in the classroom. Furthermore, as will be explained later, teacher assessment leads to a Panoptic classroom technology, with students exposed to a continuous and internalized scrutinizing examination.

Discipline

Examination, especially in the form of coursework assessment, has an inherent effect on the nature of the subject subculture. Part of the discourse of this subculture, however, is that each segmental group propounds its view of the subject as the central one: 'The modern disciplines maintain themselves by defining truth and claiming it as their own. In this way, they exclude the question of power from their own discourse – the conditions for their own existence and possibilities as bodies of knowledge' (Nicoll and Edwards 1997: 15). Claims are made not in terms of particular interpretations of the subject, but as definitions of what it is really about. An example of this is Smithers and Robinson's attempt to promote the Engineering Council's view of the nature of design and technology:

> The 'language' of technology is *essentially* the knowledge areas (including materials, electronics, instrumentation, fluids, structures) and skills (including control, measurement, assembly, construction, project management) applied to a particular class of practical problems, improving or inventing products or systems.
>
> (1992: 16, my emphasis)

Although it is clear from a footnote that the examples of knowledge and skills are taken from another Engineering Council publication, the proposed definition is presented as fact, in order to support the authors' argument that technology as defined in the National Curriculum is not really technology at all. The argument is not about what in particular we might want students to learn; it is taken for granted that we want them to learn technology, but then argued that they are not doing so because those who wrote the curriculum were in fact describing something else. Such arguments take this form because of the power invested in the conception of the subject as a discipline:

> [discipline] comes from the Latin *disciplina*, and in the Latin it has the same double meaning that it retains today, referring both to the ancient knowledge arts such as philosophy, music and rhetoric, and to the problems of power, as for instance in *disciplina militaris* (military discipline).
>
> (Hoskin 1990: 30)

In seeing subjects as disciplines it is understood that there is something central and essential about their nature (Hirst 1965); segmental struggles take on a discourse that suggests that they are more than micropolitical. This invests the dominant view of the subject with disciplinary power because keeping within the understood boundaries of the subject becomes necessary in a strong sense (Klein 1993); one has to treat the boundaries as real rather than as social constructs: 'Discipline sometimes requires *enclosure*, the specification of a place heterogeneous to all others and closed in upon itself. It is the protected place of disciplinary monotony' (Foucault 1977: 141).

Foucault is speaking literally, but we can also apply this metaphorically to the enclosure of the school subject construed as a discipline. Its boundaries delimit the subject content for both teacher and learner, they regulate the knowledge that is permitted and that which is excluded, forming a division between what pertains to the classroom and what has no place there. This requires self-discipline on the part of both teachers and learners; they have to learn not to stray from the subject, to keep formal from informal knowledge and to remain within subject boundaries. This means, among other things, that the knowledge they deal with is largely decontextualized, something that female students find particularly uncongenial (Gipps and Murphy 1994; Murphy and Elwood 1997). The conception of the school subject as an objective entity, as regulated by the requirements of assessment, perpetuates subject boundaries and keeps the learners' and teachers' attention on the subject as defined by the examination, through the discourse of disciplinary essentialism.

Because the discourse of disciplines means that only that legitimated as school knowledge has a place in the classroom, the disciplinary power of the examination is also necessary to keep the learner's attention focused on that knowledge. When they find it difficult to be interested in school knowledge for its own sake, the main reason for students to continue studying is the credentials to which, through examination, it leads (McNeil 1986; Brown 1987; Foreman-Peck and Thompson 1998). The examination, and in particular the assessment of work done in class, brings pressure to bear upon students, encouraging them to cooperate with the transmission of school knowledge from the teachers to themselves, at least to the extent that they may be able to reproduce it for assessment.

Concern about the need to get students to give their attention to the knowledge to be conveyed can, in this situation, begin to take precedence over student learning. Cusick found, for example, that educators who assumed that the school curriculum existed as an agreed body of knowledge, and who then found that students had no interest in it, responded to this lack of interest by shifting their own concerns from actually teaching 'positive knowledge' to maintaining order and control:

> Not only did those administrators spend their time on those matters [administration and control], they also tended to evaluate other elements, such as the performance of teachers, according to their ability to maintain order. They tended to arrange other elements of the school according to how they contributed or failed to contribute to the maintenance of order.
>
> (Cusick 1983, quoted in Giroux, 1985: 26)

Nespor further notes that in the context of the US elementary school:

> When a teacher's space becomes defined by the bodies of her students, the kids' bodily behaviours become the focus of attention. Teachers are held responsible for the noise and movement their kids produce rather than for what they know. The maintenance of calm and quiet serves as the index of teaching 'success'. Denscombe (1980) pointed out that noise emanating from a classroom is taken to indicate the teacher's lack of control and a concomitant absence of learning. By implication, students

who are noisy are thought to be engaged in illegitimate, non-school forms of activity.

(Nespor 1997: 123)

This phenomenon is further investigated by McNeil (1986), who studied teaching and learning styles in the social studies departments of four US schools. McNeil documents what happens in schools in which administrators give higher priority to student control than to learning, the result being the 'contradictions of control', or 'the failure of school knowledge in 'smooth-running' schools to educate' (1986: 16). She describes a vicious cycle in which:

> The teachers' fears of student disruption made them tighten control of knowledge at the expense of engaging students in the learning process. This oversimplification of topics made the students, in turn, cynical about learning and lowered their expectations that anything substantive was to be gained from the course. Their minimal responses sent signals to the teachers which seemed to confirm the teachers' low expectations of 'today's students'.

(McNeil 1986: 80)

In this situation the knowledge presented to students becomes subordinated to the need to preserve a docile classroom; this is achieved by making the content so boring that students are unable to engage with (and therefore challenge) it. Teachers, afraid of student dissent and under pressure from administrators to maintain good order in the school, manipulate the curriculum to this end. McNeil suggests that whereas in the past student discipline was seen as instrumental to mastering complex knowledge content:

> today many teachers reverse those ends and means. They maintain discipline by the ways they present course content. They choose to simplify content and reduce demands on students in return for classroom order and minimal student compliance on assignments. Feeling less authority than their Latin-grammar school counterpart, they teach 'defensively', choosing methods of presentation and evaluation that they hope will make their workload more efficient and create as little student resistance as possible.

(1986: 158)

The 'defensive teaching' strategies employed by the social studies teachers in McNeil's study took a number of forms, but all were intended to reduce control problems in the classroom. They were carried out consciously, often in the belief that good teaching was so unappreciated that to attempt it would be going against the expectations of the school. Defensive teaching was thus seen as a strategy for survival in adverse circumstances. It took the form of controlling the knowledge made available to students by presenting it in such a way that it was meaningless in any but the school-test context. Information was fragmented into lists, reducing it to 'facts', simultaneously suppressing alternative interpretations and facilitating quantifiable testing. Some topics were mystified, being presented as being very important but at the same time unknowable, with the apparent intention that students internalize the affective force of such terms as 'the gold standard', their loyalty to the system thus being enhanced without the need for understanding. Controversial areas, particularly in recent history, were omitted or played down. A final, overt, strategy in winning student compliance was defensive simplification: conceptually difficult topics were simplified so that while there was an illusion of dealing with the subject matter, the students were not required to put in the work needed for an understanding of the issues involved.

Teachers controlled curriculum content in such a way that students were given as little knowledge as possible about the injustices and inadequacies of economic and political institutions; they presented a consensus view of history, and rarely mentioned even historical dissent.[1] The possibility of social change, or even of alternative interpretations of events, was thus played down.[2] At the same time, the presentation as 'fact' of dominant group views that then conflicted with students' out-of-school experiences, led some students to distrust the knowledge presented and refuse to engage with it. Teachers' perception of this disengagement made them even more likely to resort to defensive teaching strategies to maintain classroom order, so that school and student-owned knowledge become increasingly separated:

> What is clear is that where knowledge control is used as a form of classroom control, alienation increases for all participants, further reinforcing patterns of control. Resistance to forms of control does not mean that students are escaping the effects of the way information is processed. One real effect of the alienation students feel toward school-supplied information is the opportunity cost of rejecting much course content without having any sense of how to find (or generate or evaluate) credible information on their own. The teachers seem fairly successful in placing a distance between the students' own questions and concerns and the course content. This seems to make the students withdraw into their own personal information (their 'real' knowledge) so that it will not become contaminated by school-supplied knowledge.
>
> (McNeil 1986: 188)

In this situation, the introduction of student-owned knowledge into school would require fundamental changes in teaching and learning styles; teachers would not only have to make it clear that students' owned knowledge was welcomed and valued in the classroom, but would additionally need to find ways to ensure that its legitimation did not merely incorporate more of the student's self into the disciplinary mechanisms of the school. Unfortunately this is precisely what happens, due to the Panoptic technology of high stakes continuous assessment.

Panoptic examination

The examination combines the techniques of an observing hierarchy and those of a normalizing judgement. It is a normalizing gaze, a surveillance that makes it possible to qualify, to classify and to punish. It establishes over individuals a visibility through which one differentiates them and judges them. . . . In it is combined the ceremony of power and the form of the experiment, the deployment of force and the establishment of truth. At the heart of the procedures of discipline, it manifests the subjection of those who are perceived as objects and the objectification of those who are subjected. The superimposition of the power relations and knowledge relations assumes in the examination all its visible brilliance.

(Foucault 1977: 184)

The teachers in McNeil's study were able to control not only the content of the curriculum but also the process of assessment, which took the form of tests and papers they set and marked themselves. This allowed a further layer of control: students who took notes in class would pass the tests and thus get the course credits they required for graduation. The carrot of the credential kept students' attention on the minimum required for its attainment, while at the same time giving teachers a bargaining tool: docility will be rewarded by my making it easy for you to pass the tests. In the UK, such direct strategies are not so easily available to teachers. Examinations are set externally, and even work devised and assessed by teachers is moderated by independent bodies. Teacher assessments at National Curriculum key stages, while compulsory, are given less importance than test results. Consequently, teachers cannot respond to the needs of classroom control by making the subject-matter easier and the examinations geared to those who take lesson notes. Instead, they have recourse to the disciplinary power of the examination itself, particularly its coursework component, as a means to classroom control (Torrance 1986). This increasing encroachment into the everyday experience of the classroom has given the examination increased disciplinary power (Broadfoot 1999), not only through its influence on the subject culture, but also through its scrutinizing regard of the students day-to-day learning.

At secondary level at least, this operates through the disciplinary force of students' need for credentials, set against much disengagement with the knowledge forms presented at school. The need to keep students engaged with the school knowledge to be transmitted means that teachers have to play on students' instrumental interest in what school can give them, high status examination passes or qualifications perceived as useful in the workplace (Brown 1987; Foreman-Peck and Thompson 1998). Thus an increasing proportion of the curriculum is geared to that which can be assessed for external certification, and material that would be included on pedagogic grounds, such as personal and social education (PSE) has to be incorporated into the examination system as far as possible. The problems encountered by teachers when the examining gaze is removed highlight both its force and its internalization by students.

The constancy of the examining gaze is particularly apparent in British vocational qualifications, especially the General National Vocational Qualification (GNVQ). These qualifications are competence based; there is no syllabus as such but students have to show evidence that they have acquired the specified competencies at the relevant level (Jessup 1995).

> All NVQs [National Vocational Qualifications] must be *competence-based*. This means that they must conform to a particular model of criterion-referencing . . . which involves an emphasis on outcomes and the decoupling of assessment from particular institutions or learning programmes. Anyone who can present the relevant evidence should be able to present themselves for assessment and obtain the relevant award.
>
> (Wolf 1999: 193, original emphasis)

In order to ensure that the detailed 'performance criteria' are met, students are expected to collect evidence in the form of portfolios. In the portfolio must be written evidence of attainment for each of the performance criteria required for the qualification. This means that the assembly of the portfolio comes to dominate the learning situation with the consequence that despite a strong rhetoric of empowerment and integration, the GNVQ curriculum is strongly classified (Bernstein 1971) in practice (Bloomer 1998; Helsby *et al.* 1998):

> A critical weakness of portfolio development is that, combined with the NVQ approach to coverage, it also demands a great deal of record-keeping both for students and for teachers. Student involvement in assessment may also become a form of control and exclusion. When they are having to busy themselves covering multiple criteria and aligning these with assessment specifications for the portfolio, students have little time to do anything else. When teachers are tackling the demands of this complex range of individualized activities, they cannot be concentrating on specific skill and knowledge development. With this density of activity, something has to give and it appears to have been fundamental skill development and theoretical understanding.
>
> (Spours 1997: 63)

The direct effect of this massive collection of evidence is a high dropout rate; for example, only 42 per cent of the 1994 GNVQ level 3[3] registrations completed successfully, with portfolio completion seen as a major problem (Wolf 1999). It is not surprising that, given that the main aim of most vocational students is to gain the qualification, many use coping strategies in assembling their portfolios, such as writing action plans after the work has been completed (Bates 1998; Bloomer 1998).

Bloomer (1998), Bates (1998) and Helsby *et al.* (1998) all argue that the need to provide so much evidence of 'coverage' of a field of study militates against the integrated student-centredness that is supposed to be at the heart of GNVQ. Furthermore, the 'decoupling' of learning from assessment in the GNVQ (Jessup 1995; Wolf 1999) effectively becomes unworkable because the assessment demands are so great that they end up driving the course:

> They'll tell you the assignment, give you the sheet for what it's going to be and then they'll take each part. As the time goes on, the lessons for the period of the assignment, they will explain the stages so that you can go away and do a bit of research and an elaboration on the points they've given.
>
> (Advanced GNVQ student, quoted in Bloomer (1998: 175))

Continuous assessment, whether in the form of teacher observation or portfolio completion, has a disciplinary function that could never be achieved by the terminal examination alone (Nicoll and Edwards 1997). In allowing students to meet ATs at any time, not just at specific, formalized times and places, it allows for the incorporation of the whole of a student's school experience into the scrutiny of the examination, and, through this, the operation of a Panoptic technology of observation.

Bentham's Panopticon was designed as a humane means of dealing with criminals, although it was considered to be equally applicable to the disciplinary aspects of hospitals and schools. It was intended to put the inmates under such potentially constant observation that they internalized the scrutinizing eye and came to regulate themselves. The design was simple. It consisted of a circular arrangement of single cells, each lit by a window in the outside wall and open to view on the inside. In the centre was a tower, from which the guards and others might observe the prisoners. Because this tower would be comparatively dark, a prisoner would not know at any particular moment whether he or she was in fact being watched, and would therefore have to make sure to behave at all times as the penitent prisoner the authorities required; it was believed that this would, in time, lead the prisoner truly to repent and thus become fit to be released back into society. Its major effect was:

> to induce in the inmate a state of conscious and permanent visibility that assures the automatic functioning of power. So to arrange things

that the surveillance is permanent in its effects, even if it is discontinuous in its action; that the perfection of power should tend to render its actual exercise unnecessary; . . . in short, that the inmates should be caught up in a power situation of which they are themselves the bearers.

(Foucault 1977: 201)

The effectiveness of the Panopticon highlights the importance of invisibility as a necessary condition of freedom. Prisoners would end up regulating their own behaviour simply because of the knowledge that they could be seen by their gaolers at any time. Obviously, this considerably lessens the control problems associated with incarceration:

There is no need for arms, physical violence, material constraints. Just a gaze. An inspecting gaze, a gaze which each individual under its weight will end by interiorising to the point that he is his own overseer, each individual thus exercising this surveillance over, and against, himself.

(Foucault 1980: 155)

Panopticism was, in its literal form, carried over to the building of schools, regulating the movements of the students through an architecture designed to facilitate continuous observation. Equally important, however, is the metaphoric application of a Panoptic technology in the incorporation of the examining gaze into developmental psychology and hence into the underlying methods of early childhood education. Such a gaze, introduced in the early twentieth century into initial teacher education through the ubiquitous 'child study', classifies and individualizes the child that is its object. Individualized pedagogy depends on the possibility of the observation and classification of normal development and on the idea that each child will learn what and as they are ready to (Bernstein 1975; Walkerdine 1984). Although Galton *et al.* (1999) argue that the National Curriculum and the emphasis of successive governments on whole-class teaching have eroded individualization as a dominant practice, the ideology of child-centred learning remains important to primary school teachers (Alexander 1990; Gipps *et al.* 1996). The production of learning conditions tailored to each individual requires the teacher constantly to observe the current state of the child's learning so that they may thus further the child's development. Panopticism has thus become incorporated into the underlying understanding of what constitutes good teaching and learning, as manifested in the 'invisible pedagogy' of the early years classroom (Bernstein 1975). Bernstein argues that both visible and invisible pedagogies require that:

There must be rules, formal and/or informal, whereby the social relationship is initially constituted. These rules regulate what it is to be a transmitter and what it is to be an acquirer. The acquirer is expected to learn how to be a particular type of acquirer, as much as the transmitter has learned to be a particular type of transmitter. These rules determine the hierarchical form of the transmission. They establish its rules of conduct.

(1975: 117)

In invisible pedagogies such rules are implicit, with the student's freedom of action undercut by the unstated requirement to act in certain ways; as Bernstein notes, this invisibility masks the power relationships involved. It also necessitates an internalization of the pedagogic relationship and the subject/object relations embodied therein. This internalization forms part of the Panoptic structure of the ostensibly open classroom. It is this on which National Curriculum teacher assessment of early years children is particularly based, developing and building on an already established individualizing gaze. The difficulties teachers have relate not to the gaze itself but to their ability to internalize the criteria upon which their normalizing judgements have to be based. This led, in the first few years at least, to the need to 'translate' their assessments to comply with National Curriculum requirements (Gipps *et al.* 1996).

Continuous assessment throughout the years of schooling is also based on a rationalist view of the student as knowable and classifiable. The examination, continuous or otherwise, appears objective and dispassionate, and, since the introduction (in Cambridge in the 1790s) of marks for individual questions (Hoskin 1979), turns the student into a 'case', an 'objectively' quantifiable individual:

> The examination as the fixing, at once ritual and 'scientific', of individual differences, as the pinning down of each individual in his own particularity . . . clearly indicates the appearance of a new modality of power in which each individual receives as his status his own individuality, and in which he is linked by his status to the features, the measurements, the gaps, the 'marks' that characterize him and make him a 'case'.
>
> (Foucault 1977: 192)

In this way, particularly in the early years of schooling, the practices of psychology, of the study of children and their development, have been translated into the practices of the classroom. The objectified child is to be studied so that she or he may be educated.

This belief in the necessity to cast the observing gaze over the learner-as-object leads to the incorporation of the idea of formative assessment as a central tenet of pedagogy throughout schooling. Formative assessment 'sets out to provide information for the teacher about the way a pupil undertakes particular tasks, so that the lessons learnt about the way that pupil performs can be fed back into future task performance' (Scott 1990: 18).

There is a belief that the more one knows about the mental or developmental state of the child, the better one will be able to lead them to discover or construct for themselves the knowledge that awaits them. It underlies the Socratic method, the perception of education as *educere*, as drawing out,[4] that good pedagogic practice begins with the elucidation of the students' own ideas (Driver and Oldham 1986). While this may indeed produce an effective pedagogy, it does so by positioning the learner as an object to be known, with the assumption that the more knowledge the teacher is able to amass, the more effective will be the learning process, because the closer it will be tailored to the needs of that particular child.

Teacher assessment for the National Curriculum requires summative assessment to be drawn out of formative assessment processes; the outcome of the continuous assessing gaze is to be used not only to develop further work with the student but to quantify the individual's achievement at particular points in their school career. Gipps *et al.* (1996) note that this means that some teachers are making notes about individual children's National Curriculum levels as frequently as daily or weekly. Hence:

> the school became a sort of apparatus of uninterrupted examination that duplicated along its entire length the operation of teaching. It became less and less a question of jousts in which pupils pitched their forces against one another and increasingly a perpetual comparison of each and all that made it possible both to measure and to judge. The Brothers of the Christian Schools wanted their pupils to be examined every day of the week: on the first for spelling, on the second for arithmetic, on the third for catechism in the morning and for handwriting in the afternoon, etc. . . . The examination did not simply mark the end of an apprenticeship; it was one of its permanent factors; it was woven into it through a constantly repeated ritual of power.
>
> (Foucault 1977: 186)

If we compare current practice to that of the late eighteenth century of which Foucault is writing, how much has changed? The 'ritual of power' remains, but it has become more insidious, more hidden in its forms. The rhetoric of coursework and continuous assessment is that it alleviates stress, allowing students to balance their performance in the examination hall. This is important; Pollard *et al.* (1994) found that the performance even of 7-year-olds could be affected by examination nerves and that teachers often pretended that the National Curriculum SATs were games, to minimize this effect. In making more of the students' work examinable the use of continuous assessment gives them more opportunities to show what they can do. However, because it permits more to be shown, this also means that more can be seen. Continuous assessment thus both liberates and enslaves, and in the name of liberation, the enslaving examining gaze has been allowed, even encouraged, to break its bonds. No longer is it confined to the formative judgement private to the relationship between teacher and student, or to the single all-important regard of the silent, timed paper. Examination has entered the classroom, the disciplinary gaze of external scrutiny pervading an increasing proportion of the student's school life.

This represents the dark side of humanism, that a more liberal regime, both in the prison and in the school, has as its other face a more pervasive disciplinary force. The Panoptic prison was designed to control not only the prisoner's body but their mind; its focus was cure and reform rather than retributive punishment. The prisoner is therefore positioned as a case, the restitution of liberty depending on personal factors and the length of time needed to effect reform rather than the completion of a standard length of retributive imprisonment (Foucault 1977); this feature has been retained in the cases of those sentenced to secure mental hospitals and those for whom therapy is offered as an alternative to incarceration. A more overtly caring regime thus was and remains tied to the constant pressure of the normalizing gaze. Similarly, the Panoptic effect of continuous assessment in the classroom represents a betrayal of humanism that operates through the mechanisms of humanism itself. Teachers and students are caught in a double-bind; the perceived improvement of student motivation, learning and examination results in the Panoptic classroom means that Panopticism will continue to be embraced by those on whom it exerts its disciplinary force.

At secondary level, the all-pervasiveness of the examination has been encouraged precisely because of the problem of classroom discipline, of getting disillusioned students to remain docile when confronted with knowledge made irrelevant by its incorporation into the power relations of the school. At Lacemakers, for example, the combined arts students were emphatic that it was only in this subject, in which they were encouraged to invest themselves emotionally, that they would carry on working even without a teacher being present, simply because they enjoyed it. The examination of coursework allows a disciplinary technology to pervade every aspect of classroom life. Students can be assessed not only on their final products, but also on the processes gone through in arriving at these. This extends the implicit judgements of formative assessment to the summative appraisal of the final examination. It is not merely what the student can do that is judged, but how they go about this. As Nicholl and Edwards put it, writing about the assessment of open learning at university level:

Through the examination, subjects become objects as they are made available for scrutiny, comparison and judgement. The network of observation embedded within systems of report, appraisal, marking and so forth makes the subject available for examination, categorisation and normalisation. Examination has a double effect insofar as it is a process of objectification, of persons becoming objects to be classified and measured, and of subjectification, where they become subjects who 'learn' the truth about themselves, including their capacity to be autonomous.

(1997: 18–19)

Again, the all-pervasiveness of this examination of the self is most notable in the case of vocational qualifications. The British GNVQs, for example, have an official pedagogy of student responsibility for their own learning, enforced by building action planning into the assessment process:

The importance of action plans [has been noted]: in the case of GNVQ it has been simply impossible to complete the award without one . . . Whether a candidate receives a pass, merit or distinction on their award depends on the evidence they provide of planning; of ability to gather information; and of self-evaluation.

(Wolf 1999: 198)

Helsby *et al.* (1998) further point out that the discourse of independence and empowerment, coupled with a curriculum that is in practice strongly classified and framed (Bernstein 1971), is intended to produce docile, self-controlling future workers for post-Fordist workplaces.

It is notable that whereas the extent of the examining gaze has been broadened in the case of vocational qualifications, this is not the case for their supposed academic equivalent, A levels, in which terminal examinations continue to predominate. It would seem that the working-class students at which vocational qualifications are aimed are in need of greater disciplinary surveillance and control than their middle-class counterparts. Hargreaves notes the similar function of the compilation of personal Records of Achievement (RoAs), also introduced primarily to motivate and control working-class students. He argues that because they use repeated, regular, personalized, one-to-one reviews in which students are expected to discuss emotions such as pride and disappointment, RoAs have particular disciplinary significance:

Like 'progressive' primary teaching, records of personal achievement also review and regulate personal and emotional development, but they can do these things with far greater force and effectiveness . . . [The process of compulsion, individuation and control], through the pupils' certain knowledge that there will be inescapable future reviews in an almost unending process of repeated and regulated assessment, suppresses 'deviant' conduct even before it arises.

(Hargreaves 1989: 137)

The GNVQ example illustrates the way that teachers in the UK have found that the more of school life that is incorporated into the examination technology, the more important it is that all the rest should be. Students, most of whose day is taken up with activities that come under the examining gaze, feel that work that is not treated in this way is unimportant. Coursework has been used to regulate their behaviour to such an extent that if the assessed element is not present, neither is the associated docility. It thus becomes necessary to incorporate matter that might otherwise not be examined into an assessment framework. RoAs are one way that this has been attempted; in their inclusion of students' out-of-school activities they also imply that anything that is not recorded is not worthwhile. Some schools, for example, use PSE time or work experience to produce coursework pieces for English. These strategies have the dual effect both of encouraging students to take seriously the school's version of their personal development and at the same time of taking into the realm of school knowledge that which is most clearly the students' own; their understanding of themselves.

The disciplinary force of coursework examination is therefore twofold: the constancy of its scrutiny serves to keep the students' attention on a corpus of knowledge that is itself defined through the constraining influence of that examination on subject and pedagogic subcultures. Its emphasis on the processes of learning makes it necessary to bring under scrutiny an ever greater part of the student's school experience, regulating it and incorporating it into school, rather than owned knowledge. Teacher assessment of work done in class makes it not only possible but necessary for the teacher to attempt to enter the student's head and see what they really know or understand, as demonstrated by the processes they go through in showing that knowledge or understanding. At the same time, the teacher also comes under increased disciplinary force, because of the need to conform to the prescribed curriculum demands, regarding not only the content, but also the form, of the work to be carried out. A more direct link is also established between teaching and student performance, making it easier for external agencies to make claims about teacher effectiveness. Teachers find themselves subject to a more stringently regulating power, as the demands of the examination encroach even more widely into the everyday life of the classroom. The attempt to escape from the piercing scrutiny of the examination hall has resulted in greater subjection to the less dazzling, but far more insidious gaze of continuous assessment.

Furthermore, this gaze is at the centre of many of the problems associated with the attempt to incorporate the methods of formative assessment into summative certification. For the examination that individualizes and differentiates not only requires disinterested observation, but furthermore, in its pure Panoptic form it is itself silent and unobserved: 'The observing gaze refrains from intervening: it is silent and gestureless. Observation leaves things as they are; there is nothing hidden to it in what it is given' (Foucault 1963: 107).

The teacher is simultaneously positioned as the detached, observing examiner, able to judge a student's work at any time, and the drawer-out of knowledge, the one who works alongside the student to enable each individual to produce of their best. Formative assessment requires that the teacher be concerned with the processes the student goes through, in order that such processes be developed and enhanced. Summative assessment, on the other hand, demands a detachment that is not consonant with the ideology, particularly pervasive in early years education, of the caring teacher (Walkerdine and The Girls and Mathematics Unit 1989). As the examination takes over the classroom, this contradiction becomes increasingly problematic, tying the pedagogic relationship in ever more complex knots. Scott points out, for example, that:

> Teachers teaching GCSE are confronted by two seemingly contradictory tasks – the need to initiate a formative process of assessment and learning throughout the duration of the two year course, and the requirement to undertake a summative process of assessment and reporting. . . . When is it the most appropriate time to break into the natural formative process of teaching and learning that goes on irrespective of any desire to compare pupil with pupil in a formal sense?
>
> (Scott 1990: 18–19)

As we saw in Chapter 5, D&T teachers carrying out and assessing the first D&T SAT at KS3 (assessed at age 13–14) found it difficult to work in any way 'normally' while carrying out an extended assessed task in class time. Because of its externally set and moderated nature, and because students were expected to work 'independently' at least some of the time, they saw the task as being more like a practical examination; this meant that they felt unable to teach students anything new or to help them in their work for the period (six weeks or more in some schools) that the task took to carry out (Paechter 1995c). Similarly, infant teachers carrying out KS1 SATs (assessed at age 6–7) felt that they had to change their classroom practices in a radical way, for example by asking children normally encouraged to collaborate not to talk or to help each other with the task (Pollard *et al.* 1994).

The disciplinary function of coursework examination thus takes a variety of forms, all coming together to regulate the work of both teachers and students. The observing gaze of the examination has invaded the classroom, disciplining the inhabitants into a closer attention to its interpretation of the subjects that are taught there. At the same time it forces teachers to adapt their pervasive but comparatively uncontrolling Panoptic technology of formative assessment to the end of summative certification, thus giving more overt disciplinary force to its all-seeing gaze. Students are not only positioned as objects of a differentiating scrutiny, but they are also made conscious of and overtly subjected to it. Meanwhile, the teacher-as-examiner is disciplined by the same mechanism; the need to assess both process and product constrains what they can allow into the classroom, making it increasingly important to retain control of student activity and ensure its assessability. The disciplinary function of the examination thus operates both directly and indirectly, on all parties to classroom interaction:

> the disciplinary power [is] both absolutely indiscreet, since it is everywhere and always alert, since by its very principle it leaves no zone of shade and constantly supervises the very individuals who are entrusted with the task of supervising; and absolutely 'discreet', for it functions permanently and largely in silence.
>
> (Foucault 1977: 177)

The presence of the examiner makes the demands of the examination explicit, its scrutinizing gaze constant. The examiner both carries out the scrutiny and is disciplined by its demands. Teachers' negotiated subject cultures are increasingly forced to conform to national assessment norms. The constancy of the examining embraces everything students bring to their learning, as the requirements of educational efficiency, encouraging the assessment of everything to which the school can gain access, results in the discipline of the examination being brought to bear on all aspects of student life. Where this includes PSE, or areas such as D&T, where students are encouraged to bring their own experiences and knowledge into school, whole areas of the students' world are taken over and turned into school knowledge through the disciplinary power of the examination. There is thus an inherent contradiction in any attempt to alter power/knowledge relations between teachers and students within an assessed curriculum; the technology of the examination exerts its disciplinary power and it facilitates the colonizing by the school of knowledge originally owned by the students. Both senses of discipline interact with both senses of examination in the transformation of 'owned' knowledge into school knowledge, as teachers and students are mutually disciplined by the Panoptic technology of the examination.

Notes

1 Cherkaoui (1977) notes that one reason for the founding of the Jesuit schools was the threat of the Reformation; the curriculum similarly turned away from the present, concentrating on classical literature. Their emphasis on strictness, continuous observation and rigour can also, he argues, be attributed to this fear of religious dissent.

2 McNeil notes that even at the school where fewest defensive strategies were observed and where students were encouraged to discuss controversial issues, some things such as the need to preserve 'our way of life' in the context of energy conservation were still presented uncritically.
3 Advanced GNVQ, intended, at merit and distincton level, to be equivalent to A level and thus acceptable for university entrance.
4 *Educere* is used in Latin to mean 'educate' only in a metaphorical sense. The correct literal translation is 'educare', which also means to rear or to care for.

nine

CONCLUSION

[A]s soon as there is a power relation, there is a possibility of resistance. We can never be ensnared by power; we can always modify its grip in determinate conditions and according to a precise strategy.

(Foucault 1988: 123)

The point of exposing the minutiae and multiplicities of gendered power/knowledge relations, the point, indeed, of this book, is to enable us to change them. Although it can be depressing to contemplate the intricacies with which oppressive gender relations are embedded in the power/knowledge regimes of our schools, such contemplation can be the inspiration and accompaniment of action. The more detail that we are able to see of how gender, power and knowledge interact to produce inequities within the school system, the more effective our interventions and resistances are likely to be.

In attempting such interventions, it is important to expose the multiplicity of micro-powers exercised in and around schooling. This focuses our attention away from metanarrative concepts such as reproduction and revolution and towards the multiple points at which power is exercised and thus can be resisted. It similarly indicates the ubiquitous nature of power and the many spaces within which resistance may be possible. This conception of power may be contrasted with traditional views of it as something held by a particular group and therefore as having to be seized in large, revolutionary actions (led, this being the political rather than the personal realm, by men). While macro analyses of power relations emphasize their importance in the way society is structured, and thus make plain the need for resistance, they can also lead to paralysis, in the face of the perceived magnitude of such a task, among those who wish to work for change. Further, the tendency (of the critical theorists, for example) to prescribe revolutionary stances and methods of resistance, some of which are implicitly masculine in their focus and orientation (Ellsworth 1989; Paechter 1998a), can lead to a feeling that there is nothing that most people can do from the positions they are actually in, except wait for a variety of (feminist, socialist) revolutions. We need to move away from such conceptions to think about gendered power relations as operating with much greater complexity and on a local, personal and specific level.

An emphasis on the multi-faceted nature of micro-powers has implications for possibilities of resistance. While we can alter gender relations or power/knowledge relations within any particular social situation, we have to accept that there will never be a point at which power is abolished and everyone lives in harmony. Patriarchal structures, for example, are so firmly embedded in social formations that it is unlikely that they will ever completely be removed. 'After the revolution' is a sort of never-never land to which we can aspire but which is impossible to achieve; revolutions can change power configurations but not abolish them. However, it is still important to stress that we can still regard some gendered power/knowledge configurations as better than others; if one result of the increased use of GCSE coursework is that more students enjoy their work and pass their examinations, the increased surveillance involved may be a price worth paying, especially for girls, who seem generally to be the beneficiaries of this change. Similarly, the increased take-up of physical sciences and mathematics by girls, while requiring them to work with a greater degree of decontextualization than may be comfortable, gives them access not only to the powerful pleasures of the 'mastery of reason' (Walkerdine 1988) but also to potentially more powerful future social positions. We should not just see power as a negative, but be mindful of its positive aspects, in terms both of how it makes us feel and of what it enables us to do. Power is indeed pleasurable (Walkerdine 1988).

It remains important, however, to be as clear as possible about the payoffs involved; we should be aware both of their existence and their extent. Even if we acknowledge the increase in pastoral power as an acceptable concomitant of, for example, open learning, we need to remain aware of the inescapability of that power. Liberal humanism has a tendency to ignore its own darker side, but it is essential that this be illuminated and examined, if only so that we can see why important aspirations, particularly those of liberal and rationalist feminists, have not been fulfilled (Kenway *et al.* 1998). In education in particular, a simplistic view of the operation of power has at times led to an assumption that changing the power/knowledge relations within schools is solely a matter of changing the structures of curriculum or assessment. As I have demonstrated in this book, this in itself is far from straightforward, due to the micropolitical forces at work; it is simplistic to assume that even if these are overcome there will not still be contradictions and complexities. These remain to be exposed, so that we can see more clearly the multiplicity of powers with which we are dealing, and thus the multiplicity of the points of resistance.

At the same time we need to beware of simplistic analyses which suggest that because girls are now outperforming boys in examinations at some levels, males are now the marginalized group in schools. By looking in detail at the processes by which male and female teachers and students interact we can see that boys and men remain dominant in many ways. Boys still dominate school spaces, both inside and outside the buildings (Shilling and Cousins 1990; Shilling 1991; Thorne 1993; Dixon 1997). Male teachers dominate high status, reason based subjects, and boys also gravitate towards these, particularly at A level, where they gain the same or greater percentage of grade As as do girls (Department for Education and Employment 1998). While some males, particularly those who are of Afro-Caribbean or working-class origin are, indeed, failed by schools, it remains the case that in the outside world (and in the informal social world of the classroom) they maintain their dominance over females, particularly females from the same socially marginalized groups (hooks 1982; Donaldson 1993; Kenway 1996; Kenway *et al.* 1998). Considering the relationship between gender, power and knowledge in all its complexity allows us to be aware that there are multiple ways of examining, understanding and resisting unequal and gendered power/knowledge relations. We also need to be much more aware of the spatial and bodily aspects of schooling. There is a need for more research into how gendered embodiment affects teachers' and students' perceptions of schooling and school subjects, particularly with regard to the higher status curriculum areas from which the body is officially excluded.

A further implication arising from the multifaceted nature of micro-powers is that the teacher no longer has to see her or himself as solely an agent in the reproduction of the dominant social order, something that has exercised the consciences of numerous left-wing and feminist practitioners, including myself. One can simultaneously have a role in what perpetuates a particular configuration of power/knowledge relations and be active in resisting them. How else, indeed, would it be possible for us to find a role for men (particularly for successful white men) in challenging the power/knowledge relations from which they directly or indirectly benefit? Given that so many of these relations operate at a day-to-day, micro level, it is unlikely that prevailing inequities can be altered without significant changes in everyday male behaviour. We need to acknowledge that small actions both support gendered power relations (so we do have to be aware of every little thing) and resist them (so that every little thing is important). At the same time the significance of micro-resistance means that ordinary teachers have a viable role to play; it is not necessary to be openly feminist or revolutionary to the extent of losing one's job or being pilloried in the staffroom. Because power is exercised at all times and at all levels, small daily resistances have an important contribution to make. Meanwhile we have to remain aware that these resistances are part of the larger project of changing gendered power/knowledge relations within schools. There is, of course, still a role for teachers and others involved in education within larger political movements; the macro and micro levels of resistance can work together, and those with access to a wider platform should use it. However, an awareness that these gendered power/knowledge relations are enacted in our everyday activities suggests that small changes can be fertile starting points.

On the other hand, big changes can, because of small resistances, ulti-mately result in hardly any change at all. The attempt, by UK policy-makers, to liberate the practical curriculum from both its low status and its gendered nature ultimately failed because no account was taken either of the realities of school micropolitics or the implications of the relationship between gender, status and subject marginality. Similarly, attempts to introduce inte-grated curricula without an understanding of students' relationship to the collection curriculum to which they are accustomed are likely to confuse rather than empower. In many ways the most important lesson of the research reported in this book is that it does not pay to introduce an edu-cational innovation without thinking about what it would feel like to be on the receiving end of the changes, either as a teacher or as a student.

One of the most important features of Foucault's work is the exposition and exposure of the multiple ways in which power is exercised; I have attempted to extend this analysis to examine how this particularly affects gender relations in the specific context of schooling. While the contem-plation of what is exposed may be hard to take, it is only by looking firmly at both the positive and negative aspects of the whole multiplicity of micro-powers that we can be clear what we are up against and thus find the points at which resistance can take place. Although it may not be possible, in a straightforward manner, completely to realign gendered power/knowledge relations in classrooms and staffrooms, we can at least move towards a clearer picture of them. This in itself makes continued resistance and trans-formation possible.

All those involved in the design and implementation of curriulum change need to realize that policy-makers and school managers do not hold all the power. One of the clearest lessons from the attempt to introduce integrated D&T is that even if a curriculum innovation is laid down by statute it can successfully be resisted by teachers and students. Consequently, teachers can take heart from the resistances I have reported in these pages. The power of teacher networks, especially those forged by women, can be very strong in terms both of curriculum resistance and of personal solidarity and support (Paechter and Head 1996b). Teachers need to use the points of resistance found everywhere in the system, and use them not just to retain a sense of control over the form and content of the curriculum but to implement small but important changes that together will bring us nearer to a school curriculum that is meaningful, relevant and powerful for all our children.

APPENDIX: EMPIRICAL SOURCES

Much of the argument in this book derives from three partially overlapping empirical studies, carried out in nine schools in total; two schools took part in two of the three studies. The first study looked at the issues involved in interdisciplinary GCSE coursework projects combining a range of school subjects; the second and third considered the negotiation and implementation of the newly formed subject of D&T. All three studies, therefore, were concerned with curriculum negotiation between teachers in conditions of rapid change. In all three, interviews were transcribed and analysed, along with observations and fieldnotes, using progressively focused coding techniques by which analyses from one phase of data collection are fed into and partially structure the next (Strauss 1987). Some of the data from the first two studies have also been re-analysed in the light of the findings of the third, with a view in particular to bringing out further the issues involved in the interaction of gender, power and knowledge. I am extremely grateful to all the teachers who took part in these studies for the time and energy they gave to my work. All of the names of the schools and of the teachers are, of course, pseudonyms.

The Cross-curricular Assessment Project[1]

The data on negotiating interdisciplinary coursework projects come from a case study, in the academic year 1990–91, of four secondary comprehensive schools in three LEA areas, conducted as part of a wider curriculum development project involving 29 schools and colleges in 11 LEA areas. It was mainly carried out through interviews with the teachers and students involved, observation of meetings and some lesson observation, with the focus being on the way the teachers approached the work and how it developed from initial ideas, through carrying out the work with students, to assessment and moderation. For more details of the findings of this study, see Murray *et al.* (1994) and Paechter (1995b).

In all the schools in the project there was an overall coordinator of the work; these were usually senior people, and several were already TVEI coordinators.[2] These school based people were supported by a coordinator in their LEA, although, with the gradual running-down of the local advisory service during this period, not all schools were able to retain this support throughout the project's work. In two of the LEAs involved in the detailed case study, there were support meetings between all the local project schools, so I was able to observe these and check my findings against what was happening in other schools. This, combined with my continuing work in the other 25 project schools, makes me confident in claiming that the processes that I observed are not peculiar to the four schools studied, but are generally to be found when this sort of innovation is undertaken.

A number of criteria were used to choose the four schools to be studied in depth; I had already been working with them all for at least a year. All of them had some continuing LEA support, and three of them participated in meetings with other project schools, allowing me access to a wider sample. They had all come quite a long way in developing cross-subject work, but by very different routes. At Lacemakers School, interdisciplinary work at GCSE level centred around a modular timetable, with a programme of specially devised 'supplementary modules' taken in addition to students' normal GCSE courses. This allowed the school to increase the breadth of students' studies by requiring them to study supplementary modules in those areas they had not chosen to continue to GCSE. There were three main strands of interdisciplinary work in Years 10 and 11. First, the modular setup allowed essentially separate subject work to be linked via a theme and combined to provide extra GCSE subjects; coursework completed for the main subject was also credited towards integrated humanities or environment courses. Second, in the technology/mathematics course, one subject area provided a context for work towards another subject's examination, with the staff emphasizing the links between the areas. Combined arts, the most integrated of all, was conceived of and taught as a fully interdisciplinary course, with each subject expert contributing as necessary. Altogether nine men and one woman from a variety of subject areas were involved. At Shipbuilders School there were two interdisciplinary projects. The first involved students designing and illustrating books for young children, and was taught by the English and art departments. Second, students attending the learning support department were helped to identify pieces of work from a range of subjects that could be used as English coursework pieces, either as they stood, or with some adaptation. At this school, two men and five women worked on a variety of projects, including a third which was, unfortunately, not realized. Work at Stitchers School was mainly focused around an integrated field course for about 40 Year 10 students, involving geography, mathematics, science and art teachers. This school was also involved in one of the D&T studies described below. Altogether six men and two women were involved either in the interdisciplinary or the D&T studies, or, as was the case with two of the men, in both. Finally, Stonemasons School, again also involved in the first D&T study, approached interdisciplinary work through a TVEE[3] initiative, the Flexible Learning Project. Interdisciplinary coursework was thus a second-order goal at this school; it was believed that once students began to take control of their own learning they would see for themselves the overlap between their subjects. Consequently there were no explicitly planned interdisciplinary coursework projects in Years 10 and 11, although a number of pieces of work were carried out for two or more subjects, through teacher–student negotiation. In this school I interviewed five men and two women, including those involved in D&T, although as I also spent part of a residential weekend with the D&T department I was able to talk to and observe a number of others in both formal and informal contexts.

The design and technology studies

My analysis of the implementation of D&T arises from two studies. The first study formed part of my PhD (Paechter 1993a). The second was co-directed by John Head and myself, and was funded by the Economic and Social Research Council.[4] For more details of the findings of these studies see Paechter (1993a, b, c, 1995a, b, c) and Paechter and Head (1996a, b).

In my PhD research, I looked at what was happening in two contrasting schools in one large LEA during 1990–91, the first year of National Curriculum D&T. The second study involved five schools in the London area, and covered the period 1992–94, during which the first cohort of students was first subjected to national testing, and was then expected to start working for the first GCSE in the subject. In both studies my focus was on the teachers involved in the innovation and on their reactions to it, how they negotiated its introduction and how they worked together on its realization and subsequent dissolution.

The main body of the research for both studies was carried out through semi-structured interviews and observation. Interviews were conducted periodically throughout the research with D&T staff and their line managers, including relevant LEA inspection and advisory staff. In the second study, those interviewed were encouraged to read and comment on transcripts of their own previous interviews, although in practice few took this opportunity.

In the second study, part of the initial interview with each department member was used to elicit a description of that individual's career to date, in both objective and subjective terms (Ball and Goodson 1985), and including periods spent outside the teaching profession. I saw the concept of 'career' as a major articulator between subject cultures, micropolitics and the life history of an individual. Data from this initial interview thus had significant influence on later analyses.

In both studies, departmental meetings were observed on a regular basis; in the first study I also observed part of a working weekend that the department at Stonemasons spent in a local hotel for discussion and team-building. The fieldnotes arising from these meetings were coded alongside the interviews and those involved were asked to comment on their perceptions of such meetings. Copies of the minutes of meetings (where available) were collected and analysed. Coding of data took place throughout the research, ongoing analysis forming the basis for further data collection.

Altogether seven schools were studied in the two separate research periods. The first involved Stitchers and Stonemasons schools, located in different (and contrasting) parts of the same county LEA. In both schools the staff involved came mainly from CDT and HE, although at Stitchers an art teacher taught a CDT group and supported HE classes, and there was a move to include art the following year at Stonemasons. At Stitchers, the new department was led by the male head of CDT, and at Stonemasons this role was taken by the head of HE; both coordinators had been promoted into the post. D&T was taught in both cases in a loosely coordinated way, with the contributing departments working independently for most of the time, coming together once or twice with their Year 7 groups (the only year group involved at this stage) for coordinated projects lasting at most half a term. As this study was of comparatively short duration, and as at this stage not all teachers were involved with teaching the new curriculum, I mainly interviewed the heads of the contributing subjects. However, these schools were also part of the Cross-curricular Assessment Project (Paechter 1995b), and some of the interviews conducted for this, particularly those with senior managers or with individuals involved in both projects, had a bearing on the D&T departments. Altogether, data from interviews with five men and two women were analysed for this study, alongside notes from meetings and less informal encounters with a much wider group.

The second research period was more substantial and built on the findings in the first. Five schools were selected for study, giving a range of LEA and departmental emphases, as well as differences in the gender and subject backgrounds of heads of department and members of participant groups. This gave a total number of 37 teachers (18 males, 19 females) who were the core focus of the study, as well as nine other school and LEA figures. The schools chosen were not intended to be a representative sample and did not reflect departmental makeup in England and Wales as a whole. In particular, there were more women CDT teachers and more women in management positions than we would have had with a representative sample. It was felt that this would yield richer data, particularly concerning the gender/power interface. These five departments were structured as follows.

Bursley School had a loose federation of CDT and HE, led by the head of CDT as an overall head of D&T. The head of HE left the school shortly after the study commenced and was not permanently replaced during the time we worked in the school. There were four CDT teachers, two of whom were women, and three female HE staff, although for various reasons two of these posts were mainly filled only on a temporary basis during the research period; these teachers were not formally interviewed. Hanbridge School retained separate subject departments, although the head of HE was paid at a higher scale to act as D&T coordinator. There were two female HE teachers, a CDT department with a female head and two male staff (both of whom only worked part-time in the department), two male BS teachers, one of whom was the head of that department, and two art teachers. During the study, the male head of art retired and was replaced by another male; the other art teacher was female. One male CDT teacher and the female art teacher also taught IT, within the overall D&T framework. Knype School was the most unusual in structure, having two joint heads of D&T, the male and female heads of CDT and HE respectively. There were three male CDT teachers, who were joined by a female in the second year of the study; at the same time the number of HE staff (all female) was reduced from four to three (one left and the post was advertised as being for a D&T teacher with any specialism; a woman was appointed who had a background in industrial design). This department also worked closely with the male head of BS, the male head of music and the male deputy head of art. Longshaw Girls' School had a department led by a male CDT teacher. There were two male CDT staff and one female, two female HE teachers (the head of HE was on extended maternity leave) and one male and one female BS/IT teacher. Turnhill School had a department led by the female head of IT. There were two male CDT teachers and two females teaching HE. The former head of CDT had become second in charge of technology and the former head of HE moved out of the department to other duties in the school. In the second year of the study there was also another female IT teacher.

Notes

1 This project was directed by Paul Black and Robin Murray at King's College London from 1988 to 1991, and funded by SEAC and the TVEI Unit of the Department of Employment.
2 By the time the project started work the TVEI was in its extension phase, referred to as TVEE, which had interdisciplinary work as a specific focus.
3 See note 2.
4 ESRC award number R000233548.

REFERENCES

Alexander, R. (1990) Core subjects and autumn leaves: the national curriculum and the languages of primary education, in B. Moon (ed.) *New Curriculum – National Curriculum*. London: Hodder and Stoughton, 72–9.

Arnot, M., David, M. and Weiner, G. (1996) *Educational Reform and Gender Equality in Schools*. Manchester: Equal Opportunities Commission.

Arnot, M., Gray, J., James, M., Ruddock, J. and Duveen, G. (1998) *Recent Research on Gender and Educational Performance*. London: The Stationery Office.

Ashton, N. (1986) Educated man as action man: a reply to Keith Thompson, *British Journal of Educational Studies*, 34(1): 4–22.

Askew, S. and Ross, C. (1988) *Boys Don't Cry: Boys and Sexism in Education*. Milton Keynes: Open University Press.

Attar, D. (1990) *Wasting Girls' Time: The History and Politics of Home Economics*. London: Virago Press.

Ball, S. J. (1985) English for the English since 1906, in I. F. Goodson (ed.) *Social Histories of the Secondary Curriculum*. Lewes: Falmer Press, 53–88.

Ball, S. (1987) *The Micropolitics of the School*. London: Methuen.

Ball, S. J. and Goodson, I. F. (1985) Understanding teachers: concepts and contexts, in S. J. Ball and I. F. Goodson (eds) *Teachers' Lives and Careers*. Lewes: Falmer Press, 1–26.

Ball, S. J. and Lacey, C. (1980) Subject disciplines as the opportunity for group action: a measured critique of subject subcultures, in P. Woods (ed.) *Teacher Strategies*. London: Croom Helm, 149–77.

Barnes, D. and Seed, J. (1984) Seals of approval: an analysis of English examinations, in I. F. Goodson and S. J. Ball (eds) *Defining the Curriculum*. Lewes: Falmer Press, 263–98.

Barnett, M. (1991) Technology within the National Curriculum and elsewhere, in M. Young and M. Barnett (eds) *Towards Technological Literacy*. London: Department of Policy Studies, University of London Institute of Education, 27–49.

Bates, I. (1998) Resisting 'empowerment' and realizing power: an exploration of aspects of the GNVQ, *Journal of Education and Work*, **11**(2): 187–204.

Bell, L. (1986) Managing to survive in secondary school physical education, in J. Evans (ed.) *Physical Education, Sport and Schooling.* Lewes: Falmer Press, 95–115.

Berger, J. (1972) *Ways of Seeing.* London: BBC and Penguin Books.

Bernstein, B. (1971) On the classification and framing of educational knowledge, in M. F. D. Young (ed.) *Knowledge and Control.* West Drayton: Macmillan, 47–69.

Bernstein, B. (1975) *Class, Codes and Control.* London: Routledge and Kegan Paul.

Bernstein, B. (1977) *Class, Codes and Control Volume 3.* London: Routledge and Kegan Paul.

Bernstein, B. (1990) *The Structuring of Pedagogic Discourse.* London: Routledge.

Bernstein, B. (1996) *Pedagogy, Symbolic Control and Identity: Theory, Research, Critique.* London: Taylor and Francis.

Black, P. (1990) Implementing Technology in the National Curriculum. Paper presented at the Standing Conference on School Science/Design and Technology Association Conference, 'Technology in the National Curriculum, issues in implementation', London: University of London Institute of Education, May.

Black, P. and Atkin, J. M. (1996) *Changing the Subject: Innovations in Science, Mathematics and Technology Education.* London: Routledge in association with OECD.

Black, P. and Harrison, G. (1985) *In Place of Confusion.* London: Nuffield-Chelsea Curriculum Trust.

Blackburne, L. (1992a) Inspectors told to review technology, *Times Educational Supplement.* 5 June.

Blackburne, L. (1992b). Technology review set to cut targets, *Times Educational Supplement.* 30 October.

Blackburne, L. (1992c) Technology U-turn starts, *Times Educational Supplement.* 26 June.

Blacker, D. (1998) Intellectuals at work in power: toward a Foucaultian research ethic, in T. S. Popkewitz and M. Brennan (eds) *Foucault's Challenge: Discourse, Power and Knowledge in Education.* New York: Teachers College Press, 348–67.

Blatch, T. B. (1992) Letter, *Times Educational Supplement*, 10 July.

Bloomer, M. (1998) 'They tell you what to do and then they let you get on with it': the illusion of progressivism in GNVQ, *Journal of Education and Work*, **11**(2): 167–86.

Bloot, R. and Browne, J. (1996) Reasons for the underrepresentation of females at head of department level in physical education in government schools in Western Australia, *Gender and Education*, **8**(1): 81–101.

Boaler, J. (1997) Reclaiming school mathematics: the girls fight back, *Gender and Education*, **9**(3): 285–305.

Bourdieu, P. and Passeron, J.-C. (1977) *Reproduction in Education, Society and Culture.* Beverley Hills, CA: Sage Publications.

Bowe, R. and Ball, S. J. with Gold, A. (1992) *Reforming Education and Changing Schools.* London: Routledge.

Bowles, S. and Gintis, H. (1976) *Schooling in Capitalist America*. London: Routledge and Kegan Paul.

Brittan, A. (1989) *Masculinity and Power*. Oxford: Basil Blackwell.

Broadfoot, P. (1999) Assessment and the emergence of modern society, in B. Moon and P. Murphy (eds) *Curriculum in Context*. London: Paul Chapman Publishing, 63–91.

Brown, L. M. and Gilligan, C. (1993) Meeting at the crossroads: women's psychology and girls' development, *Feminism and Psychology*, 3(1): 11–35.

Brown, P. (1987) *Schooling Ordinary Kids*. London: Tavistock Press.

Bryson, L. (1987) Sport and the maintenance of masculine hegemony, *Women's Studies International Forum*, 10(4): 349–60.

Burgess, R. G. (1988) Promotion and the physical education teacher, in J. Evans (ed.) *Teachers, Teaching and Control in Physical Education*. Lewes: Falmer Press, 41–56.

Burgess, T. (1986) *Education for Capability*. Windsor: NFER-Nelson.

Burton, L. (1986) *Girls Into Maths Can Go*. Eastbourne: Holt, Rinehart and Winston.

Burton, L. (1989) Images of mathematics, in P. Ernest (ed.) *Mathematics Teaching: the State of the Art*. Lewes: Falmer Press, 180–7.

Burton, L. and Weiner, G. (1990) Social justice and the National Curriculum, *Research Papers in Education*, 5(3): 203–27.

Butler, J. (1990) *Gender Trouble: Feminism and the Subversion of Identity*. London: Routledge.

Campbell, D. and Wintour, P. (1999) Schools told: play games to win. *The Observer*. 20 June.

Carrigan, T., Connell, B. and Lee, J. (1985) Toward a new sociology of masculinity, *Theory and Society*, 14: 551–604.

Carrington, B. and Wood, E. (1983) Body talk: images of sport in a multi-racial school, *Multiracial Education*, 11(2): 29–38.

Carroll, B. (1986) 'Troublemakers': making a name in physical education, in J. Evans (ed.) *Physical Education, Sport and Schooling*. Lewes: Falmer Press, 117–32.

Carroll, B. (1995) Gender and other factors influencing the choice of examination subjects. Paper presented at the European Conference on Educational Research, Bath, September 1995.

Cassidy, S. (1999) Science sacrificed on altar of literacy. *Times Educational Supplement*, 25 June.

Chalmers, A. F. (1982) *What is This Thing Called Science?* Milton Keynes: Open University Press.

Chapman, B. R. (1986) Reflections on 'In place of confusion', *School Science Review*, 68: 363–9.

Cherkaoui, M. (1977) Bernstein and Durkheim: two theories of change in educational systems, *Harvard Educational Review*, 47(4): 557–64.

Cherryholmes, C. H. (1988) *Power and Criticism: Poststructural Investigations in Education*. New York: Teachers College Press.

Coles, F. (1994–95) Feminine charms and outrageous arms, *Trouble and Strife*, 29–30: 67–72.

Connell, R. W. (1987) *Gender and Power*. Cambridge: Polity Press.

Connell, R. W. (1995) *Masculinities*. Cambridge: Polity Press.

Connell, R. W., Ashenden, D. J., Kessler, S. and Dowsett, G. W. (1982) *Making the Difference: Schools, Families and Social Division*. London: George Allen and Unwin.

Cooper, B. (1984) On explaining change in school subjects, in I. F. Goodson and S. J. Ball (eds) *Defining the Curriculum: Histories and Ethnographies*. Lewes: Falmer Press, 45–63.

Cooper, B. (1985) *Renegotiating Secondary School Mathematics*. Lewes: Falmer Press.

Corrigan, P. D. R. (1988) The making of the boy: meditations on what grammar school did with my body, *Journal of Education*, 170(3): 142–61.

Cross, A. and McCormick, B. (eds) (1986) *Technology in Schools*. Milton Keynes: Open University Press.

Culpin, J. (1991) Making the best of things, *Times Educational Supplement*, 18 October.

Cunnison, S. (1989) Gender joking in the staffroom, in S. Acker (ed.) *Teachers, Gender and Careers*. Lewes: Falmer Press, 151–67.

Curtner-Smith, M. D. (1999) The more things change the more they stay the same: factors influencing teachers' interpretations and delivery of National Curriculum physical education, *Sport, Education and Society*, 4(1): 75–97.

Cusick, P. (1983) *The Egalitarian Ideal and the American School*. New York: London.

Datnow, A. (1998) *The Gender Politics of Educational Change*. London: Falmer Press.

Davies, B., Evans J., Penney, D. and Bass, D. (1997) Physical education and nationalism in Wales, *The Curriculum Journal*, 8(2): 249–70.

Dearing, R. (1994) *The National Curriculum and its Assessment*. London: School Curriculum and Assessment Authority.

Deem, R. (1980) *Schooling for Women's Work*. London: Routledge and Kegan Paul.

Delamont, S. (1994) Accentuating the positive: refocusing the research on girls and science, *Studies in Science Education*, 23: 59–74.

Denscombe, M. (1980) 'Keeping 'em quiet': The significance of noise for the practical activity of teaching, in P. Woods (ed.) *Teacher Strategies*. London: Croom Helm, 61–83.

Department for Education (1993) *School Assessment Folder: Instructions for the Statutory Practical Task and Sample Test Questions*. London: School Examinations and Assessment Council.

Department for Education and Employment (1998) *Statistics of Education: Public Examinations in GCSE/GNVQ and GCE in England and Wales 1997*. London: DfEE.

Department for Education/Welsh Office (1992) *Technology for Ages 5 to 16 (1992): Proposals of the Secretary of State for Education and the Secretary of State for Wales*. London: DfE and the Welsh Office.

Department for Education/Welsh Office (1995) *Design and Technology in the National Curriculum*. London: HMSO.

Department of Education and Science/Welsh Office (1989) *Design and Technology for Ages 5 to 16: Proposals of the Secretary of State for Education and Science* and the Secretary of State for Wales (Final Report of the Working Group). London: DES.

Department of Education and Science/Welsh Office (1990) *Technology in the National Curriculum*. London: HMSO.

Dewar, A. (1987) The social construction of gender in physical education, *Women's Studies International Forum*, 10(4): 453–65.

Dewar, A. (1990) Oppression and privilege in physical education: struggles in the negotiation of gender in a university programme, in D. Kirk and R. Tinning (eds) *Physical Education, Curriculum and Culture*. Basingstoke: Falmer Press, 67–99.

Dixon, C. (1997) Pete's tool: identity and sex-play in the design and technology classroom, *Gender and Education*, 9(1): 89–104.

Donaldson, M. (1993) What is hegemonic masculinity?, *Theory and Society*, 22: 643–57.

Donnelly, J. F. (1992) Technology in the school curriculum: a critical bibliography, *Studies in Science Education*, 20: 123–56.

Driver, R. and Oldham, V. (1986) A constructivist approach to curriculum development in science', *Studies in Science Education*, 13: 105–22.

Dunford, J. (1992) Postpone technology at Key Stage 4, *Times Educational Supplement*, 11 December.

Dyhouse, C. (1977) Good wives and little mothers: social anxieties and the schoolgirl's curriculum 1890–1920, *Oxford Review of Education*, 3(1): 21–35.

Eggleston, J. (1991) A fading flower, *Times Educational Supplement*, 22 November.

Eggleston, J. (1992a) Pressed into shape?, *Times Educational Supplement*, 12 June.

Eggleston, J. (1992b) Rebuilt better than new, *Times Educational Supplement*, 18 December.

Elliott, D. J. (1996) Consciousness, culture and curriculum, *International Journal of Music Education*, 28: 1–15.

Ellsworth, E. (1989) Why doesn't this feel empowering? Working through the myths of critical pedagogy, *Harvard Educational Review*, 59(3): 297–324.

Elwood, J. (1999) Gender, achievement and the 'gold standard': differential performance in the GCSE A level examination, *The Curriculum Journal*, 10(2): 189–208.

Equal Opportunities Commission (1983) *Equal Opportunities in Craft, Design and Technology*. Manchester: EOC.

Equal Opportunities Commission (1999) Gender issues in vocational training and workplace achievement of 14–19 year olds: an EOC perspective, *The Curriculum Journal*, 10(2): 209–29.

Evans, J. (1990a) Ability, position and privilege in school physical education, in D. Kirk and R. Tinning (eds) *Physical Education, Sport and Schooling*. Basingstoke: Falmer Press, 139–67.

Evans, J. (1990b) Defining a subject: the rise and rise of the new PE?, *British Journal of Sociology of Education*, 11(2): 155–69.

Evans, J. and Davies, B. (1993) Equality, equity and physical education, in J. Evans (ed.) *Equality, Education and Physical Education*. London: Falmer Press, 11–27.

Evans, J. and Penney, D. (1995a) Physical education, restoration and the politics of sport, *Curriculum Studies*, 3(2): 183–96.

Evans, J. and Penney, D. (1995b) The politics of pedagogy: making a National Curriculum physical education, *Journal of Education Policy*, **10**(1): 27–44.

Evans, J. and Williams, T. (1988) Moving up and getting out: the classed and gendered career opportunities of physical education teachers, in T. Templin and P. Schemp (eds) *Socialisation Into Physical Education*. Uckfield: Benchmark.

Fletcher, S. (1984) *Women First*. London: The Athlone Press.

Flintoff, A. (1993) Gender, physical education and initial teacher education, in J. Evans (ed.) *Equality, Education and Physical Education*. London: Falmer Press, 184–204.

Foreman-Peck, L. and Thompson, L. (1998) Destined to fail? A study of possible factors leading to the non-completion of a General National Vocational Qualification course; completion, guidance and student perceptions, *Westminster Studies in Education*, **21**: 21–34.

Foucault, M. (1963) *The Birth of the Clinic*. London: Routledge.

Foucault, M. (1977) *Discipline and Punish*. London: Penguin.

Foucault, M. (1978) *The History of Sexuality Volume One*. London: Penguin.

Foucault, M. (1980) *Power/Knowledge: Selected Interviews and Other Writings 1972–1977*. Hemel Hempstead: Harvester Press.

Foucault, M. (1982) The subject and power, in H. L. Dreyfus and P. Rabinov (eds) *Michel Foucault: Beyond Structuralism and Hermeneutics*. Brighton: Harvester Press, 208–26.

Foucault, M. (1984) *The Use of Pleasure: The History of Sexuality Volume 2*. London: Penguin.

Foucault, M. (1988) *Politics, Philosophy, Culture: Interviews and Other Writings 1977–1984*. London: Routledge.

Frank, A. W. (1991) For a sociology of the body: an analytical review, in M. Featherstone, M. Hepworth and B. S. Turner (eds) *The Body: Social Process and Cultural Theory*. London: Sage Publications, 36–102.

Fraser, N. (1989) *Unruly Practices: Power, Discourse and Gender in Contemporary Social Theory*. Cambridge: Polity Press.

French, M. (1994) Power/sex, in H. L. Radtke and H. J. Stam (eds) *Power/Gender*. London: Sage, 15–35.

Fullan, M. G. (1991) *The New Meaning of Educational Change*. London: Cassell Educational.

Galton, M., Hargreaves, L., Comber, C., Wall, D. and Pell, A. (1999) *Inside the Primary Classroom: 20 Years On*. London: Routledge.

Gatens, M. (1991) *Feminism and Philosophy: Perspectives on Difference and Equality*. Cambridge: Polity Press.

Gillborn, D. (1990) '*Race*', *Ethnicity and Education*. London: Unwin Hyman.

Gilligan, C. (1982) *In a Different Voice: Psychological Theory and Women's Development*. Cambridge, MA: Harvard University Press.

Gilligan, C. and Attanucci, J. (1988) Two moral orientations: gender differences and similarities, *Merrill-Palmer Quarterly*, **34**(3): 223–37.

Gipps, C. and Murphy, P. (1994) *A Fair Test? Assessment, Achievement and Equity*. Buckingham: Open University Press.

Gipps, C., McCallum, B. and Brown, M. (1996) Models of teacher assessment among primary school teachers in England, *The Curriculum Journal*, **7**(2): 167–83.

Giroux, H. A. (1985) Critical pedagogy, cultural politics and the discourse of experience, *Journal of Education*, **167**(2): 23–41.

Giroux, H. A. (1988) Border pedagogy in the age of postmodernism, *Journal of Education*, **170**(3): 162–81.

Goodson, I. F. (1983a) Defining and defending the subject: geography versus environmental studies, in M. Hammersley and A. Hargreaves (eds) *Curriculum Practice: Some Sociological Case Studies*. Lewes: Falmer Press, 89–106.

Goodson, I. F. (1983b) *School Subjects and Curriculum Change*. Beckenham: Croom Helm.

Goodson, I. F. (1985) Subjects for study, in I. F. Goodson (ed.) *Social Histories of the Secondary Curriculum*. Lewes: Falmer Press, 343–67.

Goodson, I. F. (1988) *The Making of Curriculum*, Lewes: Falmer Press.

Goodson, I. F. (1992) On curriculum form: notes towards a theory of curriculum, *Sociology of Education*, **65**: 66–75.

Goodson, I. F. and Ball, S. J. (eds) (1984) *Defining the Curriculum: Histories and Ethnographies*. Lewes: Falmer Press.

Goodson, I. F., Cookson, P. Jr and Persell, C. (1997) Distinction and destiny: the importance of curriculum form in elite American private schools, *Discourse*, **18**(2): 173–83.

Goodson, I. F. with Anstead, C. J. and Morgan, J. M. (1998) *Subject Knowledge: Readings for the Study of School Subjects*. London: Falmer Press.

Gordon, T. (1996) Citizenship, difference and marginality in schools: spatial and embodied aspects of gender construction, in P. F. Murphy and C. Gipps (eds) *Equity in the Classroom: Towards Effective Pedagogy for Boys and Girls*. London: Falmer Press. Falmer/UNESCO Publishing, 34–45.

Gordon, T. and Lahelma, E. (1996) School is like an ants' nest: spatiality and embodiment in schools, *Gender and Education*, **8**(3): 301–10.

Gore, J. (1998) Disciplining bodies: on the continuity of power relations in pedagogy, in T. S. Popkewitz and M. Brennan (eds) *Foucault's Challenge: Discourse, Power and Knowledge in Education*. New York: Teachers College Press, 231–51.

Grant, M. (1984) *Presenting Design and Technology to Girls*. London: Chelsea College Centre for Science and Mathematics Education, University of London.

Green, A. (1991) The nature of technology: some lessons for the National Curriculum, *Curriculum*, **12**(1): 26–37.

Green, L. (1997) *Music, Gender, Education*. Cambridge: Cambridge University Press.

Halsey, A. H., Postlethwaite, N., Prais, S. J., Smithers, A. and Steedman, H. (1991) *Every Child in Britain*. London: Channel 4 Television.

Hamilton, D. (1989) *Towards a Theory of Schooling*. Lewes: Falmer Press.

Harding, S. (1990) Feminism, science and the anti-Enlightenment critique, in L. J. Nicholson (ed.) *Feminism/Postmodernism*. London: Routledge, 83–106.

Hargreaves, A. (1989) *Curriculum and Assessment Reform*. Milton Keynes: Open University Press.

Hargreaves, A. (1994) Restructuring restructuring: postmodernity and the prospects for educational change, *Journal of Education Policy*, **9**(1): 47–65.

Hargreaves, A., Earl, L. and Ryan, J. (1996) *Schooling for Change: Reinventing Education for Early Adolescents*. London: Falmer Press.

Hargreaves, D. J. (1994) Musical education for all, *The Psychologist*, August 1994: 357–8.

Harris, K. (1979) *Education and Knowledge*: London, Routledge and Kegan Paul.

Harrison, G. (1990) Five easy pieces? *Times Educational Supplement*, 23 February.

Hartsock, N. (1990) Foucault on power: a theory for women?, in L. J. Nicholson (ed.) *Feminism/Postmodernism*. London: Routledge, 157–75.

Head, J. O. (1997) *Working With Adolescents: Constructing Identity*. London: Falmer Press.

Head, J. O. and Ramsden, J. (1990) Gender, psychological type and science, *International Journal of Science Education*, 12(1): 115–21.

Hekman, S. J. (1990) *Gender and Knowledge: Elements of a Postmodern Feminism*. Cambridge: Polity Press.

Hekman, S. J. (1995) *Moral Voices, Moral Selves: Carol Gilligan and Feminist Moral Theory*. Cambridge: Polity Press.

Helsby, G., Knight, P. and Saunders, M. (1998) Preparing students for the new work order: the case of Advanced General National Vocational Qualifications, *British Educational Research Journal*, 24(1): 63–78.

Her Majesty's Inspectorate of Schools (1992) *Technology Key Stages 1, 2 and 3: A Report by HM Inspectorate of the 1st Year, 1990–91*. London: HMSO.

Hirst, P. H. (1965) Liberal education and the nature of knowledge, in R. D. Archambault (ed.) *Philosophical Analysis and Education*. London: Routledge and Kegan Paul, 113–38.

Hirst, P. H. and Peters, R. S. (1970) *The Logic of Education*. London: Routledge.

Hodge, G. M., Jupp, J. J. and Taylor, A. J. (1994) Work stress, distress and burnout in music and mathematics teachers, *British Journal of Educational Psychology*, 64: 65–76.

hooks, b. (1982) *Ain't I a Woman: Black Women and Feminism*. London: Pluto Press.

Hoskin, K. (1979) The examination, disciplinary power and rational schooling, *History of Education*, 8(2): 135–46.

Hoskin, K. (1990) Foucault under examination: the crypto-educationalist revealed, in S. J. Ball (ed.) *Foucault and Education*. London: Routledge, 29–53.

Ingólfur Ásegir Jóhannesson (1998) Genealogy and progressive politics: reflections on the notion of usefulness, in T. S. Popkewitz and M. Brennan (eds) *Foucault's Challenge: Discourse, Power and Knowledge in Education*. New York: Teachers College Press, 297–315.

Inner London Education Authority (1984) *Providing Equal Opportunities for Girls and Boys in Physical Education*. London: ILEA.

Jessup, G. (1995) Outcome based qualifications and the implications for learning, in J. Burke (ed.) *Outcomes Learning and the Curriculum: Implications for NVQs, GNVQs and other qualifications*. London: Falmer Press, 33–54.

Johnston, L. (1996) Flexing femininity: female body-builders refiguring 'the body', *Gender, Place and Culture*, 3(3): 327–40.

Jones, A. and Kirk, C. M. (1990) Gender differences in students' interests in applications of school physics, *Physics Education*, 25: 308–13.

Keddie, N. (1971) Classroom knowledge, in M. F. D. Young (ed.) *Knowledge and Control*. Macmillan: West Drayton, 133–60.

Kelly, A. with Baldry, A. *et al.* (1987). Traditionalists and trendies: teachers' attitudes to educational issues, in M. Arnot and G. Weiner (eds) *Gender Under Scrutiny*. London: Hutchinson, 233–42.

Kenway, J. (1996) Reasserting masculinity in Australian schools, *Women's Studies International Forum*, **19**(4): 447–66.

Kenway, J., Willis, S., Blackmore, J. and Rennie, L. (1998) *Answering Back: Girls, Boys and Feminism in Schools*. London: Routledge.

Kessler, S. J. (1990) The medical construction of gender: case management of inter-sexed infants, *Signs: Journal of Women in Culture and Society*, **16**(1): 3–26.

Kessler, S. J. and McKenna, W. (1978) *Gender: an Ethnomethodological Approach*. New York: John Wiley and Sons.

Kirk, D. (1990) Defining the subject: gymnastics and gender in British physical education, in D. Kirk and R. Tinning (eds) *Physical Education, Sport and Schooling*. Basingstoke: Falmer Press, 43–66.

Kirk, D., Macdonald, D. and Tinning, R. (1997) The social construction of pedagogic discourse in physical education teacher education in Australia, *The Curriculum Journal*, **8**(2): 271–98.

Klein, J. T. (1993) Blurring, cracking and crossing: permeation and the fracturing of discipline, in E. Messer-Davidow, D. R. Shumway and D. J. Sylvan (eds) *Knowledges: Historical and Critical Studies in Disciplinarity*. Charlottesville, VA: The University Press of Virginia, 185–211.

Landau, N. R. (1994) Love, hate and mathematics. Unpublished MA dissertation, King's College, London.

Layton, D. (1972) Science as general education, *Trends in Education* 11–15.

Layton, D. (1991) Science education and praxis: the relationship of school science to practical action, *Studies in Science Education*, **19**: 43–79.

Layton, D. (1995) Constructing and reconstructing school technology in England and Wales, *International Journal of Technology and Design Education*, **5**: 89–118.

Leaman, O. (1984) *'Sit on the Sidelines and Watch the Boys Play': Sex Differentiation in Physical Education*. York: Longman.

Lenskyj, H. (1987) Female sexuality and women's sport, *Women's Studies International Forum*, **10**(4): 381–6.

Mac an Ghaill, M. (1992) Student perspectives on curriculum innovation and change in an English secondary school, *British Journal of Educational Research*, **18**(3): 221–34.

Madaus, G. (1988) The influence of testing on the curriculum, in L. Turner (ed.) *Critical Issues in Curriculum*. Chicago, IL: University of Chicago Press, 83–121.

Manthorpe, C. (1986) Science or domestic science? The struggle to define an appropriate science education for girls in early twentieth-century England, *History of Education*, **15**(3): 195–213.

Manthorpe, C. (1989) Reflections on the scientific education of girls, in B. Moon, P. Murphy and J. Raynor (eds) *Policies for the Curriculum*. London: Hodder and Stoughton, 119–30.

Markus, T. A. (1996) Early nineteenth century school space and ideology, *Pedagogic History*, **32**(1): 9–50.

Marshall, J. D. (1990) Foucault and educational research, in S. J. Ball (ed.) *Foucault and Education*. London: Routledge, 11–28.

Massey, D. (1995) Masculinity, dualisms and high technology, *Transactions of the Institute of British Geographers*, **20**(4): 487–99.

McCormack, D. (1999) Body shopping: reconfiguring geographies of fitness, *Gender, Place and Culture*, **6**(2): 155–77.

McCormick, R. (1990) Technology in the National Curriculum: the creation of a subject by committee?, *Curriculum Journal*, **1**(1): 39–51.

McCormick, R. (1992) Technology education in the United Kingdom, in R. McCormick, P. Murphy and M. E. Harrison (eds) *Teaching and Learning Technology*. London: Addison-Wesley, 15–27.

McCulloch, G., Jenkins, E. and Layton, D. (1985) *Technological Revolution?* Lewes: Falmer Press.

McNeil, L. (1986) *Contradictions of Control*. New York: Routledge and Kegan Paul.

McNeil, M. (1993) Dancing with Foucault: feminism and power-knowledge, in C. Ramazanoglu (ed.) *Up Against Foucault*. London: Routledge, 147–75.

Measor, L. (1983) Gender and the sciences: pupils' gender-based conceptions of school subjects, in M. Hammersley and A. Hargreaves (eds) *Curriculum Practice: Some Sociological Case Studies,* London: Falmer Press, 171–91.

Medway, P. (1989) Issues in the theory and practice of technology education, *Studies in Science Education*, **16**: 1–24.

Medway, P. (1990) Technical hitch? *Times Educational Supplement*, 19 October.

Mirza, H. S. (1992) *Young, Female and Black*. London: Routledge.

Monaghan, E. J. and Saul, E. W. (1987) The reader, the scribe, the thinker: a critical look at the history of American reading and writing instruction, in T. S. Popkewitz (ed.) *The Formation of School Subjects*. London: Falmer Press, 85–122.

Morris, M. (1979) The pirate's fiancee, in M. Morris and P. Patton (eds) *Michel Foucault, Power, Truth, Strategy*. Sydney: Feral Publications, 148–68.

Murphy, P. F. (1990) Gender difference: implications for assessment and curriculum planning. Paper presented at the British Educational Research Association Annual Conference, London, September 1990.

Murphy, P. F. and Elwood, J. (1997) Gendered experiences, choices and achievement – exploring the links. Paper presented at the 23rd Annual Conference of the International Association for Educational Assessment, Equity Issues in Gender and Assessment, Durban, South Africa, June 1997.

Murray, R. with Paechter, C. F. and Black, P. (1994) *Managing Learning and Assessment Across the Curriculum*. London: HMSO.

Musgrove, F. (1968) The contribution of sociology to the study of curriculum, in J. F. Kerr (ed.) *Changing the Curriculum*. London: University of London Press.

Nash, I. (1988) Artists uninspired by 'narrow' syllabus, *Times Educational Supplement*, 10 October.

Nash, I. (1990) Technology plan angers employers, *Times Educational Supplement*, 23 February.

National Curriculum Council (1989) *Technology 5–16 in the National Curriculum*. York: National Curriculum Council.

National Curriculum Council (1990a) *Non-Statutory Guidance: Design and Technology Capability*. York: National Curriculum Council.

National Curriculum Council (1990b) *Technology in the National Curriculum*. London: HMSO.

National Curriculum Technology Working Group (1988) *Interim Report*. York: National Curriculum Council.

Nelson, M. B. (1996) *The Stronger Women Get, the More Men Love Football*. London: The Women's Press.

Nespor, J. (1997) *Tangled up in School*. Mahwah, New Jersey: Lawrence Erlbaum Associates.

Nicoll, K. and R. Edwards (1997) Open learning and the demise of discipline?, *Open Learning*, November: 14–24.

O'Grady, C. (1992) Spectre at the feast, *Times Educational Supplement*, 16 October.

Öhrn, E. (1993) Gender, influence and resistance in school, *British Journal of Sociology of Education*, **14**(2): 147–58.

Paechter, C. F. (1992a) Gendered subjects coming together: power and gender in the design and technology curriculum for England and Wales. Paper presented at the Gender and Science and Technology East and West European Conference, Eindhoven, November 1992.

Paechter, C. F. (1992b) Subject subcultures and the negotiation of open work: conflict and co-operation in cross-curricular coursework, in R. McCormick, P. Murphy and M. E. Harrison (eds) *Teaching and Learning Technology*. London, Addison-Wesley, 279–88.

Paechter, C. F. (1993a) Power, knowledge and the design and technology curriculum. Unpublished PhD thesis, King's College, London.

Paechter, C. F. (1993b) Texts, power and design and technology: the use of national curriculum documents in departmental power struggles. Paper presented at the International Conference on Design and Technology Educational Research and Curriculum Development, Loughborough, Department of Design and Technology, Loughborough Institute of Technology, August 1993.

Paechter, C. F. (1993c) What happens when a school subject undergoes a sudden change of status?, *Curriculum Studies*, **1**(3): 349–64.

Paechter, C. F. (1995a) Subcultural retreat: negotiating the design and technology curriculum, *British Educational Research Journal*, **21**(1): 75–87.

Paechter, C. F. (1995b) *Crossing Subject Boundaries: The Micropolitics of Curriculum Innovation*. London: HMSO.

Paechter, C. F. (1995c) 'Doing the best for the students': dilemmas and decisions in carrying out standard assessment tasks, *Assessment in Education*, **2**(1): 39–52.

Paechter, C. F. (1998a) *Educating the Other: Gender, Power and Schooling*. London: Falmer Press.

Paechter, C. F. (1998b) Schooling and the ownership of knowledge, *Curriculum Studies*, **6**(2): 161–76.

Paechter, C. F. and Head, J. O. (1995) Power and gender influences on curriculum implementation. Paper presented at the American Educational Research Association Annual Meeting, San Francisco, April 1995.

Paechter, C. F. and Head, J. O. (1996a) Gender, identity, status and the body: life in a marginal subject, *Gender and Education*, **8**(1): 21–30.

Paechter, C. F. and Head, J. O. (1996b) Power and gender in the staffroom, *British Educational Research Journal*, **22**(1): 57–69.

Palmer, R. (1971) *Space, Time and Grouping*. Basingstoke: Macmillan.

Parker, A. (1996) The construction of masculinity within boys' physical education, *Gender and Education*, 8(2): 141–57.

Pascall, D. (1992) Letter, *Times Educational Supplement*, 10 July.

Patton, P. (1979) Of power and prisons, in M. Morris and P. Patton (eds) *Michel Foucault, Power, Truth, Strategy*. Sydney: Feral Publications, 109–47.

Penfold, J. (1988) *Craft, Design and Technology: Past, Present and Future*. Stoke on Trent: Trentham Books.

Penney, D. and Evans, J. (1994) It's just not (and not just) cricket, *British Journal of Physical Education*, 25(3): 9–12.

Percy, P. V. (1991) *Some Outlines for the Sociological Study of Technology*. London: University of London, Institute of Education.

Pitt, J. (1991) Design and technology and social responsibility, *Design and Technology Teaching*, 24(1): 34–6.

Pollard, A., Broadfoot P., Croll, P., Osborn, M. and Abbott, D. (1994) *Changing English Primary Schools? The Impact of the Education Reform Act at Key Stage One*. London: Cassell.

Popkewitz, T. S. (1997) The production of reason and power: curriculum history and intellectual traditions, *Journal of Curriculum Studies*, 29(2): 131–64.

Prais, S. and Beadle, E. (1991) *Pre-Vocational Schooling in Europe Today*. London: National Institute of Economic and Social Research.

Pyke, K. D. (1996) Class-based masculinities: the interdependence of gender, class and interpersonal power, *Gender and Society* 10(5): 527–49.

Qualifications and Curriculum Authority (2000) *The Revised National Curriculum for 2000. What has Changed?* London: QCA.

Rafferty, F. (1992) Children 'lack basic food skills', *Times Educational Supplement*, 19 June.

Rawls, J. (1972) *A Theory of Justice*. Oxford: Oxford University Press.

Redman, P. (1997) Educating Peter: schooling, the unconscious and the production of heterosexual masculinities. Paper presented at the Transitions in Gender and Education Conference, University of Warwick, 16–18 April 1997.

Rees, C. R. (1997) Still building American character: sport and the physical education curriculum, *The Curriculum Journal*, 8(2): 199–212.

Reid, W. A. (1984) Curricular topics as institutional categories: implications for theory and research in the history and sociology of school subjects, in I. F. Goodson and S. J. Ball (eds) *Defining the Curriculum*. Lewes: Falmer Press, 67–75.

Resnick, L. B. (1987) Learning in school and out, *Educational Researcher*, 16(12): 13–20.

Riddell, S. (1992) *Gender and the Politics of the Curriculum*. London: Routledge.

Roberts, K. (1996) Young people, schools, sport and government policies, *Sport, Education and Society*, 1(1): 47–57.

Rogers, C. (1983) *Freedom to Learn for the 80s*. Columbus, OH: Charles E. Merrill.

Ruddock, J. (1991) *Innovation and Change*. Buckingham: Open University Press.

Said, E. (1986) Foucault and the imagination of power, in D. Couzens Hoy (ed.) *Foucault: A Critical Reader*. Oxford: Basil Blackwell, 149–55.

Scarth, J. (1983) Teachers' school-based experience of examining, in M. Hammersley and A. Hargreaves (eds) *Curriculum Practice: Some Sociological Case Studies*. Lewes: Falmer Press, 207–27.

Schutz, A. (1964) The stranger, in B. R. Cosin, I. R. Dale, G. M. Esland, D. Mac-Kinnon and D. F. Swift (eds) *School and Society*. London: Routledge and Kegan Paul, 27–33.

Scott, D. (1990) Issues and themes: coursework and coursework assessment in the GCSE. Paper presented at the British Educational Research Association Conference, London, September 1990.

Scraton, S. (1986) Images of femininity and the teaching of girls' physical education, in J. Evans (ed.) *Physical Education, Sport and Schooling*. Lewes: Falmer Press, 71–94.

Scraton, S. (1993) Equality, coeducation and physical education, in J. Evans (ed.) *Equality, Education and Physical Education*. London: Falmer Press, 139–53.

Shapin, S. and Barnes, B. (1977) Science, nature and control: interpreting mechanics' institutes, *Social Studies of Science*, 7: 31–74.

Sharon, D. (1989) An interdisciplinary approach, *Education*, **173**: 53–4.

Shepherd, J. and Vulliamy, G. (1983) A comparative sociology of school knowledge, *British Journal of Sociology of Education*, 4(1): 3–18.

Shepherd, J. and Vulliamy, G. (1994) The struggle for culture: a sociological case study of the development of a national music curriculum, *British Journal of Sociology of Education*, 15(1): 27–40.

Sheridan, A. (1980) *Michel Foucault: The Will to Truth*. London: Tavistock Publications.

Sherlock, J. (1987) Issues of masculinity and femininity in British physical education, *Women's Studies International Forum*, 10(4): 443–51.

Shilling, C. (1991) Social space, gender inequalities and educational differentiation, *British Journal of Sociology of Education*, 12(1): 23–44.

Shilling, C. (1992) Schooling and the production of physical capital, *Discourse*, 13(1): 1–19.

Shilling, C. (1993) *The Body and Social Theory*. London: Sage Publications.

Shilling, C. and Cousins, F. (1990) Social use of the school library: the colonisation and regulation of educational space, *British Journal of Sociology of Education*, 11(4): 411–30.

Sikes, P. J. (1988) Growing old gracefully? Age, identity and physical education, in J. Evans (ed.) *Teachers, Teaching and Control in Physical Education*. Lewes: Falmer Press, 21–40.

Siskin, L. S. (1994) *Realms of Knowledge: Academic Departments in Secondary Schools*. London: Falmer Press.

Sloboda, J. A., Davidson, J. W. and Howe, M. J. A. (1994) Is everyone musical?, *The Psychologist*, August: 349–54.

Smart, B. (1986) The politics of truth and the problem of hegemony, in D. Couzens Hoy (ed.) *Foucault: A Critical Reader*. Oxford: Basil Blackwell: 149–55.

Smithers, A. and Robinson, P. (1992) *Technology in the National Curriculum: Getting it Right*. London: The Engineering Council.

Soper, K. (1993) Productive contradictions, in C. Ramazanoglu (ed.) *Up Against Foucault*. London: Routledge, 29–50.

Sparkes, A. C. (1987) Strategic rhetoric: a constraint in changing the practice of teachers, *British Journal of Sociology of Education*, 8(1): 37–54.

Sparkes, A. C. (1990) Winners, losers and the myth of rational change in physical education, in D. Kirk and R. Tinning (eds) *Physical Education, Sport and Schooling*. Basingstoke: Falmer Press, 193–224.

Sparkes, A. C. (1991a) Alternative visions of health-related fitness: an exploration of problem-setting and its consequences, in N. Armstrong and A. C. Sparkes (eds) *Issues in Physical Education*. London: Cassell, 204–27.

Sparkes, A. C. (1991b) Exploring the subjective dimension of curriculum change, in N. Armstrong and A. C. Sparkes (eds) *Issues in Physical Education*. London: Cassell, 20–35.

Sparkes, A. C. (1993) Curriculum change in physical education: on the need to consider personal meanings, *Scottish Journal of Physical Education*, 21(3): 4–12.

Sparkes, A. C., Templin, T. J. and Schempp, P. G. (1990) The problematic nature of a career in a marginal subject: some implications for teacher education, *Journal of Education for Teaching*, 16(1): 3–28.

Spelman, E. V. (1982) Woman as body: ancient and contemporary views, *Feminist Studies*, 8(1): 109–31.

Spours, K. (1997) GNVQs and the future of broad vocational qualifications, in A. Hodgson and D. Spours (eds) *Dearing and Beyond: 14–19 qualifications, frameworks and systems*. London: Kogan Page, 57–74.

Spruce, G. (1999) Music, music education and the bourgeois aesthetic: developing a music curriculum for the new millennium, in R. McCormick and C. Paechter (eds) *Learning and Knowledge*. London: Sage Publications, 68–84.

St John-Brooks, C. (1983) English: a curriculum for personal development?, in M. Hammersley and A. Hargreaves (eds) *Curriculum Practice: Some Sociological Case Studies*. Lewes: Falmer Press, 37–59.

Stables, A. and Wikeley, F. (1996) Pupil approaches to subject option choices. Paper presented at the European Educational Research Association Conference, Seville, October 1996.

Strauss, A. (1987) *Qualitative Analysis for Social Scientists*. Cambridge: Cambridge University Press.

Swanwick, K. (1996) Music education liberated from new praxis, *International Journal of Music Education*, 28: 16–24.

Talbot, M. (1993) A gendered physical education: equality and sexism, in J. Evans (ed.) *Equality, Education and Physical Education*. London: Falmer Press, 74–89.

Taylor, S. (1989) Empowering girls and young women: the challenge of the gender-inclusive curriculum, *Curriculum Studies*, 2(5): 441–56.

Templin, T. J., Bruce, K. and Hart, L. (1988) Settling down: an examination of two women physical education teachers, in J. Evans (ed.) *Teachers, Teaching and Control in Physical Education*. Lewes: Falmer Press, 57–81.

Thomas, K. (1990) *Gender and Subject in Higher Education*. Buckingham, Society for Research into Higher Education and Open University Press.

Thomas, S. (1991) Equality in physical education: a consideration of key issues, in N. Armstrong and A. Sparkes (eds) *Issues in Physical Education*. London: Cassell, 56–73.

Thomas, S. (1993) Education reform: juggling the concepts of equality and elitism, in J. Evans (ed.) *Equality, Education and Physical Education*. London: Falmer Press, 105–24.

Thompson, K. (1984) 'Education for Capability': a critique, *British Journal of Educational Studies*, 32(3): 203–12.

Thorne, B. (1993) *Gender Play: Girls and Boys in School*. Buckingham: Open University Press.

Times Educational Supplement (1991) Leader article. What kind of technology?, *Times Educational Supplement*, 25 October.

Timpson, W. M. (1988) Paulo Freire: advocate of literacy through liberation, *Education Leadership*, **45**(5): 62–6.

Torrance, H. (1986) School-based assessment in GCSE: aspirations, problems and possibilities, in C. Gipps (ed.) *The GCSE: An Uncommon Examination*. London: Institute of Education, University of London, 30–42.

Torrance, H. (1991) Evaluating SATs – the 1990 pilot, *Cambridge Journal of Education*, **21**(2): 129–40.

Vulliamy, G. (1976) What counts as school music?, in G. Whitty and M. Young (eds) *Explorations in the Politics of School Knowledge*. Driffield: Nafferton Books, 19–34.

Walden, R. and Walkerdine, V. (1985) *Girls and Mathematics: From Primary to Secondary Schooling*. London: Heinemann.

Walker, J. C. (1988) The way men act: dominant and subordinate male cultures in an inner-city school, *British Journal of Sociology of Education*, **9**(1): 3–18.

Walker, R. (1996) Music education freed from colonialism: a new praxis, *International Journal of Music Education*, **27**: 2–15.

Walkerdine, V. (1984) Developmental psychology and the child-centred pedagogy: the insertion of Piaget into early education, in J. Henriques, W. Hollway, C. Urwin, C. Venn and V. Walkerdine (eds) *Changing the Subject*. London: Methuen, 153–202.

Walkerdine, V. (1988) *The Mastery of Reason*. Cambridge: Routledge and Kegan Paul.

Walkerdine, V. (1990) *Schoolgirl Fictions*. London: Verso.

Walkerdine, V. and The Girls and Mathematics Unit (1989) *Counting Girls Out*. London: Virago.

Weiner, G. (1993) The gendered curriculum – producing the text: developing a post-structural feminist analysis. Paper presented at the Annual Conference of the Australian Association for Research in Education, Perth, December 1993.

Welch, R. H. (1992) Letter. *Times Educational Supplement*, 29 May.

Welch, R. W. (1990) Letter. *Times Educational Supplement*, 23 November.

Whitty, G. (1985) *Sociology and School Knowledge*. London: Methuen.

Whitty, G., Rowe, G. and Aggleton, P. (1994) Discourse in cross-curricular contexts: limits to empowerment, *International Studies in Sociology of Education*, **4**(1): 25–42.

Williams, J. (1992) Letter. *Times Educational Supplement*, 10 July.

Willis, P. (1977) *Learning to Labour*. Aldershot: Gower Publishing Company.

Wolf, A. (1991) A sum of its parts, *Times Educational Supplement*, 1 February.

Wolf, A. (1999) Outcomes, competencies and trainee-centred learning: the gap between rhetoric and reality, in P. Murphy (ed.) *Learners, Learning and Assessment*. London: Paul Chapman, 191–213.

Wright, J. (1996a) The construction of complementarity in physical education, *Gender and Education*, **8**(1): 61–79.

Wright, J. (1996b) Mapping the discourses of physical education: articulating a female tradition, *Journal of Curriculum Studies*, **28**(3): 331–51.

Wynn, B. (1983) Home economics, in J. Whyld (ed.) *Sexism in the Secondary Curriculum*. London: Harper and Row, 119–215.

Young, M. F. D. (1971) An approach to the study of curricula as socially organised knowledge, in M. F. D. Young (ed.) *Knowledge and Control: New Directions in the Sociology of Education*. West Drayton: Macmillan, 19–45.

Young, M. F. D. (1976) The schooling of science, in G. Whitty and M. F. D. Young (eds) *Explorations in the Politics of School Knowledge*. Driffield: Nafferton Books, 47–61.

Young, M. F. D. (1991) Technology as an educational issue: why is it so difficult and why is it so important?, in M. Young and M. Barnett (eds) *Towards Technological Literacy*. London: Department of Policy Studies, University of London Institute of Education, 5–16.

Younger, M. and Warrington, M. (1996) Differential achievement of girls and boys at GCSE: some observations from the perspective of one school, *British Journal of Sociology of Education*, 17(3): 299–313.

INDEX

A level, 22, 35, 36, 43, 44, 148, 155
academic/practical divide, 22, 51–3, 55, 56, 57, 58, 59, 62, 64, 68
access to curriculum by students, 12, 22, 28
androcentricity, 17, 26
art and design, 51, 83, 92, 120–9, 159, 160, 162
artistic gymnastics, 97
assessability, 133, 136, 151
assessment, 79, 85, 87, 117, 130, 131, 135, 137, 141, 142, 147, 154
assessment schemes, 132–4, 135, 142
attainment, 19, 52, 136
  and 'flair' or 'brilliance,' 22, 37, 38
  and gender, 22, 35, 37, 43, 44, 155
  and hard work, 22, 37
attainment targets (ATs), 67, 103

Bernstein, Basil, 6, 7, 8, 112, 119, 142, 144–5
bodily display, 58, 62, 98, 100, 101, 102
body, embodiment, 19, 28, 30, 36, 37, 49, 55, 59, 62, 93, 97–8, 101, 103, 105, 106, 123, 124, 138, 147
  as gendered, 50, 57, 58, 155
  and power, 91, 94–5, 100

body-building, 98, 102
boundaries between subjects, 10, 15, 23, 112, 116–19, 120, 121, 125, 128, 136–8
boys, 22, 28, 30, 35, 38, 43, 44, 46, 53, 55, 57, 100, 104, 122, 155
Bursley School, 49, 51, 60, 61, 77, 79, 85, 87, 162
Business Studies (BS), 51, 83, 84, 161
Butler, Judith, 99

capability, 64, 66, 67, 81, 82
caring perspective, 17
Cartesian subject, 25
change process, 5, 11, 13, 33, 41, 49, 79, 156, 158, 160
Channel 4 Commission on Education, 82
citizenship, 94, 95, 106
class, 12, 27, 29, 44, 52, 53, 57, 58, 62, 79, 92, 94, 96, 148
classification, 6, 7, 10, 142
coeducational PE, 54, 62, 100, 104
combined arts course, Lacemakers School, 116, 119–29, 159
communicative body, 98
contextualization, 28, 69, 70, 112, 114, 115, 136

continuous assessment, 86, 132–4, 142–3, 146–7, 149
contradictions of control, 139–41
coursework, 116–19, 126–8, 135, 141, 146, 149–50, 154
craft, design and technology (CDT), 9, 34, 40, 46, 51, 61, 62, 63–90, 92, 111, 161, 162
craft skills, 51, 55, 58, 59, 69, 79, 80, 81, 82, 84, 88
credentialism, 129, 135, 137, 141–3
Cross-curricular Assessment Project, 158–61
cultural capital, 52
curriculum
    change, 4, 15, 33, 34, 75, 79, 154
    codification, 131, 132, 134
    collection curriculum, 7, 8, 112, 119, 156
    compulsory, 4, 32, 45, 49
    content, 4, 15, 45, 141
    contestation, 5, 45, 71, 77
    documentation, 69, 76, 133
    gendered, 32, 71
    implementation, 78
    negotiation, 16, 29, 45, 63–90, 103–5
    structure/form, 1, 5, 15, 35, 36, 45, 46, 73, 77–8, 154, 156

dance, 54, 61, 96, 98, 101, 104, 105, 107
Dearing curriculum review, 41, 81, 88, 89
decision-making, 31
decontextualized knowledge, 21, 22, 23, 28, 138
defensive teaching, 139–40
design and technology (D&T), 5, 9, 15, 32, 34, 40, 41, 43, 45, 46, 49–62, 63–90, 92, 111, 121, 136, 137, 150, 151, 156, 159, 160–2
design cycle, 67, 79
designing and making, 84
desire, 27
developmental psychology, 144–5

differences between subjects, *see* subject(s), differences between
disciplinary power, 141, 143
discipline, 24, 94, 123, 125, 132, 149, 151
    subject as, 10, 23, 30, 116, 135–41
discipline/examination, 134–51
disciplined body, 97, 104
disciplining of bodies, 30, 92, 93, 104, 106, 107
disempowerment of teachers, 73
disintegration of D&T, 70–89
disaffected students, 51, 58
docile bodies, 93–6, 104, 106, 123, 139, 141, 147, 149
domestic science, 46
dominating body, 98, 104
drama, 92, 120–9

educational gymnastics, 54, 60, 96, 97, 104, 105
emotion, 36
empowerment, 98, 106
    of students, 112, 119–29, 134, 142
    of teachers, 72, 87–8
Engineering Council, 70, 81, 84, 85, 137
Engineering Employers Federation, 82
English, 30, 34, 35, 38, 43, 55, 72, 133, 149, 159
Enlightenment, 21, 36, 37
environmental studies, 43, 129, 159
examination, 135, 143, 145, 147–9
examination syllabuses, 131
examinations, 22, 36, 52, 86, 128, 129, 131, 133, 135, 136, 138, 141, 147, 148, 150–1
extended D&T tasks, 85
extra-curricular activities, 52

'facts', 123
feelings, 123
female PE, 93, 95, 96–8, 106
female PE teachers, 59
femininity, 28, 36, 42, 53, 54, 58, 59, 60, 61, 98, 100, 101, 102, 105, 107

field study course, Stitchers School, 116–19, 160
food skills, 84
food technology, 43, 58, 61, 71, 84, 89
formative assessment, 133, 145–7, 149–50
Foucault, Michel, 13, 14, 16–28, 93–5, 130, 137, 141, 143–7, 153, 156
and gender, 26, 27
framing, 6, 7
Frank, Arthur, 97–8
Fraser, Nancy, 24, 26
freedom, for students, 92, 120, 122, 124–5, 128

games skills, 104
gaze
disciplinary, 20, 141, 144, 147, 149, 150–1
examining, 142, 144–7, 149–51
normalizing, 145, 147
sexualized, 58, 60, 107
gender, 14, 30, 32, 129, 154
and bodily forms, 98
and curriculum, 3, 92, 136
and D&T, 53, 54, 58, 60, 80
and educational change, 15
and marginal subjects, 46, 49–62
and music, 50, 54, 55, 57, 60
and PE, 53, 54, 57, 58, 59, 60, 61, 98
and power, *see* power, and gender
stereotypes, 98, 100, 101, 102
of students, 28, 39, 57, 121
and subject histories, 53, 92
of teachers, 12, 41, 42, 54, 60, 80, 101
gendered dichotomies within PE, 105–7
gendered nature of school subjects, 16, 28, 29, 32, 38, 41, 42, 43, 45, 136
gendered traditions in the practical curriculum, 45, 46, 80
gendered traditions of PE, 12, 45, 46, 54, 92–3, 96–8, 103, 107
genealogy, 26
General Certificate of Secondary Education (GCSE), 16, 22, 34, 35, 36, 38, 43, 45, 87, 116, 117, 150, 154, 158–60
General National Vocational Qualification (GNVQ), 44, 142–3, 148–9
geography, 10, 41, 43, 45, 49, 55, 116–19, 129, 160
Gilligan, Carol, 17, 28, 29
girls, 22, 27, 28, 30, 35, 38, 43, 44, 46, 53, 55, 122, 154, 155
and PE, 58, 100, 101, 104, 105
Giroux, Henry, 112
Goodson, Ivor, 3, 9, 10, 22, 33, 45
Green, Lucy, 54, 55, 56, 60

Hanbridge School, 72, 77, 85, 162
health, 95, 96, 103, 105
hegemonic curriculum, 23
hegemonic masculinity, 53, 58, 59, 62, 93, 99, 104, 106
Hekman, Susan, 17, 25, 28, 37
Her Majesty's Inspectorate of Schools (HMI), 81, 83
high stakes assessment, 116, 129, 132
high status subjects, 3, 7, 38, 40, 41, 45, 50, 92, 115, 116, 119, 123, 129, 135, 155
history, 41, 45, 49, 55
HMI review of D&T, 84
home economics (HE), 34, 46, 51, 58, 61, 63–90, 92, 111, 161, 162
human purposes and values, 68, 69, 70, 89, 136
humanities subjects, 41, 53, 159

identity, 50, 56
information technology (IT), 40, 41, 43, 44, 45, 51, 65, 73, 162
innovation, *see* change process
integrated codes, 112
integrated/interdisciplinary curricula, 7, 30, 41, 53, 61, 64, 66, 67, 70, 71, 72, 76, 77, 88, 89, 111–29, 142–3, 156, 158–61
interest groups, influence of, 10, 81–5

knowledge, 8, 14, 15, 67, 68, 69, 86,
    89, 112, 128, 129, 137, 140–1,
    149, 150
  forms, 6, 10, 28, 141
  as gendered, 27, 29, 37
  and power, 17, 21, 23, 26, 28, 37,
    49, 135, 141
  real-world, *see* student-owned
    knowledge
  status, 23, 49
Knype School, 73, 77, 80, 86, 87, 88,
    162
Kohlberg, Lawrence, 28

Lacemakers School, 33, 41, 43, 92,
    111, 116, 119–29, 147, 159
liberal humanism, 26, 41, 147, 154
literacy hour, 34, 39, 111, 132
Longshaw Girls' School, 59, 60, 85, 86,
    162
low status subjects, 7, 9, 15, 34, 40, 50,
    79, 91, 92, 121, 123, 156

McNeil, Linda, 139–41
male PE, 93, 95, 96–8, 100, 104
marginal subjects, 15, 34, 41, 46,
    49–63, 156
  as gendered, 45, 50
masculine curriculum, 30, 36–8, 92, 93
masculinity, 35, 36, 37, 42, 53, 57, 58,
    59, 92, 98, 99, 100, 104, 105
masculinization of curriculum, 54, 136
mathematics, 21, 22, 27, 33–4, 38–9, 43,
    55, 114, 116–19, 123, 154, 159
metalwork, 80, 82
micropolitical struggle, 31, 40, 41, 45,
    53, 75, 156, 161
micro-powers, 16, 18, 24, 153
micro-resistances, 16, 21, 33, 155–7
mind, 50, 91, 92, 93, 94, 147
mind-body dualism, 28, 36–7, 91, 93
mirroring body, 98
modern foreign languages, 49
moral judgements, 17, 24, 25, 26, 28
music, 45, 46, 49–62, 92, 162

National Curriculum Council (NCC),
    65, 75, 84, 104

National Curriculum for England and
    Wales, 9, 10, 11, 15, 30, 34, 40,
    41, 43, 44, 51, 61, 63, 65, 70, 76,
    131, 133, 137, 141, 144, 146
National Curriculum Order for Design
    and Technology (1995), 77, 88, 89,
    160–2
National Curriculum Order for Physical
    Education, 104
National Curriculum Order for
    Technology (1990), 65, 66, 76, 84,
    85, 86, 89
National Curriculum Working Group
    for Design and Technology, 63, 65,
    67, 71, 75, 89
National Curriculum Working Group
    for Physical Education, 103, 104
nationalism, 95–6
negotiation of curriculum, 5, 13,
    63–90, 136, 151, 158, 160–2
Nespor, Jan, 20, 99, 138–9
'new PE', 54, 103
'new sociology of education', 5, 10,
    12
Non-statutory Guidance for Design and
    Technology, 65, 77–8
normalization, 141, 144, 148
nostalgia, 80
numeracy hour, 34, 39, 111, 132

Olympic gymnastics, 97
open learning, 85, 88, 121, 134, 145,
    154

Panoptic classroom, 136
  examination, 134, 141–51
  space, 19
Panopticon, 18–20, 143–5
pastoral power, 23, 24, 28, 154
pedagogy, 19, 45, 130–4, 144–6, 150
  invisible, 144–5
  visible, 144
performative body, 99, 102
personal and social education (PSE),
    142, 149, 151
physical capital, 100
physical education (PE), 12, 30, 39, 42,
    45, 46, 49–62, 91–107

physical exploration and expression, 93, 104
power, 14, 16, 18, 24, 29, 141, 143, 144, 145–7, 153–6
and gender, 4, 12, 13, 27, 46, 77, 161
positional, 41, 54, 77, 121, 128
as positive/pleasurable, 26, 27, 28, 106
relations, 13, 15, 17, 19, 20, 71, 77, 134
relations between school subjects, 7, 30, 41, 43, 53, 64, 93, 112, 113, 119
relations between teachers, 7, 41, 42, 53, 64, 73, 76, 77, 93, 112, 113, 119
as repressive, 26
structures, 18, 53
power, gender and school subjects, 13, 80
power/knowledge, 4, 15, 17, 21, 23, 24, 27, 38, 64, 68, 70, 112, 119, 129, 135
and curriculum, 29, 64, 112, 128, 129
as gendered, 13, 14, 16, 29, 32, 46, 98, 153–7, 158
as pleasurable, 28, 101, 154
relations in classroom, 113, 120, 122, 124, 128, 134, 145, 150–1, 154
practical curriculum, 9, 40, 66, 67, 69, 71, 73, 79, 91, 156
practical reasoning, 117
Prais and Beadle report 1991, 82
press reports, 70, 71, 81–5
processes of schooling, 15
Programmes of Study for D&T, 67
public/private spheres, 93, 105

race, 44, 62, 100
Rawls, John, 17, 28
reason, 21–7, 32, 36, 37, 38, 42, 49, 92, 93, 145, 154, 155
Records of Achievement (RoAs), 148–9
resistance, 7, 15, 16, 18, 20, 21, 24, 25, 26, 33, 153–7

by students, 54, 105, 111, 113, 119–29, 140
by teachers, 49, 70, 74, 77, 121, 157
resistant materials, 43, 58, 71, 75, 89
resources, 4
review of D&T curriculum 1992, 71, 77
revisions to D&T curriculum 1994, 70

school architecture, 19
school knowledge, 6, 8, 23, 135–7, 139–42, 149, 151
school learning, 113, 135
School Examinations and Assessment Council (SEAC), 84
science, 22, 23, 28, 29, 30, 34, 35, 37, 38, 39, 41, 45, 46, 50, 62, 68, 71, 72, 92, 115, 116–19, 123, 129, 154, 160
self-discipline, 137
Shipbuilders School, 134, 159
Smithers and Robinson report, 81, 83, 84, 85, 137
social change, 5, 6, 113, 140
social class, *see* class
social control, 92
social processes, 5, 33
space/time, 16, 19, 20, 30, 38, 39, 121, 122, 123, 126, 128, 138, 155
sport, 54, 95, 96, 97, 98, 99, 103, 104, 105, 107
staff appointments, 72–3
staffing structures, 73
staffroom, 42
Standard Assessment Tasks (SATs), 71, 76, 77, 85–8, 146, 150
Stitchers School, 41, 72–3, 75, 116–19, 160, 161
Stonemasons School, 73, 74, 76, 78, 160, 161
struggle, 7, 45, 71, 77, 79, 82–4, 113
student
'ability', 8, 37, 40, 51, 55, 79
course choice, 112
as gendered, 43, 44, 53
enjoyment, 57, 122–4
identities, 28, 30
participation in the learning process, 112

strategies for success, 118
understanding of teacher
expectations, 116–19, 122, 124–9
student-owned knowledge, 8, 23, 68,
70, 112, 124, 126, 134, 135, 137,
140–1, 149, 151
students
and curriculum change, 111, 128,
129
and curriculum subjects, 43, 116–29
and embodiment, 92
subcultural retreat, 80, 84
subjectivity, 37
subject(s)
definition, struggles over, 11, 45, 52,
65, 66, 71, 75, 77, 81–5, 89,
103–5, 130, 136
departments, 10, 11, 30, 41
differences between, 114, 117, 118,
124, 126–7, 129
as discipline, *see* discipline, subject as
as gendered, 12, 45
identity, 7, 10, 45, 80–5
as gendered, 53
marginality, *see* marginal subjects
status, 4, 9, 15, 22, 33, 34, 35, 36,
40, 41, 43, 45, 49, 50, 51, 55, 56,
71, 79, 84, 91, 116, 117
subcultural segments, 10, 137
subcultures, 10, 11, 83, 130–4, 136,
149, 151, 161
assessment focused, 134–51
summative assessment, 133, 146,
149–50
surveillance, 19, 20, 141, 143–4, 148
as covert, 20
as overt, 20
swimming, 97

teacher(s)
agendas, 116
assessment, 145
careers, 54, 58, 72, 93, 160–1
cultures, 130–4
expectations of students, 117–19,
122, 129
identities, 42, 59, 80
as gendered, 59
morale, 76, 78, 80
perceptions of students, 55
relationship to curriculum, 69, 77,
133
status, 40, 71, 72–3, 93
teacher-student relations, 57, 64, 70,
80, 119–29, 131
Technical and Vocational Education
Initiative (TVEI), 71, 159, 160
technical subjects, 41
textiles technology, 43, 58, 61, 71, 84,
86, 89
Times Educational Supplement (TES),
83, 84
transgression, 102, 106
truth, 26, 141, 148
Turnhill School, 55, 57, 72, 73, 74, 75,
162

vocational education, 35, 44, 56, 89,
142–3, 148
skills, 81, 82, 84

Walkerdine, Valerie, 19, 21, 22, 27, 32,
36, 37, 55, 114, 115, 154
woodwork, 80, 82

Young, Michael, 5, 115

A CURRICULUM FOR LIFE
SCHOOLS FOR A DEMOCRATIC LEARNING SOCIETY

John Quicke

> . . . a quality and 'mould-breaking' book which develops a coherent, continuous, authoritative argument, and expresses, with sustained and impressive clarity, the moral-political perspective that John Quicke has adopted . . . There are few authors who could achieve the integrated reach that is achieved in this book.
>
> Professor Andrew Pollard, University of Bristol

- What kind of curriculum do we need for life in the 21st century?

This is the central question which this book sets out to address. It is widely recognized that we need to reconsider the school curriculum. Schools need to teach literacy, numeracy and other skills but what else do children need to learn for life in present day and future society?

The book seeks to counter the incoherence and fragmentation of much curriculum thinking. It has a clear rationale – an explicit political and ethical framework – which underpins discussion and draws upon theory and research in a number of disciplines – social science, psychology, philosophy and politics. A 'curriculum for life' is proposed as an alternative to the present National Curriculum. It is focused on themes like social development, thinking skills, parenting, citizenship and work related learning. How and what to teach about these and other themes is highly contested and in the book a number of such themes are explored in the light of a particular conception of society and democracy. In this way it is hoped that a morally and intellectually serious debate about the curriculum can be generated.

The book will be of particular interest to teachers studying for advanced degrees, researchers and policy makers who are concerned with curriculum development in a changing society.

Contents

Introduction: the curriculum and reflexive modernity – Education for self-identity – Becoming a 'good' learner – Towards a collaborative culture of professionalism – Pupils' cultural practices and collaborative group work – Teaching for cultural pluralism – Gender politics and school achievement – On learning and democracy in families – Reworking the work ethic – Science and the risk society – Schools for a democratic learning society – References – Index.

192 pp   0 335 20297 7 (Paperback)   0 335 20298 5 (Hardback)

THE CURRICULUM EXPERIMENT
MEETING THE CHALLENGE OF SOCIAL CHANGE

John Elliott

This book focuses on the interface between curriculum policy/practice and social change in technology-driven advanced societies, and the challenges this presents for education in the 21st century.

The book begins with both an autobiographical account of the experience of curriculum change in England over the past 40 years and an analysis of a major issue which emerged during that period, namely, the teacher's role in curriculum development. It then moves on to look at what the author believes to be a current manifestation of contemporary curriculum policy and practice in England: student disaffection from schooling. It is argued that the now widespread phenomenon of 'disaffection' can be explained by the failure of curriculum policy making to respond to the complexity of social change in an advanced modern society.

Drawing on the experience of attempts at radical innovation in the curriculum within the UK and other OECD countries, the author develops a framework for curriculum policy making and development which he argues will enable education to meet the challenges of social change. In the process, he undertakes a critique of the currently fashionable school effectiveness and improvement movements and argues that they are underpinned by outmoded views of the roles and functions of schools.

Contents
Introduction – Institutions in the mind: autobiographical fragments – The teacher's role in curriculum development: an unresolved issue in English attempts at curriculum reform – The curriculum dimensions of student disaffection – Social complexity, subsidiarity and curriculum policy-making – School effectiveness research and its critics: alternative visions of schooling – Culture, education and distributive justice – Environment and school initiatives (ENSI): an international innovative curriculum experiment – The politics of environmental education: a case story – What have we learned from action research in school-based evaluation? – References – Index.

224 pp   0 335 19429 X (Paperback)   0 335 19430 3 (Hardback)

EDUCATIONAL RESEARCH FOR SOCIAL JUSTICE
GETTING OFF THE FENCE

Morwenna Griffiths

This is a book for all researchers in educational settings whose research is motivated by considerations of justice, fairness and equity. It addresses questions such researchers have to face. Will a prior political or ethical commitment bias the research? How far can the ideas of empowerment or 'giving a voice' be realized? How can researchers who research communities to which they belong deal with the ethical issues of being both insider and outsider?

The book provides a set of principles for doing educational research for social justice. These are rooted in considerations of methodology, epistemology and power relations, and provide a framework for dealing with the practical issues of collaboration, ethics, bias, empowerment, voice, uncertain knowledge and reflexivity, at all stages of research from getting started to dissemination and taking responsibility as members of the wider community of educational researchers.

Theoretical arguments and the realities of practical research are brought together and interwoven. Thus the book will be helpful to all researchers, whether they are just beginning their first project, or whether they are already highly experienced. It will be of great value to research students in designing and writing up their theses and dissertations.

Contents

Part I: Introduction and context – Taking sides, getting change – Research for social justice? Some examples – Part II: Theoretical frameworks for practical purposes – Truths and methods – Facts and values: power/knowledge – Living with uncertainty in educational research – Educational research for social justice: a framework – Part III: Practical possibilities – Getting started: the research process – Getting justice: empowerment and voice – Better knowledge – Educational research at large – Appendix: Fair schools – References – Index.

176 pp   0 335 19859 7 (Paperback)   0 335 19860 0 (Hardback)